JOSEPH CONRAD:
THE
MODERN IMAGINATION

JOSEPH CONRAD:
THE
MODERN IMAGINATION

C. B. Cox
Professor of English, University of Manchester

J. M. DENT & SONS LTD, LONDON
ROWMAN & LITTLEFIELD, TOTOWA, N.J.

Acknowledgements

I am grateful to the many people with whom I have talked about Conrad over the years, and particularly to A. E. Dyson, Professor John Jump, Professor Norman Sherry and Jacques de Villiers. I must especially thank Vedah Moody (a graduate at Manchester working on Conrad for her Ph.D.), with whom I have had many stimulating discussions. In the academic year 1972–3 I took a seminar on Conrad at Manchester University, and my book has profited considerably from the criticism and ideas of my students. The many articles and books on which I have drawn are referred to in the text; I have been particularly influenced by the writings on Conrad by James Guetti, J. Hillis Miller and Ian Watt. An early version of the opening chapter was published in the *Bulletin of the John Rylands University Library of Manchester*, and the chapters on *Lord Jim* and *The Secret Agent* have appeared in *The Critical Quarterly*.

I must also thank Shelagh Aston and Nancy Walsh, two of the English departmental secretaries at Manchester, who typed the manuscript so efficiently while at the same time coping with a host of administrative and student problems.

Extracts from *Joseph Conrad's Letters to Cunninghame Graham*, ed. C. T. Watts (1969), and *The English Mind*, ed. H. S. Davies and George Watson (1964), are reprinted by kind permission of Cambridge University Press; from *Poets of Reality*, by J. Hillis Miller (1966), by kind permission of the Belknap Press of Harvard University Press; and from *Conrad's Polish Background*, ed. E. Najder (1974), by kind permission of Oxford University Press.

C. B. C.

Page references for quotations from Conrad are taken from the *Collected Edition of the Works of Joseph Conrad*, J. M. Dent and Sons Ltd, 1946–55.

Contents

To Jean

Chapter 1

The Question of Suicide

> In a vivid insight, a flash of black lightning, he saw that all life was
> parallel: that evolution was not vertical, ascending to a perfection,
> but horizontal. Time was the great fallacy; existence was without
> history, was always now, was always this being caught in the
> same fiendish machine. All those painted screens erected by man
> to shut out reality—history, religion, duty, social position, all
> were illusions, mere opium fantasies.
>
> JOHN FOWLES, *The French Lieutenant's Woman*

I

In February, 1878, Joseph Conrad's uncle, Thaddeus Bobrowski,
received an urgent telegram from France: 'Conrad wounded, send
money—come'.[1] Bobrowski, who had assumed control of Conrad's
upbringing after the death of both parents, had been under the impression that Conrad was sailing somewhere in the Antipodes. He hurried
to Marseilles, where Conrad had entered upon his sea career four years
previously. There he spent two weeks sorting out his nephew's affairs,
particularly by paying his debts.

What events had precipitated this crisis? In his later years Conrad
led his family and friends to believe that the scar on his left breast
resulted from a duel. In the semi-autobiographical *The Arrow of Gold*
(1919), M. George (Conrad's nickname in Marseilles) fights a duel
with a Captain Blunt, and is shot through the left side of the breast. The
cause of the duel is Rita, a brilliant, cold, neurotic adventuress, with
whom they are both in love. In the copy of *The Arrow of Gold* owned
by Richard Curle, a young admirer, Conrad wrote that 'all the per-
sonages are authentic and the facts are as stated'.[2] In a review of 1919,[3]
Sir Sidney Colvin, at Conrad's instigation, emphasized the factual
history behind the novel, particularly of the duel which ends the book.

1

It was not until 1957, when a letter of Bobrowski describing Conrad's attempted suicide was published in Poland, that the truth fully emerged. This letter was quoted at length in Jocelyn Baines's excellent biography of 1960, and, although some hero-worshippers have demurred, the evidence now published of three separate references in Bobrowski's writings seems conclusive. The main letter was sent to Stephen Buszczyński, a close friend of Conrad's father. It describes how Conrad had lost a large sum of money through smuggling and gambling:

> Having managed his affairs so excellently he returns to Marseilles and one fine evening invites his friend the creditor [Mr. Fecht] to tea, and before his arrival attempts to take his life with a revolver. (Let this detail remain between us, as I have been telling everyone that he was wounded in a duel. From you I neither wish to nor should keep it a secret.) The bullet goes durch und durch near his heart without damaging any vital organ. Luckily, all his addresses were left on top of his things so that this worthy Mr. Fecht could instantly let me know, and even my brother, who in turn bombarded me. Well, that is the whole story! [4]

As is usual in many attempted suicides, witness Sylvia Plath, it is possible that Conrad hoped his self-injury would not prove fatal. He did not shoot himself in the head, and he arranged for a friend to arrive soon afterwards. His self-wounding may have represented a cry for help.

Was there a woman in the case? We shall probably never know. Bobrowski mentions no such person, and there is psychological evidence that Conrad's amorous adventures in Marseilles had more existence in his imagination than in fact. It seems certain, therefore, that Conrad lied to his family and friends about his career in Marseilles, just as in his early days he lied to Bobrowski to obtain additional advances of money.

2

After the attempted suicide in Marseilles, Conrad suffered from fits of depression and nervous breakdowns, of varying importance, for the rest of his life. The injury he sustained while working as first mate on the *Highland Forest* on his way to Samarang in 1887 was followed by a sudden collapse of will, by inexplicable periods of powerlessness, and this pattern was repeated during many later crises of illness. Paul Langlois, who met Conrad in Mauritius in 1888, called him a 'neurasthénique', and noted a tic of the shoulder and the eyes. He was easily startled by the least unexpected thing, the fall of an object onto the floor, or a banging door.

In letters to friends Conrad continually deplored his mental condition, using powerful language that on occasions must have thrown the recipients into consternation. In 1896 he wrote to Edward Garnett, his publisher's reader: 'I have long fits of depression, that in a lunatic asylum would be called madness. I do not know what it is. It springs from nothing. It is ghastly. It lasts an hour or a day; and when it departs it leaves a fear'. [5] And in 1898 to Garnett again: 'I feel suicidal'. [6] Words such as 'weariness', 'depression', 'paralysis' and 'suicide' crop up again and again, giving evidence to his continual struggle against the urge to self-destruction. At times, his letters breed, as from a dunghill, images of disgust and horror at his own mental condition. 'Difficulties are as it were closing round me,' he wrote to Cunninghame Graham, the explorer, in 1900, 'an irresistible march of blackbeetles I figure it to myself. What a fate to be so ingloriously devoured'. [7] And to a distant relative, Marguerite Poradowska: 'Comme tout est noir noir noir ... j'ai des accès de melancholia qui me paralysent la pensée et la volonté'. [8] Literary composition in particular turned his brain into a quagmire, in which he struggled heroically against paralysis of the imagination. In 1898 he wrote to Cunninghame Graham of his 'nerve-trouble—a taste of hell': 'An extreme weariness oppresses me. It seems as though I had seen and felt everything since the beginning of the world. I *suspect* my brain to be yeast and my backbone to be cotton. ... It seems to me I am disintegrating slowly. Cold shadows stand around. ... My brain reduced to the size of a pea seems to rattle about in my head. I can't rope in a complete thought; I am exhausted mentally and very depressed'. [9] In 1903 he told John Galsworthy: 'I am trying to keep despair under. Nevertheless I feel myself losing my footing in deep waters. They are lapping about my hips'. [10]

After he completed *Under Western Eyes* in 1910 the nervous tension laid him up for three months. The manuscript of the novel lay on a table at the foot of his bed, and in his delirium he held converse with the characters. He even accused his doctor and Jessie, his wife, of trying to put him in an asylum. After he had recovered he wrote to Norman Douglas: 'I feel like a man returned from hell and look upon the very world of the living with dread'. [11] It is arguable that after this terrifying nightmare Conrad deliberately repressed the sensitive, imaginative side of his nature, and forced his mind into safer, more normal channels of thought. This provides one explanation for the comparatively superficial quality of his post-1910 writings, and the naive falsification of the profundities of his major works in the author's notes he wrote in his later years.

With this background it is not surprising that in Conrad's fiction suicide and thoughts of suicide repeatedly occur. There are fifteen actual suicides in the fiction, though in this number I include Peyrol (*The Rover*) and Lord Jim, who could be called voluntary martyrs to an ideal. The others are Kayerts ('An Outpost of Progress'), Decoud (*Nostromo*), Captain Whalley ('The End of the Tether'), Renouard ('The Planter of Malata'), Heyst (*Victory*), Susan ('The Idiots'), Brierly (*Lord Jim*), Winnie Verloc (*The Secret Agent*), Erminia ('Gaspar Ruiz'), Sevrin ('The Informer'), Ziemianitch (*Under Western Eyes*), De Barral (*Chance*) and Jörgenson (*The Rescue*). In *Chance*, Flora is first seen by Marlow on a cliff top contemplating whether or not to throw herself over. Other characters, such as Alice Jacobus in 'A Smile of Fortune', talk about suicide, and many vigorous male characters, such as Cosmo in *Suspense*, and M. George himself in *The Arrow of Gold*, experience inexplicable hours of mental paralysis, of impotence when they are overwhelmed by a *tedium vitae*. Even Nostromo nearly jumps overboard from his schooner when he first sees the new lighthouse on the Great Isabel being built near the spot where he has hidden the silver. Conrad writes: 'The man, subjective almost to insanity, looked suicide deliberately in the face'.

The reasons for the suicides vary considerably. Some, such as Winnie Verloc's jump into the sea, are acts of desperation by people trapped in an impossible situation. Captain Whalley's suicide is a calculated manœuvre in his struggle to provide financially for his daughter. Renouard is a masochistic, enraptured lover, who swims out to sea and oblivion when rebuffed by Felicia Moorsom, his *belle dame sans merci*. But the most interesting examples are Brierly and Decoud, who appear to choose suicide deliberately and consciously as a proper response to the meaninglessness of their lives. These two suicides reflect the temptation to which Conrad himself was attracted.

When in Mauritius he filled in a playful questionnaire prepared by the daughter of his host, he answered the question 'Que désirez-vous être?' with 'Should like not to be'.[12]

4

3

A variety of interpretations for Conrad's depression have been put forward. In 1890 he obtained command of a steam-boat in the Upper Congo, an ill-fated expedition which ruined his health. He was also profoundly shocked by the exploitation of the natives. This experience certainly had a lasting effect on his imagination, which is recorded in *Heart of Darkness*. But it is wrong to ascribe his later nervous problems solely to this adventure. His numerous childhood illnesses and complaints, together with his lifelong periods of breakdown, prove the existence of more deeply ingrained causes.

Conrad was born Teodor Jósef Konrad Korzeniowski in 1857 near Berdichev in the Polish Ukraine. He was the son of a poet and man of letters. In 1862 the family was sent into exile at Vologda in Russia, a punishment for their Polish nationalist activities. In a letter of 1862, Conrad's father described the appalling conditions of their exile: 'The climate consists of two seasons of the year: a white winter and a green winter. The white winter lasts nine-and-a-half months and the green one two-and-a-half. We are now on the onset of the green winter: it has already been raining ceaselessly for twenty-one days and that's how it will be to the end. . . . The population is a nightmare: disease-ridden corpses'. [13] Evelina, Conrad's mother, soon showed symptoms of an advanced stage of tuberculosis, and she died when he was seven. His father, Apollo Korzeniowski, died only four years later, after spending his last years absorbed in morbid religiosity and a cult of his dead wife. These early experiences must have put a great strain on Conrad's over-sensitive nature. For some time he had no friends of his own age, and he developed habits of solitude, a depressive sense of loneliness which he carried with him to his grave.

Conrad's decision at the age of sixteen to leave Poland and become a sailor was naturally opposed by his family. It has often been argued that this created in him a sense of betrayal and that he never overcame his guilt at his desertion of his country. According to this theory, in his heart he knew he had abandoned the cause for which both his parents sacrificed their lives. The desire for atonement and self-justification, therefore, dominated his life. Baines sees Lord Jim's jump over the side of the *Patna*, or Razumov's betrayal of Haldin in *Under Western Eyes*, as, possibly, unconscious symbolical representations of Conrad's action in leaving Poland. He draws attention to Conrad's use of the word 'jump' to describe his own case: 'I verily believe mine was the only case of a boy of my nationality and antecedents taking a, so to speak, standing jump out of his racial surroundings and associations'. [14] Parallels can be drawn between Jim's efforts to vindicate himself after his desertion of the *Patna* and Conrad's own life. His sense of exile is recreated in 'Amy Foster', in which Yanko Goorall, from Austrian Poland, is treated with cruelty and incomprehension when he is shipwrecked on the Kentish coast.

This theme of betrayal can be over-emphasized. Conrad's letters do not suggest a mind ridden by guilt complexes about Poland. He enjoyed the prospect of a return visit in 1914, and often wrote easily and sensibly about the folly of Poland's messianic ambitions. If we are looking for psychological explanations for his depression, then his sexual problems are probably more important. These have been astutely analysed by Thomas Moser in *Joseph Conrad: Achievement and Decline* (1957) and by Bernard Meyer in *Joseph Conrad. A Psychoanalytic Biography* (1967), though the latter is carried away by his theories. Conrad's misogyny is evident throughout his life and works. The examples in *Chance* are particularly notorious. He could not write satisfactorily about a physical relation between a white man and woman, and this explains why his worst short story is 'The Return'. It also partly explains why *The Rescue*, particularly the sections dealing with Lingard's infatuation with Mrs Travers, gave him such difficulties in composition, so that it took him twenty years to complete. He was imaginatively more comfortable with miscegenation, as in *An Outcast of the Islands*, but even in this novel the sexual embrace soon produces disgust and impotence in the man. There is no doubt that Conrad himself had strong heterosexual desires, for he was constantly infatuated with women. He made a fool of himself in Mauritius over Eugénie Renouf, who was already engaged; and over the seductive American, Jane Anderson, when he was an old married man. Yet the early death of his mother appears to have retarded his development, leaving behind an unconscious fear of incest with a white woman of his own family. His marriage with Jessie, so different in background from himself and out of touch with his intellectual pursuits, suggests that sexual arousal depended to some extent for him on an element of miscegenation. It is not surprising that after his successful proposal of marriage to Jessie he disappeared for three days, apparently too afraid to return.

At the core of these psychological disturbances there seems a basic uncertainty about his own identity. In many of his stories a kind of dismemberment of personality takes place. Just as Virginia Woolf divided herself up into six characters in *The Waves*, so Conrad is repeatedly concerned with two characters who reflect the composite nature of a contradictory identity. The best-known example is 'The Secret Sharer', where Leggatt is an alter ego, an unrealized potentiality in the character of the captain-narrator. There is also Kurtz in *Heart of Darkness*, who in certain ways reflects the unconscious urges of Marlow's soul. The breakdown of such composite personalities into separate identities reflects Conrad's difficulty in creating a synthesis for the warring elements in his own nature. He often uses the image of the mirror, like a man obsessively scrutinizing his face in search of his real self. In *Victory*, as Axel Heyst's infatuation with Lena begins to trouble his pose of stoical indifference, he turns to his mirror:

> He got up then, went to a small looking-glass hanging on the wall, and stared at himself steadily. It was not a new-born vanity which induced this long survey. He felt so strange that he could not resist the suspicion of his personal appearance having changed during the night. What he saw in the glass, however, was the man he knew before. It was almost a disappointment—a belittling of his recent experience. (p. 90)

Heyst is awakening to his double personality, to the strength of his repressed emotions, but the mirror tells him nothing. Its firm reflection is too familiar, too precise, for the uncertainties in his soul. In his fiction Conrad seeks technical devices to mirror the hidden elements in the psyche. In 'The Secret Sharer', the Captain is struck by the similarity between himself and Leggatt: 'It was, in the night, as though I had been faced by my own reflection in the depths of a sombre and immense mirror.' He sees the secret self for which Heyst was searching. A comparable fascination with mirrors as a means of representing a split personality occurs in the poetry of Sylvia Plath. This uncertainty about identity is endemic in modern literature, of course, and in this way Conrad reflects the malaise of the contemporary disintegrating personality. His own jumps from Poland to France to England, from aristocrat to seaman to novelist, made him a living embodiment of this breakdown. His life and art testify to a continual, by and large unsuccessful search for a stable identity.

Also, he had to endure the problems of an alien language. Although fluent in Polish and French, he spoke English with a heavy accent, and never overcame his deficiencies. G. B. Shaw said that his style was too pure for English, too impossibly free of local idiosyncrasies. Conrad, then, was digging his language out of a foreign quarry. This made him doubtful about the mimetic function of words, and in this he is characteristically modern in outlook. Words for him have moved a few steps away from reality, and so on occasions he turns to image and symbol for a more mysterious and complex means of communication. Like Nabokov, he understood the fallibility of words, their different roles in different languages. He chose English for his fiction probably because for ten years he had grown accustomed to the language; perhaps he wanted to hide his fiction in a form unavailable to his Polish family. But, whatever the hidden reasons, the writing of English involved him in the radical problems of identity which haunt the twentieth-century imagination. George Steiner's comments on Nabokov also apply to Conrad:

> A great writer driven from language to language by social upheaval and war is an apt symbol for the age of the refugee. No exile is more radical, no feat of adaptation and new life more demanding. It seems proper that those who create art in a civilisation of quasi-barbarism which has made so many homeless, which has torn up tongues and peoples by the root, should themselves be poets unhoused and wanderers across language.[15]

4

Although his childhood and his self-imposed exile must count as major sources for his depressions, just as important was his conscious philosophy, his personal response to what he considered as the absurdity of the universe. His suicidal tendencies were nourished by a nihilism derived from his reading of books (particularly Schopenhauer) and from the climate of thought in the late nineteenth century. His doubts about his own identity were linked to philosophical scepticism about the nature of reality.

Conrad often explained the grounds of his pessimism in his letters. That the world must eventually cool down and disintegrate destroyed for him the illusion of progress. In 1898 he wrote to Cunninghame Graham:

> Of course reason is hateful—but why? Because it demonstrates (to those who have the courage) that we, living, are out of life—utterly out of it. The mysteries of a universe made of drops of fire

and clods of mud do not concern us in the least. The fate of a humanity condemned ultimately to perish from cold is not worth troubling about. If you take it to heart it becomes an unendurable tragedy. If you believe in improvement you must weep, for the attained perfection must end in cold, darkness and silence. In a dispassionate view the ardour for reform, improvement for virtue, for knowledge, and even for beauty is only a vain sticking up for appearances as though one were anxious about the cut of one's clothes in a community of blind men. Life knows us not and we do not know life—we don't know even our own thoughts. Half the words we use have no meaning whatever and of the other half each man understands each word after the fashion of his own folly and conceit. Faith is a myth and beliefs shift like mists on the shore; thoughts vanish; words, once pronounced, die; and the memory of yesterday is as shadowy as the hope of to-morrow— only the string of my platitudes seems to have no end. As our peasants say: 'Pray, brother, forgive me for the love of God.' And we don't know what forgiveness is, nor what is love, nor where God is. Assez.[16]

'We, living, are out of life'. This sense of a divorce between man and 'reality', of the inadequacy of our thought processes to comprehend our experience, is crucial in Conrad's best work (as in many twentieth-century writers). In *Chance*, Marlow comments on our 'inability to interpret aright the signs which experience (a thing mysterious in itself) makes to our understanding and emotions. . . . Our experience never gets into our blood and bones. It always remains outside of us.' It is not surprising that Conrad was fascinated by X-rays, for their hidden existence suggested to him the unknown realities of matter behind the illusory forms available to our senses. After attending a demonstration of a Röntgen X-ray machine, he wrote to Garnett:

The secret of the universe is in the existence of horizontal waves whose varied vibrations are at the bottom of all states of consciousness . . . there is no space, time, matter, mind as vulgarly understood, there is only the eternal something that waves and an eternal force that causes the waves—it's not much—and by the virtue of these two eternities exists that Corot and that Whistler . . .[17]

Conrad is saying that the human world, including the first productions of art, has developed from undifferentiated matter. This applies to the forms observed by the senses, to the structures of behaviour demanded by society, to the rational formulations of the mind. Behind such human ideas of order lies inert matter, formless, the primal darkness which transcends even the most basic categories of time and space. For many of Conrad's characters, the climax of their experience occurs when they journey into the darkness before creation; the best-known example is Decoud's ride in the open boat across the blackness of the Placid Gulf towards his eventual suicide.

This central feature of Conrad's art has been brilliantly analysed by Royal Roussel in *The Metaphysics of Darkness* (1971). He demonstrates how for Conrad this darkness lies far behind all material things, as long as they continue to possess qualities of weight and mass. Stripped of all accessory details, the darkness stands as an indefinite, silent immensity, still as death. Objects like silver in *Nostromo* or the Russian plains in *Under Western Eyes* exist, in one form or another, from generation to generation. The human mind is vulnerable and infinitely precarious, whereas matter can be altered, but never annihilated. Decoud's suicide results from loss of faith in the world presented to him through his senses. The awareness of the eventual annihilation of the individual mind and all its constructs breeds a sense of ultimate illusion, of a universe absurd and meaningless.

In a letter to Cunninghame Graham in 1897, Conrad compares the universe to a knitting machine in a manner which would not seem inappropriate in one of Ted Hughes's nightmare poems:

> There is a—let us say—a machine. It evolved itself (I am severely scientific) out of a chaos of scraps of iron and behold!—it knits. I am horrified at the horrible work and stand appalled. I feel it ought to embroider—but it goes on knitting. You come and say: 'this is all right; it's only a question of the right kind of oil. Let us use this—for instance—celestial oil and the machine shall embroider a most beautiful design in purple and gold.' Will it? Alas no. You cannot by any special lubrication make embroidery with a knitting machine. And the most withering thought is that the infamous thing has made itself; made itself without thought, without conscience, without foresight, without eyes, without heart. It is a tragic accident—and it has happened. You can't interfere with it. The last drop of bitterness is in the suspicion that you can't even smash it. In virtue of that truth one and immortal

which lurks in the force that made it spring into existence it is what it is—and it is indestructible!

It knits us in and it knits us out. It has knitted time, space, pain, death, corruption, despair and all the illusions—and nothing matters. I'll admit however that to look at the remorseless process is sometimes amusing.[18]

This is the paralysing vision with which Conrad was wrestling during his great creative years. The same kind of torment has had something to do with the suicides of modern artists such as Virginia Woolf, Hart Crane, Sylvia Plath or John Berryman; it influenced the breakdowns of T. S. Eliot and Robert Lowell. Such pessimism is not a peculiarly modern phenomenon; but post-Darwin the primal darkness has taken one step nearer. In *Poets of Reality* (1966), J. Hillis Miller writes: 'The special place of Joseph Conrad in English literature lies in the fact that in him the nihilism covertly dominant in modern culture is brought to the surface and shown for what it is'.[19] As in Stein's words in *Lord Jim*, society is a house of cards poised over an abyss. The Victorian illusion that mind can understand and control matter, can create a permanent civilized order, is shattered. Instead the eternal knitting machine annihilates mind. It knits us in and it knits us out.

Conrad would have agreed with the American poet Louis Simpson's scorn in 'Moving the Walls' for the Victorian attempt to transform leviathan into a museum-piece:

> Idiots.
> We too are all for reducing
> The universe to human dimensions.
> As if we could know what is human!

5

But how can human art fail to reduce the universe to human dimensions? What kind of artistic vision is appropriate to Conrad's pessimism? The withering paradox, with which Conrad struggled so desperately, is that the artist must be engaged in making shapes to prove that shapes cannot be made, in giving form to the formless. Like T. S. Eliot when he was composing *The Waste Land*, Conrad is seeking a *modus vivendi* to save him from silence in art and suicide in life.

In *The Limits of Metaphor* (1967), James Guetti explores how writers such as Melville, Conrad and Faulkner cope with this modern situation, and how they adequately express the inadequacies of language. Their narrative techniques exhibit a fundamental imaginative instability, a failure to compose experience in any way or to create coherent metaphorical structures of any sort. Ishmael, Marlow, Quentin Compson surround problematic experience with disparate allusions and suggestions, never emphasizing a single perspective as definite, and constantly relying, at crucial moments, upon the nearly simultaneous use of separate kinds of language and upon similes of the greatest but vaguest dimensions. Uncertain about the mimetic function of words, feeling that artistic consciousness is always, in a sense, outside 'life', Conrad seeks for imaginative formulations to prevent his readers from resting at ease in illusion. In *Heart of Darkness* we sense the inadequacy of language to express the existences that lie outside the thinking mind. Marlow is engaged on a quest, on a search into the interior for truth. This arouses an expectation in the reader of an approaching revelation, but the outcome frustrates this desire. For Conrad, a prime purpose of the novelist should be manipulation of the reader's responses. The breakings of time scheme, the multiple points of view, the device of the reflector within a reflector, ensure that no coherent interpretation can be imposed on the novel. Perspectives shift, waver, disperse, like mist on water.

According to Conrad, one possible response to the suicidal claims of moral nihilism is a stoical recognition of the precarious status of mind. The artist builds in language an acknowledgement of our incomprehension, a form of poised irresolution. Modern art, as Frank Kermode has written, goes out into the neutral air, remains in an area of non-commitment. In Conrad's greatest works there is no conclusive resolution of meanings; endlessness is made an end. Hillis Miller describes how the novels hover between contradictions, light and darkness, motion and stillness, personality and anonymity, nothingness and substance, speech and silence, meaning and meaninglessness, servitude and freedom, time and eternity.

It is this 'stoical recognition of the precarious status of mind' which has fascinated me in Conrad, and made me want to write a book about him. This recognition is a basic element in the modern imagination, and, in my opinion, it has now become a necessary constituent in the sensibility of all intelligent human beings who respond truthfully to their environment. Yet even today, after so many great works of art have embodied this point of view, there is an intense emotional resistance to the complex difficulties involved in this stance. I admire Conrad for his courage in making his own journey into the darkness, and for his search for a kind of sensibility that might survive in the universe of the knitting machine. This quest is inadequately reflected in his non-fictional writings, which particularly in his last days tend to simplify his essential vision. I have chosen to examine the major novels at length, because it is only here that we can see the full expression of Conrad's modern imagination. I begin with *Lord Jim*, because this novel offers for inspection all the central problems.

Conrad's efforts to put this new sensibility into words are not always successful. He found the full artistic expression of his inner-most being an incalculable strain on his resources of nervous energy, and even his greatest works include major flaws when the tired imagination chooses the easy way out. Like T. S. Eliot, he was often unsure about the effects he intended to achieve. Nor is there a clear development of ideas throughout his work. As he seeks for a *modus vivendi*, he veers and tacks, and perhaps occasionally makes some headway. But in *The Secret Agent* he is blown back to a position of extreme pessimism, and in *The Arrow of Gold*, *The Rescue*, *The Rover* and *Suspense* he indulges in sentimental evasions. His major weakness is that, by and large, he fails to find imaginative forms to express a person's commitment to a loving relationship with another human being. This is perhaps why his work has tended to be less popular with women. But in his great novels he offers to the twentieth century what Ian Watt has called 'bifocal vision'. His art presents to us a way of responding to life which accepts the validity of incompatible modes of apprehension, which commits itself to meaning in an apparently meaningless universe. To this I shall return in my last chapter.

6

In numerous fictions, Conrad looks for an answer to nihilism in the sense of community and solidarity inspired by life on ship-board. As we have seen, he himself was far from being the extrovert adventurer and seaman of popular legend; he had a difficult, unstable character, which in later years depended for support on the common sense and equanimity of his wife. Yet his sea years proved the strength of his will to survive. Conditions at sea were brutally hard, and involved a self-discipline extending over months and years. From the age of twenty, when he joined the English freighter, *Mavis*, he had to make his way among strangers whose language he only gradually acquired. He was deservedly proud of his extraordinary success in eventually qualifying for his master's certificate in 1886.

He began his first novel, *Almayer's Folly*, in 1889, and managed to persuade Fisher Unwin to publish it in 1895. This was followed by a second apprentice work, *An Outcast of the Islands*, in 1896, and by his acknowledge masterpiece, *The Nigger of the 'Narcissus'*, in 1897. These three novels represent one kind of progression in Conrad's writing, from the outcasts of the two early novels to the triumphant vindication of the seaman's code in the character of Singleton in *The Nigger of the 'Narcissus'*. I shall deal with them briefly, for they do not embody in any complete way the profoundly modern sensibility of Conrad which is my prime concern.

Almayer's Folly, which includes some pretentious over-writing, is a story of decadence and breakdown, of exhaustion and frustration. Almayer has married a Malay girl, and taken charge of a river trading post, where he dreams of luxury and riches. But he is incompetent, a pathetic failure whose visions end only in opium-smoking, and his eventual death. My memory of this novel is of the omnipresence of the jungle, so heavy, drowsy and vast that it reduces the characters to insignificance. In *A Reader's Guide to Joseph Conrad* (1960), Frederick R. Karl draws attention to the similarities between the poetic language of the 1890s and Conrad's early work. In the writings of Arthur Symons and Ernest Dowson, there is the same assortment of exhausted objects: 'the drear oblivion of lost things'. Almayer's ruined business premises, surrounded by the oppressive atmosphere of the jungle, provide Conrad with an image for his despair. Karl writes:

> Among Conrad's contemporaries, this imagery had of course gained prominence—in the necropolis of James Thomson's nocturnal imagination, in Dowson's personal laments, in Beardsley's nihilistic sketches, in the pessimism of John Davidson's distorted visions; it would reappear in Housman's *A Shropshire Lad* (1896) and come to fruition in Conrad's own 'Heart of Darkness' (1899), in which a personal malaise became objective and gained epic proportions.[20]

An Outcast of the Islands is similarly full of images of desolation, of a sense of debility and impotence. Willems is a study of a man who falls from power into a wasted life of treachery and self-disgust. He is seduced by Aissa, a native girl, and this 'abominable desire' destroys his character. The whole movement of the novel is towards death. The jungle towers over the characters, emphasizing their isolation and futility.

The Nigger of the 'Narcissus' escapes from this fetid atmosphere, and Conrad's style becomes more restrained and precise. The crew in this novel are faced by two tests, to survive the storm and to overcome the subversive anarchy symbolized by the waster, Donkin, and the sick negro, James Wait. In the storm, one of Conrad's greatest descriptive pieces, the ship becomes an archetype for human society on its journey through an inexplicable universe: 'Nothing seems left of the whole universe but darkness, clamour, fury—and the ship. And like the last vestige of a shattered creation she drifts, bearing an anguished remnant of sinful mankind, through the distress, tumult, and pain of an avenging terror.' The sea and the storm represent Nature's insane violence in her dealings with man: 'A big, foaming sea came out of the mist; it made for the ship, roaring wildly, and in its rush it looked as mischievous and discomposing as a madman with an axe.' The crew survive this ordeal, and at the end, after they have been paid off in London, the narrator pays tribute to their courage and endurance. For a moment the world of greed and suffering is magically transmuted by the light of their heroism:

> The dark knot of seamen drifted in sunshine. To the left of them the trees in Tower Gardens sighed, the stones of the Tower gleaming, seemed to stir on the play of light, as if remembering suddenly all the great joys and sorrows of the past, the fighting prototypes of these men; pressgangs; mutinous cries; the wailing of women by the riverside, and the shouts of men welcoming victories. The sunshine of heaven fell like a gift of grace on the mud of the earth, on the remembering and mute stones, on greed, selfishness; on the anxious faces of forgetful men. And to the right of the dark group the stained front of the Mint, cleansed by the flood of light, stood out for a moment dazzling and white like a marble palace in a fairy tale. The crew of the 'Narcissus' drifted out of sight. (p. 172)

Conrad's suicidal despair finds relief, just for a moment, in this 'gift of grace'. But the novel is not just a simple justification of the community of the ship. James Wait's sickness tempts the crew in insidious ways which point forward to the complexities of Conrad's later fiction. Their duty as seamen is corrupted by pity for the malingerer, and they

are lost in moral ambiguities which finally seduce even their Captain.
There is a sense that the order of the ship necessitates a withdrawal of
human sympathies, and that its straightforward concept of duty can
satisfy only simple, unimaginative men like Singleton. In *Typhoon*, in
which Captain MacWhirr represents the stolid, dutiful seaman, the
hurricane breaks in upon the orderly arrangements of his privacy with
a threat that undermines, though only temporarily, his sense of the
fitness of things. The ship's discipline may represent only a form of
human illusion by which men evade the ultimate realities of an absurd
universe. This is the frightening possibility which Conrad examines
with such honesty and subtlety in his major fictions. In the novels from
Heart of Darkness (1899) and *Lord Jim* (1900) to *Under Western Eyes*
(1911), he still feels affection for men who submit themselves to the
demands of hard work, but their integrity no longer provides him with
final solutions for his own quest into the nature of moral reality.

7

Conrad's modern imagination presents difficult problems to the critic.
What can rational criticism say about literature which, to a certain
degree, denies the validity of reason? Recently a university professor
began a lecture on Samuel Beckett by pointing out that his enterprise
would seem absurd to Beckett. This did not prevent him from con-
tinuing with fifty minutes of polished exegesis. *Heart of Darkness*, for
example, rejects the simplistic interpretation of critics. Baines's
biography is excellent in its treatment of the life, but almost always
inadequate in its critical commentary on the fiction. After quoting
Conrad telling Cunninghame Graham that the idea behind *Heart of
Darkness* is so wrapped up that his friend may miss it, Baines writes:

> So wrapped up is it that one wonders whether Conrad was always
> clear as to his intention and whether one is justified in trying to
> unravel the story to the extent of imparting a coherent meaning to
> it.[21]

Here Baines fails to comprehend an art concerned to express a profound
metaphysical scepticism, to be coherent about what must remain
incoherent. On another occasion Baines writes straightforwardly in a
manner characteristic of much Conrad criticism about how in Patusan
Lord Jim was 'blameless' to let the desperado Gentleman Brown go
free. Baines thinks that when Brown betrays this trust, Jim is absolutely

right to deliver himself up to Doramin, knowing that Doramin would exact death as retribution for Brown's killing of his son: 'Some critics have asserted that Jim's life ended in defeat but despite the reference to his "exalted egoism" which recalls Brierly's suicide there can be little doubt that Conrad approved of Jim's action'. [22] Conrad might have replied: 'If only issues were so simple!' In *Lord Jim* Conrad creates multiple points of view towards Jim's martyrdom, in order to disturb his readers into a lively sense of the uncertainties involved in moral action. Talking of 'The Secret Sharer', Baines says that 'Conrad had no wish to condemn Leggatt but considered him an honourable man who had done something that other honourable men might equally well have done under similar circumstances'. [23] Conrad is not thinking in these terms. Baines's language is too assertive, too categorical, in its discussion of motivation. He is out of touch with an artistic sensibility that feeds on irresolution, that makes art out of uncertainty, and considers human rationality an illusion.

The suicide of Brierly in *Lord Jim* provides me with a brief illustration of Conrad's approach to moral questions. The story is mediated to us through the subtle, wavering narration of Marlow; and Marlow himself is not a first-hand observer of many important details. The account of the drowning is told to him two years later by Mr Jones, Brierly's mate, whose selection of material is influenced by prejudice and sentimentality. The suicide remains mysterious, held at a distance because only known through these partial explanations. This element of mystery is also evoked by certain bizarre effects. Just before he jumps overboard, Brierly sets the log, and even puts in a drop of oil. His efficiency does not desert him even at the end, and yet ironically his suicide undermines his belief in confident service of the social order imposed by ship routine. The detail of the oil adds a little touch of absurdity, a hint that human habits of order are laughable illusion.

Both Marlow and Jones introduce doubt into their narration: 'He was *probably* holding silent enquiry into his own case', says Marlow about Brierly's behaviour in the courtroom. After describing how Brierly put four iron belaying-pins in his pockets to weigh him down, Jones interjects: '*Maybe* his confidence in himself was just shook a bit at the last'. These uncertainties can be seen in the following paragraph:

> The sight of that watery-eyed old Jones mopping his bald head with a red cotton handkerchief, the sorrowing yelp of the dog, the squalor of that fly-blown cuddy which was the only shrine of

his memory, threw a veil of inexpressibly mean pathos over Brierly's remembered figure, the posthumous revenge of fate for that belief in his own splendour which had almost cheated his life of its legitimate terrors. Almost! Perhaps wholly. Who can tell what flattering view he had induced himself to take of his own suicide? (p. 64)

The story comes through a 'veil'. The mean pathos is 'inexpressible'. Such words, often repeated, reflect the impossibility of complete communication. And the final sentence is a question. We can never know Brierly's state of mind, for Marlow's supposition may be quite wrong.

We must speak in terms of probabilities. Brierly says to Marlow about the *Patna*: 'Such an affair destroys one's confidence'. Apparently Jim acts as a mirror for Brierly, as he does for Marlow. They recognize in him hidden aspects of their own nature. Jones finds words for Marlow's own view of Brierly: 'Ay, Ay! neither you nor I, sir, had ever thought so much of ourselves'.

And so we come to the enigma. Brierly's suicide, like Jim's own decision to die, results apparently from a consciousness of his own unworthiness. Is it true, therefore, that the order of society is suited only to less imaginative natures? Are Brierly and Jim superior because of their awareness of their inadequacy? Is all human activity a sham, only acceptable to the deluded and the hypocritical? Is the man who commits suicide the man who sees most? The novel offers no complete resolution, hovering uncertainly around these uncertainties. For a critic to offer some final conclusion about Brierly's conduct is to abuse the novel's essence as a work of art. *Lord Jim* dramatizes the claims both of a complete moral nihilism and a commitment to ideals of service to the community; the novel never rests finally in any decisive posture. Yet both alternatives exist in their own powerful right; Marlow acknowledges the values of scepticism, yet lives on and continues in the quest for meaning, for acceptable standards of loyalty. The determination to go on with the exploration into the nature of moral reality is itself a kind of positive virtue.

As his best, Conrad insists that we must live with our uncertainties, and not evade our enigmas. Confronted by the mystery of human experience, he offers us strange high-sounding phrases whose implications are deliberately left unclear. These we take away with us, finding in them what satisfaction we can—'The horror! The horror!', 'in the destructive element immerse', 'heart of darkness'.

Chapter 2

The Metamorphoses of Lord Jim

> the solving emptiness
> That lies just under all we do . . .
>
> PHILIP LARKIN, 'Ambulances'

I

At times we might wonder if Conrad believed with Pythagoras in the transmigration of souls. In *Lord Jim* we recall how, on his arrival back in port, the German Captain of the *Patna* is transformed first into a trained baby elephant walking on hind-legs, then into a sixteen-hundredweight sugar-hogshead wrapped in striped flannelette, and finally into an immense green-and-orange beetle burrowing into a ramshackle gharry as if it were a ripe cotton-pod. The Captain then vanishes for ever, flying into space like a witch on a broomstick.

The status of these several metamorphoses varies. The elephant is merely a fanciful analogy which occurs to Marlow, while the sugar-hogshead is a temporary hallucination of Archie Ruthvel, the principal shipping-master. We can put these aside, perhaps, as temporary freaks of mind occasioned by the German's huge bulk. But the gaudy beetle is less easy to categorize, for the whole passage infiltrates in a disturbing way into the supposedly realistic form of Marlow's narration. The Captain takes off into an extraordinary world whose comic absurdity might seem more appropriate to *Alice's Adventures in Wonderland*. He shuffles his feet as if to free his ankles from some invisible and mysterious grasp (mysterious, of course, is one of Conrad's favourite words); he makes himself so warm his bullet head positively smokes. His disappearance seems a magical event. Apparently the gharry vanishes too, for Marlow tells us he never again came across the sorrel pony with its slit ear or the lackadaisical Tamil driver afflicted by a sore foot. This bizarre episode appears to Marlow 'like one of those grotesque and distinct visions that scare and fascinate one in a fever'.

Conrad's characters make a habit of vanishing or of appearing from nowhere. In *Victory*, Heyst's servant, Wang, habitually materializes and dematerializes. His departures suggest a 'vanishing out of existence rather than out of sight, a process of evaporation rather than of movement'. Some examples in *Lord Jim* are comparatively trivial. After introducing Marlow, Stein's Javanese servant disappears 'in a mysterious way as though he had been a ghost only momentarily embodied for that particular service'. This detail recalls boys' adventure stories, the world of Sax Rohmer and Fu Manchu, but serves a purpose in creating a suitably weird atmosphere for Stein's ambiguous pronouncements on life and romance. Tamb' Itam, Jim's servant in Patusan, possesses a similar oriental facility for disappearing and then springing up close to people as if from the ground. Another example is Cornelius, the stepfather of Jewel who is Jim's native mistress. Cornelius is one of several characters transformed like the German Captain into a repulsive beetle. After the emotional interview during which Marlow fails to convince Jewel of Jim's reliability, Cornelius bolts out, vermin-like, from the long grass growing in a depression of the earth, as if when out of Marlow's purview he inhabits some other dimension of being.

Both Stein and Jim participate in the Conradian vanishing act. In the famous interview with Marlow, Stein's head occasionally disappears in a cloud of smoke from his pipe, and, when he is at last ready to communicate his suggested cure for Jim's malady, he drifts off away from the lamp into 'shapeless dusk', 'as if these few steps had carried him out of this concrete and perplexed world'. Jim performs this trick at the end of his harrowing breakdown in Marlow's room after the verdict has deprived him of his mate's certificate. As the noise and glare of a thunderstorm grow in intensity, Jim rushes out onto the verandah:

> The growl of the thunder increased steadily while I looked at him, distinct and black, planted solidly upon the shores of a sea of light. At the moment of greatest brilliance the darkness leaped back with a culminating crash, and he vanished before my dazzled eyes as utterly as though he had been blown to atoms. (p. 177–8)

Conrad's characters vanish or change shape because they exist as fictional images whose status remains perpetually in doubt. In *Lord Jim* they usually appear through the reflector of Marlow's imagination, dressed in the forms of language deemed appropriate by him at some given moment; but as artist and narrator Marlow is not sure in what genre he is composing his story, and so his images are constantly changing, like patterns in a kaleidoscope. When reading Conrad we often feel that his characters exist only in the consciousness of a beholder, and that their shape and quality depend on the perceiver's method of apprehension. When they depart from the scene of the narrative, they seem to walk out of life. What language or imagery is appropriate for a phenomenon such as the German Captain? His vanishing act is a joke, a sport of Marlow's imagination, but his freakish metamorphoses are a sign of Conrad's uncertainty about the modes of language suitable for reality. Human beings are indeed 'mysterious' to Conrad, and no one kind of description is adequate. The German Captain cannot be satisfactorily presented in the conventional words of realism. Conrad sees him as an extraordinary, inexplicable lump of flesh, as peculiar and crazy in his human manifestation as if he had jumped onto the earth from a distant planet. In *Through the Looking-Glass* Tweedledee asks Alice where she supposes she would be if the King stopped dreaming about her. 'You'd be nowhere. Why, you're only a sort of thing in his dream', he tells her. This appears to be the status of the German Captain (as of Patusan), who once outside Marlow's dream steps off the earth into nothingness. Marlow writes in a tone of ironic astonishment, and in this he appears at one with his creator. It is no more surprising that the Captain should fly off on a broomstick than that he should be there at all. We know that he is disgusting and contemptible, and it is worth emphasizing here, before we lose ourselves in too much epistemological uncertainty, that the moral perspective in this instance is clear. But when we seek for an authoritative viewpoint about the proper kind of imagery to embody these mysteries, we find ourselves confronted only by enigma.

The Pythagorean transformations are by and large a manifestation of Marlow's wit, except for the disappearing acts of Stein and Jim, with which I shall deal later. Many commentators on this novel take Marlow's words too literally, presuming that his narrative is uniform in tone and that he speaks truth. This approach ignores his many references to literary types, and his constantly questioning attitude towards every manipulation of language he employs. In *The Metaphysics of Darkness*, Royal Roussel points out that, as with Kurtz, Marlow's interest in Jim is an expression of his own concerns. Jim is a test case most obviously for Marlow's allegiance to the group and the ethos defined by the phrase 'one of us'. Yet Jim's symbolic quality refers also to Conrad's problems as an artist:

> In the pattern that dominates Conrad's fiction of this period, a pattern in which the voyage of the adventurer becomes a metaphor for the act of writing, Jim's symbolic quality will inevitably have an aesthetic reference as well. He is ... both sailor and artist, and in the *Patna* incident Conrad has given us an analysis not only of the destruction of Jim's dreams of heroism, but of the dissolution of a certain kind of art which is implicit in his dreams.[1]

Jim himself wants to play the romantic lead in a boy's adventure story, confronting savages and quelling mutinies, and he discovers his vocation for the sea after a course of light holiday literature. He wants to live as a butterfly, as if, in Gentleman Brown's words, he 'were one of those people that should have wings so as to go about without touching the dirty earth'. But Marlow is unsure what role Jim is playing, and in what kind of play.

2

Each of T. S. Eliot's *Four Quartets* includes a section discussing the problem of how far words are valid as an expression of thought and emotion, and it is not surprising that a similar concern should appear in *Lord Jim*. As Jim and Marlow try to understand his 'jump', to find an appropriate form in which to comprehend this enigmatic event, they are led to question whether words can ever prove adequate to the task. At first Jim thinks that 'only a meticulous precision of statement would bring out the true horror behind the appalling face of things'. But, as the Inquiry proceeds on its quest for facts, Jim changes his mind: 'The sound of his own truthful statements confirmed his deliberate opinion that speech was of no use to him any longer.' This authorial insight into Jim's mind is granted to us by the anonymous narrator who is responsible for the opening chapters. Appropriately only a couple of sentences after this rejection of speech by Jim, Marlow is introduced, to offer us his own strange arrangements of language as a means of encompassing reality. For Marlow the Inquiry's questions beat futilely around the well-known fact, as instructive as the tapping with a hammer on an iron box when the object is to find out what is inside.

To the reader Marlow is at various times garrulous, contradictory and ambiguous. As he seeks for the right formula to help Jim after the verdict, he reflects: 'And a word carries far—very far—deals destruction through time as the bullets go flying through space.' At other times we wish he would speak to us with this kind of directness and force; his equivocations frustrate our desire to understand. It is appropriate that several of the characters he describes to us cannot speak English properly. The half-caste master of the brigantine that transports Jim to Patusan uses a flowing English which 'seemed to be derived from a dictionary compiled by a lunatic'. The obscurity of Stein's famous pronouncements is considerably increased by his distortion of conventional usage.

In Patusan, Marlow virtually admits that his arrangements of words are an evasion of reality; this is one of the most revealing scenes in the novel. Jewel has been recounting to him the horror of her mother's death, made so painful by Cornelius outside the room, banging at the door for admittance. The story has the power to drive Marlow out of his conception of existence, 'out of that shelter each of us makes for himself to creep under in moments of danger, as a tortoise withdraws into its shell':

> For a moment I had a view of a world that seemed to wear a vast and dismal aspect of disorder, while, in truth, thanks to our unwearied efforts, it is as sunny an arrangement of small conveniences as the mind of man can conceive. But still—it was only a moment: I went back into my shell directly. One *must*—don't you know?—though I seemed to have lost all my words in the chaos of dark thoughts I had contemplated for a second or two beyond the pale. These came back, too, very soon, for words also belong to the sheltering conception of light and order which is our refuge. (p. 313)

According to this confession, words constitute our refuge against chaos. The world is palpably not just a sunny arrangement of small conveniences, and when Marlow says this he appears to be ignoring completely the tragedy of Jim's leap from the *Patna*. Like so many of his remarks, what he says 'in truth' is clearly not true. Here with Jewel, he acknowledges that his words are a mechanism for escape from reality. I agree with Peter K. Garrett, who argues that this speech marks a kind of development in Marlow's consciousness:

> Marlow's retreat is not simply a relapse into 'agreeable somno-
> lence'; the change in his state of consciousness is reflected in the
> irony with which he preserves self-awareness even as he reinstates
> the necessary illusions.[2]

For Garrett, his ability to maintain this tension causes his values to
appear as earned, not blindly acepted.

At several significant moments both Marlow and Jim can find no
words to express their feelings. Marlow can find nothing to say to help
Jim while he struggles to regain his composure after the verdict. Jim's
final messages, in speech and writing, are incomplete. Yet the total
experience of the novel does not support a negative attitude towards
language. We can adequately acknowledge, with a verbal paradox, that
words are inadequate. The existence of the novel presupposes there is
some virtue in seeking appropriate form, even if the quest can never be
finally successful. Although life is an irrational chaos, with no possibility of a discovery of an organizing image, Conrad believes the
determination to search for one witnesses to a desirable framework of
mind. Otherwise, why write a novel?

3

Throughout his career Conrad usually drew back from bruising
contact with the dislocated horrors of absurdist art. Like Marlow, he
seeks images that will make sense of his experience. He welcomes the
sheltering concepts of light and order, the life illusion which may keep
back the tempting overtures of suicide. But there are moments when he
seems quite close to Kafka. One of these occurs when Marlow visits the
chief engineer of the *Patna*, who is in hospital suffering from *delirium
tremens*. He informs Marlow that the ship was full of reptiles, and
invites him to inspect the millions of pink toads under his bed. For him,
Nature has proved untrustworthy; its phenomena may seem rational
under normal conditions, but at any moment may metamorphose
themselves into menacing shapes. In his delirium he inhabits a universe
whose forms he cannot control, and which seems determined to
destroy him. That his hallucinations have some general applicability to
the human condition is shown by Marlow's reactions. For an instant he
almost enters the nightmare; his imagination transforms the engineer
into the non-human. The sick man's arm, thin like a tentacle, claws at
Marlow's shoulder, while a wolfish howl tears at his soul. He perceives

behind the eyes a spectral alarm: 'a nondescript form of a terror crouching silently behind a pane of glass'. Normal sight seems false covering behind which lurks a terror that ordered language cannot describe. At the scene's climax, the horror breaks out from behind the glassy gaze, and surges forward to claim the world for its own. The face 'decomposed'; the man's normal 'old-soldier' aspect appears to have been just painted illusion. As the engineer yells out for help, Marlow feels that ordinary life has receded into the distance: 'a dresser, aproned to the chin, showed himself in the vista of the ward, as if seen in the small end of a telescope.' Perspectives change, as if, like K. in *The Trial*, Marlow had opened a door and found behind it a scene of abnormal cruelty; or as if he had woken to find himself metamorphosed into a huge insect. Nature is out of the control of the ordering devices of the mind. When Marlow leaves, he tells the resident surgeon that the engineer's evidence is not in the least material to the inquiry. Maybe not, but his fantasies proffer an interpretation of reality that the whole novel cannot so easily shrug away.

A similar kind of perspective image, reminiscent of Lewis Carroll, occurs in the verandah scene. As Marlow writes letters, waiting for Jim to control himself, he recalls Chester's offer to take Jim to the guano island:

> All at once, on the blank page, under the very point of the pen, the two figures of Chester and his antique partner, very distinct and complete, would dodge into view with stride and gestures, as if reproduced in the field of some optical toy. I would watch them for a while. No! They were too phantasmal and extravagant to enter into any one's fate. (p. 174)

Like a novelist, Marlow wonders where next to send his hero. A few moments later Jim performs the vanishing act described earlier in this chapter. When he reappears Marlow will transform him first into a water-clerk, and then into the hero of Patusian. His fictional roles shrink or expand, as under some optical toy, through Marlow's manipulations. At first the grotesqueries of Chester and Holy-Terror Robinson are rejected for the security of the position of water-clerk. When this proves impossible, Marlow invents a romantic paradise of adventure, closely in accord with Jim's dream. But at the end the extravagant, diabolical figure of Gentleman Brown can no longer be kept at the wrong end of the telescope. His grotesque menace breaks through the illusions of heroic action.

On occasions Jim appears like a tragic hero, surrounded by immensity, assaulted by mysterious forces from sea and sky. Conrad's ability to recreate the energies of Nature in a colourful, forceful style confers an heroic status on the sailors who struggle with her moods. We think of Singleton in *The Nigger of the 'Narcissus'* or MacWhirr in *Typhoon*, and even Jim at times appears to symbolize solitary man opposing a malevolent universe. We sympathize with him because he will never abandon his dreams of heroic endeavour. We see him poised against the hugeness of the sky, the fury of the storm. But among tragic heroes Jim is closest to Hamlet, and it is appropriate that Stein should quote from that play in his famous scene with Marlow. Jim's imagination paralyses his ability to act, and like Hamlet he seems at times trapped in a universe whose salient characteristics are those of comic burlesque rather than tragedy. Jim himself is conscious of this absurdity as he watches the crew's attempts to launch a boat from the *Patna*. Three times they push out the boat, and three times it swings back in again, driving them back, helpless and jostling against each other. Jim, as reported by Marlow, thinks the wind is converting their desperate exertions into a bit of fooling, 'fit for knockabout clowns in a farce'. He is caught in a situation of low comedy, a kind of cosmic joke hatched in hell. Marlow comments: 'In this assault upon his fortitude there was the jeering intention of a spiteful and vile vengeance; there was an element of burlesque in his ordeal—a degradation of funny grimaces in the approach of death or dishonour.' The poor donkeyman dies of a heart attack because of his fear, fooled into killing himself by the supposed certainty that the *Patna* will sink. Jim finds this droll: if only the man had stayed in bed and told the crew to go to the devil when they rushed into his bunk with their story of the collision, he would have survived. Later in the open boat, the men seem cut off from the rest of mankind, in their extremity a prey to burlesque meanness, to the 'Irrational that lurks at the bottom of every thought, sentiment, sensation, emotion'.

Jim is forced continually into the company of grotesques. There is the German Captain, whose vanishing act I have already discussed. There is Chester, the West Australian, with his crazy dream of a rich guano island (a parody of Stein's romantic idea of Patusan), and his companion, the senile Holy-Terror Robinson, 'as patient and still as a worn-out cab-horse'. Egstrom's partner, Blake, for whom Jim works as a water-clerk, upbraids his associate constantly, screaming like an outraged cockatoo. On his death-bed Gentleman Brown glares at

Marlow 'like some man-beast of folklore'. On these occasions Jim appears to inhabit a society of demented creatures.

   This mixture of the tragic and the farcical reflects the violent, disjointed, extravagant nature of much modern literature. Thomas Mann once remarked that in his lifetime the traditional categories of comedy and tragedy had disappeared, leaving the grotesque as the dominant literary mode. We see this process at work in the *Patna* incident. Marlow tells us: 'It was tragic enough and funny enough in all conscience to call aloud for compassion. . . .' A similar mixture of forms occurs in the verandah scene. The thunderstorm provides a tragic backcloth for Jim's suffering. But as the rain falls, a perforated waterpipe performs outside the window 'a parody of blubbering woe with funny sobs and gurgling lamentations, interrupted by jerky spasms of silence'. It chokes and splashes 'in odious ridicule of a swimmer fighting for his life'. As elsewhere in Conrad, inanimate objects behave with malevolent intention, like goblins cruelly parodying the misery of humans. Even at this climax, the Absurd must have its due.

4

As he tries to find language for his uncertainties, to reveal disorder through orderly syntax, Conrad often turns to patterns of light and darkness. His imagination seeks to comprehend Jim not only through the forms of tragedy or burlesque, but also as a composition of gleams and shadows. In his Preface to *The Nigger of the 'Narcissus'*, Conrad argues that fiction must be impressionistic:

> All art, therefore, appeals primarily to the senses, and the artistic aim when expressing itself in written words must also make its appeal through the senses, if its high desire is to reach the secret spring of responsive emotions. It must strenuously aspire to the plasticity of sculpture, to the colour of painting, and to the magic suggestions of music—which is the art of arts. And it is only through complete, unswerving devotion to the perfect blending of form and substance; it is only through an unremitting never-discouraged care for the shape and ring of sentences that an approach can be made to plasticity, to colour, and that the light of magic suggestiveness may be brought to play for an evanescent instant over the common-place surface of words: of the old, old words, worn thin, defaced by ages of careless usage. (p. ix)

This passage draws attention to Conrad's faith in the power of art to communicate some kind of meaning. His scepticism makes him treat the human rage for order ironically, but he believes that meaning can be apprehended in gleams and hints. His eloquence implies a positive faith in words which works against completely nihilistic interpretations. Dissatisfied with rational discussion of motives (at many crucial moments we are told little about Jim's inner state of mind), Conrad conveys his impression through arrangement of visual effects. Marlow often explains that he found it easier to conceive Jim not through language but as a gleam of light. After their meal in the club, Marlow experiences one of these flashes of insight:

> He heard me out with his head on one side, and I had another glimpse through a rent in the mist in which he moved and had his being. The dim candle spluttered within the ball of glass, and that was all I had to see him by; at his back was the dark night with the clear stars, whose distant glitter disposed in retreating planes lured the eye into the depths of a greater darkness; and yet a mysterious light seemed to show me his boyish head, as if in that moment the youth within him had, for a moment, gleamed and expired. (p. 128)

Jim often appears like this as a speck in a dark void. A suitable painting to accompany Conrad's fiction would be a huge canvas completely black, except for in the centre a gleam of fierce light. As Jim stands on the verandah, Marlow tells us: 'through the open door the outer edge of the light from my candle fell on his back faintly; beyond all was black; he stood on the brink of a vast obscurity, like a lonely figure by the shore of a sombre and hopeless ocean.' Later, as Marlow leaves him for the last time, Jim gradually diminishes in size, until at last he is only 'a tiny white speck that seemed to catch all the light, left in a darkened world' (p. 336). The amount of symbolism in these descriptions is not constant. They are based on real observation, and intended as impressionist pictures. On one occasion, the prevailing pattern is reversed, and Jim is seen as a point of blackness against a sea of light. These scenes are imbued with an attractive grandeur. Darkness is mysterious, and the gleams of light, the individuals whose wills oppose annihilation, shine the brighter by contrast. There is nothing sordid or distasteful about such descriptions of Nature. They suggest compassion for Jim's solitude and insignificance in the cosmos. For Marlow the search for understanding of another human being is like plunging your gaze to the bottom of an immensely deep well: 'What is it that moves there? you ask yourself. Is it a blind monster or only a lost gleam from the universe?' Such gleams give us a moment of truth, 'like a twist of lightning that admits the eye for an instant into the secret convolutions of a cloud'. What lies behind appearances may be either nightmare or vision; both possibilities are entertained by the novel and there is no final reconciliation.

5

In *Lord Jim*, therefore, Conrad is exploring the adequacy of literary forms, indeed of language itself, and engaging in the modernist's quest for a new kind of fiction. This search is mirrored in Jim's own adventures, as he seeks for heroic action, for a true relation to the community, for his proper identity. The book asks questions about the nature of perception and of moral will to which it cannot give conclusive answers. This seems to me the correct approach to all the uncertainties and ambiguities of the narrative.

And so we return to the central episodes, like Marlow unable to resist the desire to understand, to explain. What exactly happens on the occasions when Jim is paralysed by fear? What light, or darkness, is thrown on these questions by Stein? Conrad felt that the novel divided itself unfortunately into halves. What impulses persuaded him to send Jim to the shadowy jungles of Patusan? The word 'Patusan' almost echoes 'Patna'; what is the relation between the two adventures?

The anonymous narrator of the first four chapters is more certain than Marlow in his judgments: 'He was an inch, perhaps two, under six feet', he begins, with an affirmative use of the verb 'to be'. We start with a confident sense of our location in historical time and space, and we realize that Jim has a representative status. He is just under six feet, just below the ideal requirements for the romantic hero. This confidence remains undisturbed until the fourth chapter. The narrator provides us with useful entertaining information about the duties of water-clerks, and we appear to exist in an understandable world, where the mind may satisfy curiosity by the accumulation of facts. The narrator speaks with assurance, as if he were Captain Marryat recounting the exploits of Peter Simple. The description of the snug backwater inhabited by Jim's father is amused and tolerant; this is a safe world, in which author and reader share a common faith in bravery, discipline and heroism. In these chapters Jim's progress reads like a *Bildungs-*

roman. He journeys through life in search of self-fulfilment, on a quest for the moment of discovery when he will enter into his true manhood.

Our doubts about Jim's fitness for the role of romantic hero are alerted by his moment of irresolution on the training-ship, when he fails to go to the help of two men thrown in the water by a collision. After it is all over, the narrator describes to us how Jim began to dream again of heroic adventures: 'Not a particle of fear was left'. This is the first time the word 'fear' is used. Previously Jim's paralysis of mind has been depicted as like a moment of vision: 'There was a fierce purpose in the gale, a furious earnestness in the screech of the wind, in the brutal tumult of earth and sky, that seemed directed at him, and made him hold his breath in awe. He stood still. . . .' 'Awe' is the word first used, not 'fear', and we may think that Jim's imagination has grasped a truth beyond the reach of the other boys. It is like the moment on the *Patna* when the brutal malevolence of the gale flings itself at Jim as if it had burst through something solid. At this moment his vision goes beyond conventional appearance; he acknowledges the power of death. He sees that Nature's ultimate purpose is to destroy him, and he is transfixed by this knowledge. Most of us do not *know* we are to die in the way Jim now perceives his destiny. We evade this reality by deluding ourselves with work or passion or ambition. The scene takes place in the 'falling darkness at the end of a winter's day'. For a second or so, the cutter, about to rescue the drowning men, is held perfectly still, under the spell of wind and tide. Above on deck, Jim is similarly motionless as if under the same spell. As elsewhere in Conrad, the action freezes into stasis at some crucial moment in the psychological drama. In a lightning flash, the Conradian hero realizes that existence is not moving inevitably towards a different future, but is always now. Time and progress are great fallacies, behind which remain the elemental images. Nature is brutal, and this cannot change an inch or an ounce. Previously Jim had enjoyed looking down on life from the fore-top, admiring the variety of ships and houses from a distance. Now he sees the truth. It is only later that the idea is inserted into our minds that all this may have been simply fear.

At the beginning of the second chapter, the narrator tells us that these glimpses of 'earnestness' in the anger of the sea occur only rarely. Just now and then a sinister violence of intention appears on the face of facts, an indefinable something 'which forces it upon the mind and the heart of a man, that this complication of accidents or these elemental furies are coming at him with a purpose of malice'. The aim of Nature is simply to smash, to destroy, to annihilate all he has seen, known, loved, enjoyed or hated, by the simple and appalling act of taking his life. Only the imaginative man sees this truth, for, says the narrator, imagination is the enemy of man and the father of all terrors. On the second occasion when Jim glimpses this reality he is disabled by a falling spar, and his lameness persists, even in Patusan. Once more the symbol draws attention to itself; the imaginative man is necessarily lamed by his special quality of insight. The same phenomenon occurs in other novelists of Conrad's time. Sensitivity to the realities of the post-Darwin world makes a man unfit for action, and this is symbolically represented by physical disability. There is Ralph Touchett's tuberculosis in Henry James's *The Portrait of a Lady*, or Rickie Elliot's club foot in E. M. Forster's *The Longest Journey*.

After his injury, Jim is left behind in a hospital at an Eastern port. Here perhaps the moral perspective is clear. At first, he regards the easy-going seamen of these Eastern seas with disdain. The narrator detects for us in this happy-go-lucky throng 'the soft spot, the place of decay, the determination to lounge safely through existence'. But soon Jim is bewitched by the eternal serenity of the East, by the temptation of infinite repose. He takes a berth as chief mate of the *Patna*.

6

As the *Patna* travels towards the hidden wreck, the regularity of the propeller's beat seems part of the scheme of a safe universe. On the bridge Jim feels 'penetrated by the great certitude of unbounded safety and peace that could be read on the silent aspect of nature like the certitude of fostering love upon the placid tenderness of a mother's face'. Man seems to be in control of the universe; the chart pegged out with four drawing pins is said to be as level and smooth as the glimmering surface of the waters. When they hit the wreck, it is as if a thunder had growled deep down in the water. Suddenly the calm sea, the sky without a cloud, appear 'formidably insecure in their immobility, as if poised on the brow of yawning destruction'. In one sense, Jim's romantic quest ends here, with the invasion of his life by a horror that lies behind the smoothness of appearances. It is a moment of recognition, of insight into ultimate reality.

About this moment the official Inquiry demands facts, the kind of facts we have been given by the anonymous narrator about Jim's early upbringing. Jim, like Conrad himself, realizes that facts explain nothing. As we have seen, it is time for the assurance of the anonymous narrator to be superseded by the twisting, sinuous account of Marlow. The chronological sequences are broken; the reader is perplexed by the convolutions of the narrative. Not until chapter seven do we learn that the bulkhead held out and the pilgrims were saved. The Victorian trust in an explicable orderly universe is deliberately flouted; we are left without bearings in an epistemological wilderness.

At first Jim behaves well. It is the sight of the bulge in the bulkhead that starts his imagination off in horror at the imminent death of the pilgrims. A flake of rust as big as the palm of his hand falls off: 'the thing stirred and jumped off like something alive while I was looking at it', he tells Marlow. Matter once more seems actively malevolent, determined on his destruction. His fear dries his mouth, and makes his knees wobble. These details are worth remembering, for they prove that he is instinctively prone to paralysing fear. Yet Jim insists, and we believe him, that at this time he did not think of saving himself. His imagination is obsessed by pictures of the drowning pilgrims, the horror of panic, the trampling rush, the pitiful screams, the boats swamped: 'eight hundred people and seven boats—and no time.' We must accept that Jim never doubted that at any second the ship would sink. Marlow tells us that in similar circumstances he would have been certain. As Jim is sure there is no time to do anything about the bulk-head, he stands impotent, watching the crew trying to launch a boat. After minutes of paralysis, he recalls his intention to cut the life-boats clear; and whipping out his knife he slashes at the ropes so that the boats will not be dragged down with the ship. Many critics of *Lord Jim* ignore this action. At least Jim did *something* to help the pilgrims. In his study of this novel, Tony Tanner mentions that Jim stood stock still for 27 minutes, whereas when the *Patna* was unloaded, it took only 25 minutes to carry off the pilgrims.[3] This seems to me unfair. Jim presumed the ship would sink at any second; he knew there were insufficient places in the boats. The real indictment becomes apparent when we hear the lies concocted by the German Captain. They could have launched the boats quietly; they could have tried to send off some of the pilgrims from the stricken ship. But presumably Jim would need the assistance of the crew for this. Instead he remains transfixed, and waits to be drowned. And then he moves: 'Something had started him off at last, but of the exact moment, of the cause that tore him out of his immobility, he knew no more than the uprooted tree knows of the wind that laid it low.' It is right for his move to be compared to a natural catastrophe, for as we assess its significance we are asking questions about the essence of life, the meaning of Nature. The voices below, like messages from his unconscious self, call on him to jump. As the squall bursts upon them, he obeys. He seems to make no conscious decision, but is strangely passive, a slave to unconscious demands. '"I had jumped . . ." He checked himself, averted his gaze . . . "It seems", he added.' Could this act be defined as a justified assertion of the will to live, the complete opposite of his suicidal martyrdom in Patusan? I do not see him clear, says Marlow. Should he have stayed on board to wait for an heroic death? He should certainly have opposed his will to that of the crew.

As the squall approaches, the men in their extremity appear to have broken through a veil, to have penetrated to a metaphysical blackness at the heart of things. It is no wonder the chief engineer eventually goes mad. Before the crash the *Patna* sails across the calm ocean in a dream-like movement 'as if the days were falling into an abyss for ever open in the wake of the ship'. Now, as the squall approaches, Jim falls into the abyss. The squall flies over the waters with conscious malevolence, like some voracious beast of the apocalypse. It eats up the sky, and swallows the stars. Jim accuses this infernal thing of sneaking up behind, to trap him like a beast. The wind and rain strike together with a peculiar impetuosity 'as if they had burst through something solid'. Jim jumps, as if into a well, into an everlasting deep hole. The storm is characterized first by stillness, without thunder or noise of wind, and then by blackness. The experience for Jim is as if his senses had been extinguished. At this moment of recognition, the ear cannot hear and the eye cannot see. The information offered by the senses is useless, its normal patterns of apprehension a forgotten illusion. His identity is snuffed out, vanishes. Later in the open boat, he feels like a man walled up in a roomy grave: 'No concern with anything on earth. Nobody to pass an opinion. Nothing mattered . . . No fear, no law, no sounds, no eyes—not even our own—till sunrise at least.' It is a searing unforgettable experience, which in future throws on all sensory stimuli an air of unreality.

The retired sailor who receives Marlow's packet of information about Jim's last days is sure that Jim is to be condemned. He maintains that 'we must fight in the ranks or our lives don't count'. Marlow has moments when he agrees. Curiously if the *Patna* had sunk immediately after Jim jumped, then he would not have seemed so guilty. Action is judged by society, and by Marlow, to some extent, according to consequences. Marlow feels that the real significance of the crime is in its being a breach of faith with the community of mankind, and from this point of view Jim was no mean traitor. Jim makes too much of his disgrace, while it is the guilt alone that matters. But he cannot accept that he is guilty. For the rest of his life he must struggle with a ghost, must prove to himself that the common view of him as a coward is untrue. Marlow wonders whether this conduct amounted to shirking his ghost or facing him out: 'It might have been flight and it might have been a mode of combat'.

7

Albert Guerard thinks that on a first reading we sympathize with Jim's jump, but on subsequent readings we recognize his guilt, and may feel that Marlow is too lenient. Most damning is the testimony of the French lieutenant who was on board the ship that rescued the *Patna*, and towed it into port. He is placid, reliable, stolid, imperturbable, as incapable of an emotional display as a sack of meal. Conrad applies to him one of his favourite words: immobility. Like many of Conrad's minor characters, the French lieutenant emerges from the shadows around the main events of the story like some ancient genie endowed with strange powers of insight. His immobility separates him from the perplexities of ordinary mortals, so that Marlow finds in him something occult, mysterious, almost miraculous. He is like a quiet village priest to whom it may be appropriate to confess one's sins. On the back of his hand there is a starred scar, the effect of a gunshot, and at the side of his temple a seam of an old wound from a spear or a sabre. Tony Tanner points out that Conrad, like Hemingway, uses the scar as a symbol of manhood: 'For Hemingway mutilations represent "the castigation that everyone receives who goes there long enough"— "there" being the testing arena of action.' [4] The French lieutenant has been tried and tested, and he proves this when he tells Marlow how for thirty hours he stayed on the *Patna*'s bridge while she was towed, in danger at any moment of a plunge to the bottom. As Marlow watches him, he undergoes a moment of vision, a sudden awareness of the surpassing worth of these steady, reliable men who are the raw material of great reputations.

And so when Marlow self-indulgently invites the French lieutenant to take a lenient view of Jim's case, his response takes on a priest-like symbolical status. The previously drowsy lieutenant suddenly assumes a new personality. His eyes become two tiny rings around the profound blackness of the pupils; his sharp glance is like a razor-edge on a battle-axe. He is transformed into an executioner, taking away Jim's last hope of a reprieve. Although he acknowledges that all men suffer from funk, he insists that we must control our cowardice through the habit and discipline of duty:

> 'I contended that one may get on knowing very well that one's courage does not come of itself. . . . There's nothing much in that to get upset about. One truth the more ought not to make life impossible. . . . But the honour—the honour, monsieur! . . . The honour . . . that is real—that is! And what life may be worth when' . . . he got on his feet with a ponderous impetuosity, as a startled ox might scramble up from the grass . . . 'when the honour is gone—*ah ça! par exemple*—I can offer no opinion. I can offer no opinion—because—monsieur—I know nothing of it.' (p. 148)

He speaks for all the men who without hope of glory or riches control their fears in the service of ship or country. Marlow is embarrassed, humiliated by the power of this testimony, and for many readers these words provide an authoritative moral perspective.

Immediately afterwards we are told the slightly absurd story of little Bob Stanton, who was drowned trying to save an hysterical lady's maid who refused to leave a sinking ship. At this moment we may feel Jim's cowardice is firmly established. Jim tries to argue that it was difficult for him to make a decision, that 'there was not the thickness of a sheet of paper between the right and wrong of this affair'. After we have been told about the French lieutenant and little Bob Stanton, we may wish to underline Marlow's exasperated retort: 'How much more did you want?'

And so we may settle down comfortably, and think we have a secure perspective. But even in the two scenes describing Bob Stanton and the French lieutenant doubts have not been entirely removed. Bob Stanton's wrestling match with the lady's maid is like some grim farce written by a malevolent spirit, and when eventually he gives up, and stands watching her, and waiting for the ship to sink, we wonder if he had not carried altruism beyond the limits of good sense. At the end of Marlow's colloquy with the lieutenant, the two seamen face each other mutely, 'like two china dogs on a mantelpiece'. As with so many Conrad analogies, this comparison introduces a hint of absurdity into their confrontation. Are we really to accept the inarticulate, ox-like Frenchman as a fitting representative of Conrad's ideal? Has he not sacrificed his imaginative life, the quick of his personality, to a fixed standard of conduct? Are we to accomplish our salvation only by dullness?

So we oscillate, waver, falter, between several contradictory images of Jim, as we try to decide for ourselves in what light he should be judged. Several times Marlow admits he wants to find excuses for Jim because he dare not confront the moral disturbance aroused in him by the *Patna* story. Jim should be of the right sort, 'one of us'; he should exemplify honest faith and instinctive courage: 'the kind that is not disturbed by the vagaries of intelligence and the perversions of—of nerves, let us say': in other words, the kind not to be disturbed by the mental problems that plagued Conrad during his own sea career.

Marlow knows that ideas are dangerous, that they undermine the few simple notions you must cling to if you want to live decently and would like to die easy. Jim's defection casts doubt on 'the sovereign power enthroned in a fixed standard of conduct': 'Was it for my own sake I wished to find some shadow of an excuse. . . ?' asks Marlow. It could be argued that his whole narrative is a form of evasion. His attempt to understand, his obsession with Jim, reflects his desire to escape from the horror in the thought that he would not trust Jim in charge of his deck. He prefers the surface, the ordered world of language, and a few simple notions of conduct. Brierly cannot cope with this double awareness, this double range of values. When his arrogance recognizes its hypocrisy in the reflecting mirror of Jim's cowardice, he knows what he must do. The only possible response is suicide.

If these last sentences suggest that suicide is a rational response, we go too far. As we read Conrad, we continually move towards some fixed point of view, and then find our confidence betrayed by the sudden introduction of a quite different outlook. Marlow has courage in his response to the moment of recognition; for Brierly the experience is so unique he kills himself. We must return to the central scenes, and think it all out again. I do not agree with Guerard that on a second reading we necessarily think Marlow is too lenient. We may start by admiring Jim's martyrdom in Patusan, and by condemning his cowardice in jumping from the *Patna*. We may end by thinking his death a self-indulgent renunciation, a shocking betrayal of Jewel, and his jump from the *Patna* a natural response to an impossible situation. This seems to me to have some elements of truth. But we have to accept that our glimpses through the mists of Jim's mind exist only for a moment, and are soon blotted out. In our dilemma we may go with Marlow to Stein for elucidation.

8

Stein is a white magician, a Prospero. He describes to Marlow the occasion of his greatest success as a romantic adventurer, when he defeated the ambush prepared by his enemy, and then captured the rare butterfly, which he saw sitting on a heap of dirt. In this enterprise he performs the heroic role of Jim's dreams. On that day Stein has nothing to desire. He possesses the love of a woman, a child, friendship, and has triumphed both as adventurer and scholar. Now in his retirement he might seem a living symbol of the complete man, the unified sensibility. His collection of beetles, horrible miniature monsters, looking malevolent in death and immobility, is balanced by his cabinet of butterflies, frail images 'of something as perishable and defying destruction as the delicate and lifeless tissues displaying a splendour unmarred by death'. He has conquered the base world of the German Captain, Cornelius and Gentleman Brown; he has acknowledged the claim of the ideal.

Stein has sometimes been regarded as a spokesman for Conrad, as an embodiment of final wisdom, but in my view this is quite wrong. As with Prospero in Shakespeare's *Tempest*, there are moments, particularly near the end, when the magic of his intelligence appears ineffective. His words are inconclusive, his understanding a fleeting gleam of light, or perhaps a contact with ultimate darkness. Who can say? Marlow's interview with him is one of Conrad's greatest pieces of writing, a poetic evocation of the ambiguous status of romance: '"He is romantic—romantic",' Stein says of Jim. '"And that is very bad— very bad. . . . Very good too", he added. "But *is he*? I queried".' Pinter could not have written a wittier piece of inconsequential dialogue.

In his past exploits, Stein has displayed an intrepidity of spirit and a physical courage that Marlow says was 'like a natural function of the body—say good digestion, for instance—completely unconscious of itself'. Jim's fear, as we have seen, is similarly presented as a natural phenomenon. This might suggest that because bravery and cowardice are instinctive, they merit neither praise nor blame. Are we to judge action solely by results? Such questions are left in doubt. One curious effect of Conrad's ambiguities is that it is difficult to believe Stein's story of the ambush. There is no evidence in the text to suggest he is exaggerating. But in a novel that treats romance so ironically, Stein's tale sounds like a fantasy. Even if his story is accepted as true, it exists as a transient gift of Nature, and it is not surprising that with the death of his wife and child Stein soon loses this brittle security. As he himself says, his good fortune flared violently, like a match, only to be immediately blown out.

Stein's house is like a magic cavern, a mysterious dark underworld, as if Marlow were Ulysses or Aeneas seeking wisdom among the ghosts of the dead. Stein believes that Nature is a great harmony, a balance of colossal forces, but in this order man is *not* a masterpiece. Perhaps in his case the artist was a little mad, and so man must remain always dissatisfied, restless. Jim's sickness, or madness, like that of Stein himself, is that he is romantic.

What does this mean, and what is the remedy? asks Marlow. Stein replies there is no cure, and the problem is how to live: 'that is the question'. He then performs his vanishing act. He moves into 'shapeless' dusk, as if these few steps had carried him out of this concrete and perplexed world: 'His tall form, as though robbed of its *substance*, hovered *noiselessly* over invisible things with stooping and *indefinite* movements; his voice, heard in that remoteness where he could be glimpsed mysteriously busy with *immaterial* cares, was no longer *incisive*, seemed to roll voluminous and grave—mellowed by distance [my italics]'. The words I have italicized suggest that Stein exists in a world beyond human concepts of matter, beyond time and space. It is as if he hovers in that area of consciousness the other side of the pane of glass, of which Jim became aware when the squall struck the *Patna*. In this darkness Stein seems at home. In his letters Conrad writes often with a feeling of horror of the insubstantiality of matter, of the meaninglessness of human forms of apprehension; but in his fiction the blackness behind existing shapes is not completely alien. In Stein's house, as elsewhere in Conrad, the experiences of metaphysical darkness, of 'sensory deprivation', can appear as an awareness of satisfying truth. And so Stein's voice from this darkness is no longer incisive, but rolls voluminous and grave, like some song of incredible beauty in one of Mahler's symphonies. Conrad deliberately abandons rational articulation, to create a form of words close to music, or perhaps a symbolist poem. The shadow prowling among the graves of butterflies speaks in

broken, cryptic phrases; his departures from conventional usage draw
attention to the imprecision of the words:

> 'Yes! Very funny this terrible thing is. A man that is born falls
> into a dream like a man who falls into the sea. If he tries to climbs
> out into the air as inexperienced people endeavour to do, he
> drowns—*nicht war?* . . . No! I tell you! The way is to the destruc-
> tive element submit yourself, and with the exertions of your hands
> and feet in the water make the deep, deep sea keep you up. So if
> you ask me—how to be?' (p. 214)

At this moment Stein promises revelation. His voice leaps up extra-
ordinarily strong, and he appears suddenly in the bright circle of the
lamp, extending his hand at Marlow's breast like a pistol. But his
twitching lips utter no word, and the hand falls: 'The light had
destroyed the assurance which had inspired him in the distant shadows'.
He sits down, and repeats his formula: 'And yet it is true. . . In the
destructive element immerse . . . That was the way. To follow the
dream and again to follow the dream—and so—*ewig*—*usque ad
finem* . . .' English, German, Latin—the words will not suffice.

This movement from assurance to silence, from darkness to light,
forms the context in which Stein's pronouncements must be judged.
Their quality seems to me the quality of the whole novel. The words
constitute a fragile hovering, a fluttering of language which perhaps
holds meaning, perhaps does not. We are not allowed to settle for
either affirmation or negation. Stein presumably suggests that we must
adapt ourselves to circumstances, to the nature of the destructive element in which we must live. Romantics who try to escape will drown.
But this paraphrase is clearly inadequate when we consider the musical
reverberations of the prose. The repetition of the word 'dream' makes
our destiny a mystery without solution, and the call to follow the
dream appears to contradict the advice to immerse ourselves in the
destructive element. We are to immerse ourselves, to involve ourselves
completely, in something which will destroy us. We are also required,
like a butterfly, to climb above the dirt of the beetle's destructive
world. The phrases float in our consciousness with the tantalizing
inconclusiveness of Sibyl's leaves.

So the scene ends, *sub specie aeternitatis*. As Stein escorts Marlow
through the dark and empty rooms, the two men gather into themselves the prevailing images of light and darkness. They are escorted
by gleams from Stein's two-branched candlestick:

> They glided along the waxed floors, sweeping here and there over
> the polished surface of the table, leaped upon a fragmentary curve
> of a piece of furniture, or flashed perpendicularly in and out of
> distant mirrors, while the forms of two men and the flicker of two
> flames could be seen for a moment stealing silently across the
> depths of a crystalline void. (p. 216)

Once again Conrad prefers the pictorial to the analytic, impressionism
to incisive statement. This is the way humans impinge upon the dark
night of chaos—by just a gleam, just a momentary interruption of the
all-pervading blackness.

9

The first stage of Marlow's investigation into Jim's case ends when on
the verandah Jim vanishes as the darkness leaps back after the lightning flash. It could be argued that the story should end there, with
perhaps a few additional paragraphs outlining his gradual failure to
accept the humiliations imposed on him as a water-clerk. But Marlow
is not willing to abandon him, and with Stein creates for him a new
role. They send him to Patusan, and it is as if the old Jim had vanished
to be reborn in a different time and space.

Patusan, where Jim must now pursue his dreams, is a country
outside civilization, like some primitive Shangri-la. Three hundred
miles beyond the end of telegraph cables and mail-boat lines, Marlow
tells us, 'the haggard utilitarian lies of our civilization wither and die,
to be replaced by pure exercises of imagination, that have the futility,
often the charm, and sometimes the deep hidden truthfulness of works
of art'. Marlow's description of Patusan often suggests to the reader, as
here, that this is a false but attractive world of artistic illusion. Apart
from Jim, the people of this country exist as if under an enchanter's
wand. As Tony Tanner has shown, they are not human beings, but
creatures of a fairy-tale, fixed in their symbolic postures. Jewel represents the pure and beautiful heroine, while Cornelius stands for the
traditional villain, the black filth in the abyss which Jim prefers to
forget. Tamb' Itam is the surly and faithful servant, Dain Waris the
noble friend. Above the landscape sits the immense and magnanimous
Doramin, together with his little motherly witch of a wife, gazing
down on Jim's escapades with the immobility and mystery of two
Henry Moore statues.

Marlow's response to this enchantment is ambiguous, and more than once he contradicts himself. The brig-master, who transports Jim to Patusan, says he will never again ascend to Patusan, but, in his wonderful suggestive misuse of English, he also explains that Patusan is 'situated internally'. The journey seems both an ascent towards an ideal and a return to the womb.

The sense that Jim is being reborn into another existence is particularly forced home to us by Jim's brave jump out of the stockade, reversing his cowardly desertion of the *Patna*. This is followed by Marlow's description of him stuck in the river mud, as if buried alive.

> He made efforts, tremendous sobbing, gasping efforts, efforts that seemed to burst his eyeballs in their sockets and make him blind, and culminating into one mighty supreme effort in the darkness to crack the earth asunder, to throw it off his limbs—and he felt himself creeping feebly up the bank. (p. 254)

After this rebirth he has the happy notion of going to sleep. He tells Marlow he did sleep, perhaps for a minute, perhaps for twenty seconds, and he recollects the violent convulsive start of awakening. This extraordinary detail leaves the reader gasping in unbelief. At this moment of extreme danger, he fell asleep? Conrad's symbolizing habits have taken over, drawing attention to the status of the narrative as psychological myth. The exterior situation is transformed into illustrative material for Jim's inner needs.

In these sections Marlow tries out different artistic genres. At first he compares Patusan to a star of the fifth magnitude, where Jim could leave his earthly failings behind him. In spite of his lack of the requisite six feet for heroic stature, in this climate he can ascend to a world of epic achievement. When he tells Marlow of his defeat of Sherif Ali, he bursts out 'into a Homeric peal of laughter'. He has transformed himself into a suitable companion for Ajax and Achilles. His success was extraordinary: '"Immense!" he cried aloud, flinging his arms open.' After this Homeric style opening Marlow tries his hand at a love story. Jim and Jewel are 'like knight and maiden meeting to exchange vows amongst haunted ruins'. The landscape changes appropriately, the starlight 'good enough for that story, a light so faint and remote that it cannot resolve shadows into shapes, and show the other shore of a stream'. But the stream rolls silent and black as the Styx, and we are transported into an underworld, as if the chivalry of knights and maidens exists only in limbo. The shadowy world of Jewel and Jim rests on the other side of death, their love, like that of Dante's Paolo and Francesca, a wandering of lost spirits no longer allowed to return to the light of ordinary earth. They seem creatures of another essence, of myth.

After trying out epic and romantic language, Marlow next turns to tragedy as the appropriate form. Jewel has asked him to reveal to her the secret which haunts Jim's imagination. Marlow thinks Jewel will never understand:

> Who would remember him? He had what he wanted. His very existence probably had been forgotten by this time. They had mastered their fates. They were tragic. (p. 316)

What does this mean? Why, when Jewel is made wretched by Jim's hidden guilt, should Marlow pronounce that the lovers had mastered their fates? The eventual death of Jim and breakdown of Jewel prove he is wrong. Marlow appears bewildered by Patusan, committing himself to definitions which give only temporary satisfaction.

Many important scenes take place under the moon. Above the chasm between the hills the moon floats away 'like an ascending spirit out of a grave': 'It robs all forms of matter—which, after all, is our domain—of their substance, and gives a sinister reality to shadows alone'. It is cold and pale, like the ghost of dead sunlight. The descriptions are romantic, and yet sinister, as if Jim has walked into the regions of the dead. He is ruler here, but, as Marlow notes, he is himself captive to the necessities of the Patusan environment. This ambivalent mixture of fascination and enslavement is typical of Shangri-la stories. When Marlow quoted Brierly's remark that Jim should creep twenty feet underground, Stein looked up with interested attention. By sending him to Patusan, he has in effect dispatched him to the other side of the Styx. By the solitary grave of Jewel's mother, Marlow responds to the strange attraction of this underworld:

> In the darkened moonlight the interlaced blossoms took on shapes foreign to one's memory and colours indefinable to the eye, as though they had been special flowers gathered by no man, grown not in this world, and destined for the use of the dead alone. Their powerful scent hung in the warm air, making it thick and heavy like the fumes of incense. The lumps of white coral shone round the dark mound like a chaplet of bleached skulls, and everything around was so quiet that when I stood still all sound and all movements in the world seemed to come to an end. (p. 322)

Lord Jim is a proper ruler of this static domain, where people cannot escape from symbolic postures, where under the blight of romance the complexities of human life are simplified. At the first bend of the river leading to Patusan, he loses sight of the sea 'with its labouring waves for ever rising, sinking, and vanishing to rise again—the very image of struggling mankind'. Outside this enchanted land, 'the empty ocean, smooth and polished within the faint haze, seemed to rise up to the sky in a wall of steel.' Jim is cut off from reality, whose difficulties he has put behind him in his search for the heroic. When Marlow returns to the ocean, he responds to an invigorating atmosphere that vibrates with the toil of life: 'This sky and this sea were open to me . . . I let my eyes roam through space, like a man released from bonds who stretches his cramped limbs, runs, leaps, responds to the inspiring elation of freedom.' He rejects the limitations of romance.

And so when Gentleman Brown, with his desperadoes, invades Patusan, the event only confirms that Jim's success was an illusion. From the beginning the paradise has not been without its snakes. The natives are divided by bitter factions, by horrible cruelties; these are not creatures of dignified pastoral innocence. Jim ignores Cornelius, pretends he does not exist, and so we feel Cornelius is right to call him a child. In truth Jim cannot eradicate his disgrace from his mind, cannot escape. Gentleman Brown, with his appropriate name, acts as a mirror for the dark side of Jim's consciousness, his involvement with the beetles which he has tried to forget. When Brown asks Jim whether he himself 'didn't understand that when "it came to saving one's life in the dark, one didn't care who else went—three, thirty, three hundred people"—it was as if a demon had been whispering advice in his ear.' This assumption of common experience sickens Jim, and paralyses his power to act decisively. Dain Waris is killed, and the romance is shattered. Jim feels that he can only conquer his fatal destiny by suicide, so that 'the dark powers should not rob him twice of his peace'. He allows Doramin to kill him, and Marlow understands, with sad irony, that for Jim the sacrifice might seem 'an extraordinary success': 'For it may very well be that in the short moment of his last proud and unflinching glance, he had beheld the face of that opportunity which, like an Eastern bride, had come veiled to his side.' Perhaps at the last Jim felt himself metamorphosed into a hero suited to the fancies of Scheherazade.

But, as might be expected, Marlow ends with questions. We remember the broken grief of Jewel, deserted for Jim's exalted egoism.

If we try to sort out the enigma, we fall into simplification. The last word about Jim can never be said. Marlow informs us: 'Are not our lives too short for that full utterance which through all our stammerings is of course our only and abiding intention? I have given up expecting those last words, whose ring, if they could only be pronounced, would shake both heaven and earth.' And he goes on: 'it is not my words that I mistrust but your minds.' With justification he foresees how the critics of the novel will label and categorize where he has remained satisfied to explore the abyss to seek the grain of truth in the illusion.

Stein himself becomes speechless at the moment when, returning to the lamp-light, he should say the last words about romanticism. Jim himself wants to send a message back to the human beings of middle earth. As Marlow's boat prepares to take him away from Patusan for ever, Jim raises his voice: '"Tell them . . ." he began. . . . "No—nothing," he said, and with a slight wave of his hand motioned the boat away.'

Chapter 3

Heart of Darkness: A Choice of Nightmares?

He that can with *Epicurus* content his Ideas with the *Films* and *Images* that fly off upon his Senses from the *Superficies* of Things; Such a Man truly wise, creams off Nature, leaving the Sower and the Dregs, for Philosophy and Reason to lap up. This is the sublime and refined Point of Felicity, called, *The Possession of being well deceived*; The Serene Peaceful State of being a Fool among Knaves.

SWIFT, A Tale of a Tub

I

Kurtz's native woman appears to Marlow as a wild and gorgeous apparition. She is savage and superb, he tells us, wild-eyed and magnificent. She treads the earth proudly, her body covered with barbarous ornaments, her hair arranged in the shape of a helmet. For Marlow she embodies the spirit of the dark forests: 'And in the hush that had fallen suddenly upon the whole sorrowful land, the immense wilderness, the colossal body of the fecund and mysterious life seemed to look at her, pensive, as though it had been looking at the image of its own tenebrous and passionate soul.' She regards the pilgrims on Marlow's steamer without a stir, 'like the wilderness itself, with an air of brooding over an inscrutable purpose'.

If we compare this splendid savage with Kurtz's European fiancée, his Intended, it may seem that we are setting side by side dynamic energy with sterile hypocrisy, life with death. The savage is tragic and fierce; we may take it for granted that Kurtz has enjoyed sexual orgies with her in his role as a worshipped god to whom human sacrifices are offered. Her Dionysiac passions might seem more attractive in their vitality than the living tomb the Intended has created for herself in Brussels. As often in Conrad, objects associated with human beings take on appropriate characteristics. The Intended lives in a house in a street as still and decorous as a well-kept alley in a cemetery. Her tall marble fireplace has a cold and monumental whiteness, and her grand piano gleams like a sombre and polished sarcophagus. She has chosen for herself a graveyard, where she can exist in comfort only through a lie; her condition symbolizes that of Western Europe. In contrast, the savage lives out her sexual urges as naturally as if she were a wild beast.

Yet there is something detestable, even loathsome, about this primitive creature. The youthful Russian, whom Kurtz befriends in the forests, tells Marlow how she wanted him killed for taking rags from the storeroom to mend his clothes. The unspeakable rites in which she has participated presumably include torture and killings. Co-habitation with this superb but mindless creature degrades Kurtz; for Conrad's total response to her, as to the wilderness, mixes together the attractive and the repellent.

The novel can be interpreted in a Freudian manner as a journey into the wilderness of sex, a fantasy shaped by Conrad's own divided impulses. The pilgrims penetrate down a narrow channel to find, in the darkness, a violent orgiastic experience. Kurtz, the outlaw-figure, has dared to transgress the restraints imposed by civilization. He repre-sents Marlow's shadow self, the secret sharer, and the voyage of exploration is a night journey into the unconscious, or a discovery of the Freudian Id. From this point of view, the imprecision of Conrad's language in descriptions of the wilderness could be a sub-conscious evasion of the truth, a fascinated hovering around a subject whose realities he dare not fully acknowledge. Elsewhere, as Bernard Meyer has shown, Conrad's reaction to sex seems masochistic and fearful. The helmet-like hair is characteristic of other Conrad heroines, notably Felicia Moorsom in 'The Planter of Malata', whose lover enjoys self-abasement before her power. Should we interpret the whole fearful journey, therefore, as a sign of Conrad's repressed nightmares, his desire for a sexual initiation whose demands might prove him impotent?

When such Freudian interpretations are put forward as complete explanations, they become reductive. Conrad's impressionist method gathers into itself a wealth of possible meanings of which the Freudian constitute only a part. Nor do I agree with E. M. Forster or F. R. Leavis, who find the treatment of the wilderness too imprecise. The darkness exists as a literary symbol, whose paraphrasable meanings can never do full justice to the richness of this poetic meditation on human existence. The novel contrasts the savage woman with the Intended, Western civilization with primitive Africa, the language of the rational mind, of concrete imagery and recognizable forms, with a mystery at the heart of consciousness beyond expression in words. Like Marlow, we are offered a choice of nightmares, but the strategy of the novel suggests that final commitment is possible only for the simple and the deluded. The story is a powerful fable of the divided consciousness, of the warring values of passion and restraint.

2

Conrad's own experience of the Congo covered only six months, from June to December, 1890. From his notebook and letters we can glimpse why the adventure was so traumatic. At Matadi, about forty miles up the river, he watched the Africans organized into chain-gangs, driven to the point of exhaustion. He records with horror his disgust for the Belgians' vile scramble for loot. On 3rd July, 1890, he writes in his notebook: 'Saw at a campᵍ place the dead body of a Backongo. Shot? Horrid smell.' He was quickly shipped out of the country with the fever and malarial gout which remained with him for the rest of his life.

Like Conrad, Marlow enrols as a servant of a Trading Company in Brussels, the 'city that always makes me think of a whited sepulchre'. In the office he is received by the enigmatic ladies, knitting black wool, who guard the door of Darkness. They are like the Fates, Clotho and Atropos, spinning and breaking the thread of each man's life. In many respects Marlow's journey down the Congo parallels the classic expedition to the underworld, passing through the circles of Hell, the Company Station, the Central Station and the Inner Station, where he meets Kurtz, the devil incarnate.

But such correspondences should not be pushed too far. Conrad's intention is to surround his story with an aura of poetic allusion, rather than to compose an explicit allegory. On a first reading Marlow's journey towards 'the centre of the earth' grips our attention like a conventional thriller; the setting is exotic, and we are carried forward through moments of danger, escapes, unexpected attack. But even on a first reading we are disturbed by a pervasive irony. The journey appears to be a kind of parody of the romantic quest for the Grail. Marlow ironically calls his debased, greedy companions 'pilgrims', and the manager even builds an Arthurian round-table to prevent his subordinates from quarrelling about precedence. Marlow seems to be the one true pilgrim, determined to make contact with the reality of Kurtz. The quest comes to represent for him retrospectively the culminating point of his experience: 'It seemed somehow to throw a kind of light on everything about me—and into my thought.' He embarks on an intellectual journey into the secret meanings of consciousness. But, as always, Marlow's narration is tortuous and ambiguous, and we are not sure whether he finds the Grail. The anonymous narrator informs us, as the story is told to a group of friends on the cruising yawl on the Thames, that we are about to hear 'one of Marlow's inconclusive experiences'.

James Guetti's *The Limits of Metaphor* includes a brilliant analysis of *Heart of Darkness*. He points out that the title itself can be interpreted in two different ways. Heart of darkness may suggest that the wilderness has a heart, which the reader, guided by Marlow, may discover. At the centre of existence we may find the secret meaning of the pilgrimage. But heart of darkness may also imply that the real darkness is in the heart, and that we journey from the known to the unknown. We are led towards an ultimate darkness, a condition of meaninglessness, which negates all civilized values.

Marlow's uncertainties are seen in his contradictory use of the word 'reality'. When trying to repair the battered, tin-pot steamboat, for example, he tells us:

> I don't like work—no man does—but I like what is in the work, —the chance to find yourself. Your own reality—for yourself, not for others—what no other man can ever know. They can only see the mere show, and never can tell what it really means. (p. 85)

Only a few pages later he describes how the wilderness, 'the overwhelming realities of this strange world of plants, and water, and silences', regarded the pilgrims with a vengeful aspect. His own absorption in the work of keeping the steamboat afloat helped him to avoid the frightening stillness of the forest:

> When you have to attend to things of that sort, to the mere incidents of the surface, the reality—the reality, I tell you— fades. The inner truth is hidden—luckily, luckily. But I felt it all the same; I felt often its mysterious stillness watching me at my

monkey tricks, just as it watches you fellows performing on your respective tight-ropes for—what is it? half-a-crown a tumble—. (pp. 93–4)

Is work 'monkey-tricks' or self-discovery? Is the wilderness the primary reality, and Marlow's occupation on the steam-boat merely an artificial fiction which conceals the truth from him? The novel oscillates, wanders, between these two definitions of 'reality'.

As in *Lord Jim*, the quest is both a search for moral enlightenment and an investigation into the appropriateness of aesthetic forms. As he turns his gaze away from the brooding stillness of the forests, Marlow knows that Kurtz has dared to commit himself to a barbarism both seductive and dangerous: it may be imprudent to look below the surface. At the same time, Marlow understands that it is probably impossible to find a suitable language to describe the wilderness; words are part of the world of surfaces. 'What was in there?' Marlow asks himself quite early in his adventures: 'somehow it didn't bring any image with it—no more than if I had been told an angel or a fiend was in there.' As he journeys down the coast of Africa on his way to the Congo, he notes that the landscape is 'featureless'; his artistic problem is that the wilderness impresses him as a kind of disembodied presence.

In *The Great Tradition*, F. R. Leavis takes for granted that symbols work only when anchored to a record of immediate sensations, when they totally coincide with the concrete presentment of incident, setting and image. Because of this assumption, he condemns the imprecision of parts of *Heart of Darkness*, and draws attention to the intrusion of words such as 'incomprehensible', 'inscrutable', or 'mysterious', whose 'actual effect is not to magnify but rather to muffle':

> He [Conrad] is intent on making a virtue out of not knowing what he means. The vague and unrealizable, he asserts with a strained impressiveness, is the profoundly and tremendously significant.[1]

But, as I argued in my first chapter, Conrad is deliberately creating a kind of writing which draws attention to its own inadequacies. He is seeking for an artistic form to capture an awareness beyond the area of immediate sensation. This language must in some ways remain 'featureless', because no images taken directly from the senses will suffice. The temptation for the artist, as Conrad sees it, would be to offer his readers an organizing metaphor by which they could comprehend both his values and his aesthetic forms, a heart for his awareness of darkness. It is a tribute to his courage, both as man and artist, that in this story he resists the seduction of the ultimate symbol. Marlow acknowledges that he can only achieve ordered awareness of the surfaces of life, and that the essence, the wilderness, must escape his definitions. He repeatedly uses the words 'as if' to suggest that his similes carry only a provisional status. The 'as if' construction gives Conrad the freedom to shape experience in terms of human language, and yet still to imply doubt about its final validity.

This insistence on the failure of civilized language is a central purpose of the novel, illustrated not only when Marlow despairingly admits that words cannot express his experience but also in the symbolism. On several occasions the representatives of Europe shoot into the wilderness. The French man-of-war shells the bush, incomprehensibly firing into a continent. Its tiny projectiles screech feebly, and nothing happens. The pilgrims let loose a volley at Kurtz's natives, and again their efforts seem absurd: 'The pilgrims had opened with their Winchesters, and were simply squirting lead into that bush.' Representative of Africa is the old hippo who roams at night over the station grounds. The pilgrims empty every rifle they can lay their hands on at him, but he bears a charmed life. This uselessness of European weapons parallels the failure of civilized discourse to make any impression on the wilderness. The mystery defies the usual conventions of storytelling.

Heart of Darkness includes a famous description of Marlow's indirect method of narration. The anonymous narrator on the yawl tells us:

> The yarns of seamen have a direct simplicity, the whole meaning of which lies within the shell of a cracked nut. But Marlow was not typical (if his propensity to spin yarns be excepted), and to him the meaning of an episode was not inside like a kernel but outside, enveloping the tale which brought it out only as a glow brings out a haze, in the likeness of one of these misty halos that sometimes are made visible by the spectral illumination of moonshine. (p. 48)

Marlow knows he cannot penetrate to the centre, to the heart. In this sense his journey to Kurtz can never end in a final, satisfying discovery; yet he can create 'a glow', 'a haze', so that his listeners may progress in some degree towards an apprehension of his experience. He deplores that 'it is impossible to convey the life-sensation of any given epoch of one's existence—that which makes its truth, its meaning—its subtle and penetrating essence. It is impossible. We live, as we dream—alone. . . .' But his journey, and his decision to tell his tale, arouse a hope that we may achieve some insight, that the heart may not be entirely impenetrable. As he speaks to his companions on the cruising yawl, it is for the anonymous narrator like listening to the voice of darkness. He feels faintly uneasy, as the narrative shapes itself 'without human lips in the heavy night-air of the river'. Guetti defines Marlow's final reality as 'a state of suspension between the disciplined world of mind and language and the world of essences at the centre of experience'. Perhaps this 'suspension' justifies the Buddha-like pose Marlow assumes while telling his story. Both forms of morality, both kinds of language, make their separate claims, and the man of vision must accept the burden of the double consciousness.

3

Peter Garrett makes a clear contrast between the two forms of narrative. At first the sordid farce of imperialism is presented in an imagistic manner, but as the narrative progresses the centre of attention shifts to the wilderness. Imperialist corruption is anatomized in sharp, visual images, and a clear moral viewpoint is presented, a scheme of values preserved by Marlow in his devotion to the work ethic. In contrast, the wilderness is evoked in portentous, rhetorical language which creates an indefinitely metaphysical meaningfulness, an inner 'reality' which threatens all moral significance. The tale expresses an unresolved tension between the two.

Conrad's disgust at what he witnessed in the Congo, his savage contempt for the Belgian colonists, gives *Heart of Darkness* an important public dimension. Many writers on Conrad have assumed this social and economic commentary to be central to the story, and have considered Kurtz as the supreme example of European hypocrisy. This sense of outrage invests the scenes at Matadi with a symbolic status as horrifyingly representative of civilized lunacy. The European machines prove useless, like beasts dying in an alien environment. A boiler wallows purposelessly in the grass; an under-sized railway-truck lies on its back, like a dead carcass of some animal, with its wheels in the air. Dull detonations mark the attempt to blast away the rock for a railway, but the explosion is described as ridiculous and ineffective like some incident in Kafka. No change appears on the face of the rock: 'The cliff was not in the way or anything; but this object-less blasting was all the work going on.' The unhappy savages die off in the grove of death, like souls in the gloomy circle of some Inferno. Conrad's language is bitter and furious at this wanton smash-up, this dehumanization of landscape and people.

The white human beings who greedily scramble for the ivory are all hollow men. The fastidious chief accountant is a hairdresser's dummy who has avoided the surrounding horror by merging his identity in his elegant clothes and the correct entries in his accounts. The brick-maker, who never makes bricks, is called 'a papier-mâché Mephisto-pheles'; Marlow expects that if he poked his finger through him he would find nothing inside but a little loose dirt. We suspect that the manager is never ill because he has no innards upon which the germs could latch. After Marlow has overheard their conversation, the manager and his uncle depart 'tugging painfully uphill their two ridiculous shadows of unequal length, that trailed behind them slowly over the tall grass without bending a single blade'. These men are ghosts, whose fantastic invasion can effect no permanent change on the wilderness.

Conrad expresses profound compassion for the sick negroes, and later even for the starving cannibals. This should be remembered when he is accused of an absolute nihilism. This care for humanity, mediated through the thoughts of Marlow, is linked with the work-ethic. We admire Marlow because he feels such sympathies, and because he can manage the steam-boat. While the pilgrims fire uselessly into the bush, he disperses the attacking natives by pulling the boat's whistle.

Such work is not just a keeping up of appearances, an evasion of the wilderness, but retains its own value. Like Marlow, we respect the cannibals, who 'were men one could work with'. The Russian's book, *An Inquiry into some Points of Seamanship*, strikes Marlow as 'unmis-takably real'. The author's singleness of intention, 'an honest concern for the right way of going to work', makes these pages 'luminous': 'I assure you to leave off reading was like tearing myself away from the shelter of an old and solid friendship.' The prevailing irony makes this tattered manuscript in the heart of a wilderness seem also absurd and irrelevant. But the darkness cannot always extinguish these lights. The two sets of values, darkness and light, strive unsuccessfully for a complete mastery. As he contemplates the contemporary hell which is London, the growing darkness over the Thames from which the story emerges, Marlow prays that we may live on in the light created by real men: 'We live in the flicker—may it last as long as the old earth keeps rolling!' Civilization, to which the anonymous narrator gives a more fulsome tribute, is not without its virtues, and involves the metamorphosis of darkness into light. As J. Hillis Miller points out in *Poets of Reality*, it is a process of transforming everything unknown, irrational or indistinct into clear forms, named and ordered, given a meaning and use by man. To be safe, we must have a blind devotion to immediate practical tasks, to the needs of this ordered world. Marlow's greatness is that he is not content just to be safe, and that, in contrast with the pilgrims, he craves speech with Kurtz. At the same time, his cult of efficiency, his successful caring for the people in his charge, is far from a despicable illusion.

4

Conrad's description of the wilderness depends on incremental repetition, on the resonance of drawn-out brooding sentences, on interweavings of darkness and light. The reader must respond to the strange music of the rhythms, to a sense of great tracts of time and unknown mysteries. The fascination of the abomination, to which a decent Roman citizen might have responded in Britain centuries ago, is present in the wandering ritualistic style. Many writers on this story have missed this crucial element, and concentrated solely on the sense of moral outrage.

The first blacks seen by Marlow on his journey to the Congo possess a 'wild vitality, an intense energy of movement, that was as natural and true as the surf along their coast'. Like Kurtz's mistress, they exist in a natural relation with the land. They belong, Marlow thinks, to 'a world of straight-forward facts', in contrast to the absurd endeavours of the Europeans to civilize the darkness. As he proceeds along the river, the drums speak to him with 'a sound weird, appealing, suggestive, and wild—and perhaps with as profound a meaning as the sound of bells in a Christian country'. He gradually assumes that the wilderness is alive, either making an appeal or offering a menace. Conrad tries to express the *force* of this silent presence:

> The great wall of vegetation, an exuberant and entangled mass of trunks, branches, leaves, boughs, festoons, motionless in the moonlight, was like a rioting invasion of soundless life, a rolling

wave of plants, piled up, crested, ready to topple over the creek, to sweep every little man of us out of his little existence. And it moved not. A deadened burst of mighty splashes and snorts reached us from afar, as though an ichthyosaurus had been taking a bath of glitter in the great river. (p. 86)

Conrad is trying to suggest a menacing force which encircles all forms of civilization, a presence of universal destruction we acknowledge but cannot control or even properly understand. The creature in the river typifies this sort of mental image, for he is a denizen of another earth. He recalls for Marlow a memory of an ichthyosaurus; he is bathing not in water but in the glitter of the moonlight. The burst of splashes is deadened, muted, as if our apprehension of these realities must inevitably reach us from an inaccessible distance. In *Four Quartets*, T. S. Eliot describes a stillness 'heard, half-heard, between two waves of the sea'. The wilderness is similarly only partially apprehended. Marlow feels bewitched, 'cut off for ever from everything you had known once—somewhere—far away—in another existence perhaps'. They are 'wanderers on prehistoric earth, on an earth that wore the aspect of an unknown planet'. The stillness does not in the least resemble a peace: 'It was the stillness of an implacable force brooding over an inscrutable intention.' These sentences bring into our mind the smallness of our forms of apprehension, our distinctions and categories. The mystery breathes around us, stirring up strange fears, promising strange freedoms. The natives howl and leap in the wilderness, betraying to Marlow remote kinship with this wild and passionate uproar. By concentrating on his work he resists the temptation to go ashore for a howl or a dance. The wilderness is an immensity of natural chaos, just beyond the reach of consciousness. Marlow says: 'The inner truth is hidden—luckily, luckily. But I felt it all the same.'

The quest ends in white fog, warm and clammy, more blinding than the night. The eyes of the pilgrims are of no more use to them than if they had been 'buried miles deep in a heap of cotton-wool'. This vivid, nightmare experience symbolizes the blotting out of all civilized distinctions, an entry into a non-mental world. These moments are the culmination of all Marlow's descriptions of the wilderness. Because of his sense of the insecurity of intelligence, Conrad invites his readers to participate vicariously in a condition devoid of sensation, a blacking out of perception in a trance where unknown realities may make their presence felt. When Marlow hears the loud cry of desolation of the savages, it is 'as though the mist itself had screamed'. This is a moment of revelation, an epiphany of the Savage God. In this all-embracing mist Europe's lights seem momentary flickers about to be snuffed out by a darkness both liberating and destructive.

5

Kurtz has responded to this vision. As an emissary of science and progress, he travelled to Africa to campaign for the ideal. He is a painter, writer, musician and political orator, apparently combining in himself the values of a high culture. But away from society he is liberated to do anything, either good or evil. He shakes himself free from restraints, and becomes his own diabolical God: 'He had kicked himself loose of the earth . . . he had kicked the very earth to pieces. He was alone, and I before him did not know whether I stood on the ground or floated in the air.' The wilderness has found him out, has whispered things to him about himself, has patted him on the head, turned him bald, 'and, behold, it was like a ball—an ivory ball'. With a perverse sense of humour, the darkness has metamorphosed Kurtz into the object for which he craves, the ivory, and has infiltrated itself into his blood and bones. What, then, is the value of his freedom? It is on this issue that all the critics disagree.

Writing in 1932, Joseph Warren Beach adopted a straightforward moral stance: 'Kurtz is a personal embodiment, a dramatization of all that Conrad felt of futility, degradation and horror in what the Europeans in the Congo called "progress", which meant the exploitation of the natives by every variety of cruelty and treachery known to greedy man.' [2] A completely opposite view is taken by K. K. Ruthven, who thinks of Kurtz as a hero. In 'The Savage God: Conrad and Lawrence',[3] he draws attention to the way much twentieth-century art has been fascinated by the primitive. A destructive hatred of civilization, most obvious in D. H. Lawrence, seems in many ways vindicated by the findings of Frazerian anthropology and Freudian psychology. The new discoveries in both these areas defend the integrity of the prelogical, analogical or illogical qualities of consciousness: the whole man is said to thrive in a primitive environment. From this point of view, *Heart of Darkness* is an attack on the values of Western society, and an annunciation of the Savage God. The choice of nightmares is between a bad Europe and a bad Africa. But whereas Europe is a sepulchre, Africa is horrific and vital. Marlow, according to this theory, remains solidly Victorian in his adherence to the work ethic, while Conrad's heroes, such as Kurtz, immerse themselves in the destructive element. Kurtz releases his *id* from European restraint; he is a pioneer in a psychic wilderness. Ruthven believes Conrad was in sympathy with Kurtz, who as pioneer must die before his emancipation from European values is complete.

Lionel Trilling does not go to this extreme, but he too sees Kurtz as a hero of the spirit. He admits that for him it is still ambiguous whether Kurtz's famous deathbed cry: 'The horror! The horror!' refers to the approach of death, or to his experience of savage life:

> Whichever it is, to Marlow the fact that Kurtz could utter this cry at the point of death, while Marlow himself, when death threatens him, can know it only as a weary grayness, marks the difference between the ordinary man and a hero of the spirit. Is this not the essence of the modern belief about the nature of the artist, the man who goes down into that hell which is the historical beginning of the human soul, a beginning not outgrown but established in humanity as we know it now, preferring the reality of this hell to the bland lies of the civilization that has overlaid it? [4]

Trilling compares *Heart of Darkness* to Thomas Mann's *Death in Venice*, in which Aschenbach's submission to his lust for a beautiful young boy, the conquest of his ethical reason by Dionysian eroticism, is taken by us not as a defeat but as a kind of terrible rebirth.

These views, particularly those of Ruthven, give insufficient emphasis to the moral condemnation of Kurtz. He has exploited the natives most shamefully. His megalomania as he lies dying strikes Marlow as at times contemptibly childish. He dreams of kings meeting him at railway-stations on his return from some ghastly Nowhere, where he would have accomplished great things. He is avid of lying fame, of sham distinction, of all the appearances of success and power.

The wilderness whispers to Kurtz with an irresistible fascination because he is 'hollow at the core'. Does this mean that he is another hollow man, like the brick-maker and the manager? Clearly not, for these characters have not the courage to respond to the darkness. Their death-in-life condition makes them impervious to its attractions; unlike Marlow, they feel no temptation to set off for a howl or a dance. Like so many of Marlow's pronouncements, this use of 'hollow' echoes ambiguously through the novel. Kurtz's identity reduces itself to a voice, to a display of rhetoric. This is true of his seventeen-page report to the International Society for the Suppression of Savage Customs, whose enthusiastic idealism we may treat with contempt. Its final scrawled note: 'Exterminate all the brutes!' blows the rhetoric away like smoke in a sudden gust of wind.

But Kurtz's personal rhetoric seduces the innocent Russian by its strange charm, its revelation of infinite possibilities. Marlow himself is appalled by the strange effect of Kurtz's words: 'They had behind them, to my mind, the terrific suggestiveness of words heard in dreams, of phrases spoken in nightmares.' The rhetoric, like Kurtz, wanders in freedom, untrammelled by conventional moral or practical norms. He has achieved a diabolical, Faustian liberty, which rejects European ideas as limiting illusions. His rhetoric may lack the honesty to fact exemplified in the lucid prose of *An Inquiry into some Points of Seamanship*. He is indeed a natural extremist, who, as the journalist tells Marlow after his return to Europe, could have used his eloquence for any cause. But at crucial moments, as when he confronts death itself, his vision comprehends the disparity between the lies of civilization and the primal realities of Africa.

When Kurtz drags himself from the steamboat, and crawls on all fours down the trail towards the savages, Marlow acts with great courage by pursuing him into the wilderness. He acknowledges that he might succumb to its temptations, and he dreams of living alone and unarmed in the forests to an advanced age. But it is his duty to bring the devil back to the security of the steam-boat, to make the shadow submit to the orderly world of civilization. His success ends with the death of Kurtz, and we sense that Marlow, at least temporarily, has overcome the dragon in the abyss of his own consciousness.

The most fantastic creature in the forests is the Russian, who because of his patchwork clothes resembles a harlequin. His face is like the autumn sky, overcast one moment and bright the next. His naïve enthusiasm for Kurtz is another element in the riddle. 'This man has enlarged my mind', he tells Marlow. Are we entitled to sneer? His existence is fabulous, and Marlow expects him instantly to disappear. To the harlequin, Kurtz has discoursed on everything, even love, and the rhetoric—so false?—has aroused in the Russian a fanatical loyalty. He retains a purity, a selflessness which Marlow envies: 'He surely wanted nothing from the wilderness but space to breathe in and to push on through.' The harlequin introduces a further dimension. Kurtz is degraded, exalted, tragic; Brussels is civilized, hypocritical, dead. The harlequin represents the pure spirit of youth, still free from the corruption of both sets of values.

The strain breaks Marlow, and illness takes him to the borders of death. After his recovery, his experience at first makes it impossible for him to reconcile himself to the workaday world of Brussels. Like Gulliver, he feels contempt for the inferior humans who hurry through the streets with their insignificant and silly dreams. He himself is haunted by a different kind of dream, by an awareness which makes Brussels, the sepulchral city, a place of folly and pretence. What is the nature of this dream? Marlow admits that the essentials lie deep under the surface, beyond his reach and beyond his power of meddling. He is trying to tell us a dream, and therefore 'making a vain attempt, because no relation of a dream can convey the dream-sensation, that commingling of absurdity, surprise and bewilderment in a tremor of struggling revolt, that notion of being captured by the incredible which is of the very essence of dreams . . .' He remains suspended between two irreconcilable worlds.

And so the narrative circles back to its beginnings, for no awakening from the nightmare is possible. Marlow is back on the Thames, telling his story, surrounded by memories of times when Britain herself was lost in savagery, and thinking that civilization is a continual, unsuccessful journey to conquer a wilderness. The last episode of his adventure, when he returns some relics of Kurtz to his Intended, gathers into itself all the ambiguities concerning the heart of darkness.

6

F. R. Leavis dislikes this final scene with the Intended. The irony, in his view, lies in the contrast between her innocent nobility, her purity of idealizing faith, and the corruption of Kurtz. 'Nobility' seems to me the wrong word to use for the Intended, and I do not agree that there is nothing ironical in the presentment of her. We have already seen how her home is a graveyard. It is appropriate that Marlow should lie to her, should tell her Kurtz's last words were her name, for her life is based on hypocrisy, like the European civilization in which she has been nurtured. Her devotion has transformed the reality of Kurtz into a false ideal, and this self-deception is a psychological necessity for her.

This quality of illusion horrifies Marlow. As he talks to her, he feels surrounded, menaced, by the wilderness. Her low voice is accompanied in his mind by whispers from the heart of darkness, the faint ring of incomprehensible words cried from afar. He feels panic as if he had blundered into a place of cruel and absurd mysteries not fit for a human being to behold.

In other words, he has journeyed once more towards the heart of darkness. The Intended puts out her arms as if after a retreating figure, and her gesture recalls that of Kurtz's mistress, when the steamboat was carrying him away. She is metamorphosed into the savage, for she too is a tragic figure, the prey of an incomprehensible passion. When Marlow lies to her about Kurtz's last words, he is astonished by her response:

> I heard a light sigh and then my heart stood still, stopped dead short by an exulting and terrible cry, by the cry of inconceivable triumph and of unspeakable pain. (pp. 161–2)

The wilderness claims her, for her tragic ecstasy is Dionysiac in its fervour beyond the power of words. Her triumph and pain exemplify for Marlow 'The horror! The horror!', at the end of his pilgrimage. He leaves her in her graveyard, where she can resist the darkness in her heart only because of his reverberating lie.

Chapter 4

The Ghosts of *Nostromo*

The hills are shadows, and they flow
  From form to form, and nothing stands;
  They melt like mist, the solid lands,
Like clouds they shape themselves and go.

TENNYSON, *In Memoriam*

I

Sir John, chairman of the railway company, arrives at night at the surveying camp in the hills, just too late to see the last dying glow of sunlight upon the snowy flank of Higuerota, the highest mountain. The chief engineer, as he waits for the expected diligencia, responds in a conventionally romantic way to the magnificent sunset, which he compares to 'a piece of inspired music'. Afterwards, late at night, the two men pace to and fro discussing their work, both confident they can overcome all the problems, natural and human, that beset the railway. But as they stand, dwarf-like, beneath the basalt walls of precipices, we are reminded of the insignificance of man in the universe. 'We can't move mountains!' declares the chief engineer:

> Sir John, raising his head to follow the pointing gesture, felt the full force of the words. The white Higuerota soared out of the shadows of rock and earth like a frozen bubble under the moon. All was still, till near by, behind the wall of a corral for the camp animals, built roughly of loose stones in the form of a circle, a pack mule stamped his forefoot and blew heavily twice. (p. 41)

This incident illustrates in simple form the problems of reading *Nostromo* (1904). In *The Turn of the Novel*, Alan Friedman argues that in much of Conrad's fiction 'form might be defined as the arousing and confusing of desires'.[1] In a letter to Richard Curle of 1923,

Conrad explained how he was trying to compose fluid narratives, 'depending on grouping (sequence) which shifts, and on the changing lights giving varied effects of perspective'. [2] In the description of the meeting between Sir John and the chief engineer, we begin with a conventional attitude to natural beauty—'inspired music'—and then proceed to the faith of these practical men of affairs that they can conquer all natural obstacles in the service of material interests. This confidence is already cast in an ironic light because we have been told of the subsequent riots in Sulaco; it also seems misplaced in the setting of the mountains, which throughout the novel symbolize the indifference of Nature to the futility of man. This is straightforward enough, but what are we to make of the comparison of Higuerota to a frozen bubble? The perspective suddenly shifts once again, and we see that under the moon, in the immensity of space, all the forms of Nature are insubstantial, as transient as a bubble. Then immediately our perspective is drawn back to the particular scene, to the pack-mule stamping and blowing, one detail among the hundreds that give a rich actuality to Conrad's creation of Costaguana.

In this short scene, therefore, our visual perspective rapidly changes, and this reflects shifting attitudes to man, society and Nature. The sequence is 'fluid' in that we are not allowed to settle for any one point of view. Positive actions, colourful people, warm feelings, are constantly framed in a vision which seems to negate their existence; the narrative creates different and opposing areas of value, but offers no final reconciliation.

This is one reason why the last two chapters are so unsatisfactory. A linear sequence of events, describing Nostromo's courtship of Giselle, ends with his death, shot by her father, Giorgio Viola. This gives a false appearance that the story is concluded, and the clash of values resolved. In Alan Friedman's view, Conrad is divided against himself, involved in a struggle between his technical effort to close the experience, and his refusal to do so. His true imaginative vision is represented by the early sections, which bewilder and disturb the reader. The novel falls down when Conrad allows himself to be trapped in space and time. At his best his imagination feeds on ironic evasions. The chronological dislocations give a sense of the richness of history and the multiplicity of events; at the same time they place the reader in what Albert Guerard has called a vertiginous stance. [3] The first part of the novel frustrates the normal objectives of the reader to an astonishing degree, not allowing him to identify himself with one character or to locate himself firmly in time or place.

Nostromo presents at least two irreconcilable points of view. At one extreme there is a profound scepticism which pervades the descriptions of landscapes and people, and which seems akin to that of Decoud when he commits suicide; at the other extreme this pessimism is countered by the human and moral claims most finely represented by Mrs Emilia Gould.

2

In the opening chapter, Conrad describes how in Sulaco at midday the sun withdraws from the Placid Gulf the shadow of the mountains, and the clouds roll out of the lower valleys to blot out the peaks of the Sierra: 'The Cordillera is gone from you as if it had dissolved itself into great piles of grey and black vapours that travel out slowly to seaward and vanish into thin air all along the front before the blazing heat of the day.' This 'as if' fancy imaginatively enacts a process of dissolution to which all the people and landscapes of the novel are forced at times to submit. Just as Higuerota is transformed into a bubble, so the characters become ghosts, or dissolve into shadows, as though human beings were no more than flickering images cast on a screen by some eternal cine-camera.

This pervading sense of human insubstantiality is particularly noticeable at moments involving crowds in times of crisis. The individual is caught up in an historical process which is determined to extinguish his identity. This is brilliantly symbolized in the fourth chapter, as Giorgio, the old Garibaldini, gazes across the plain where Nostromo is pursuing the rioters:

> On this memorable day of the riot his arms were not folded on his chest. His hand grasped the barrel of the gun grounded on the threshold; he did not look up once at the white dome of Higuerota, whose cool purity seemed to hold itself aloof from a hot earth. His eyes examined the plain curiously. Tall trails of dust subsided here and there. In a speckless sky the sun hung clear and blinding. Knots of men ran headlong; others made a stand; and the irregular rattle of firearms came rippling to his ears in the fiery, still air. Single figures on foot faced desperately. Horsemen galloped towards each other, wheeled round together, separated at speed. Giorgio saw one fall, rider and horse disappearing as if they had galloped into a chasm, and the movements of the ani-

mated scene were like the passages of a violent game played upon the plain by dwarfs mounted and on foot, yelling with tiny throats, under the mountain that seemed a colossal embodiment of silence. Never before had Giorgio seen this bit of plain so full of active life; his gaze could not take in all its details at once; he shaded his eyes with his hand, till suddenly the thundering of many hoofs near by startled him. (pp. 26–7)

This game of killing is placed at such a distance it seems without purpose. Human beings in *Nostromo* are often reduced in size, to dwarfs as here, or to insects. Giorgio himself at the time of his wife's death is compared in his movements to a mouse, and Nostromo with Decoud on the lighter in the darkness of the Placid Gulf thinks they are like beetles. As he gazes on the animated scene, Giorgio, like the narrator of the novel, cannot take in all the details at once, cannot impose form on this confused tableau. The fallen rider vanishes as if he had never existed. Above, the white dome of Higuerota stands as a colossal embodiment of Nature's silent, unmoved response to the anguish of human beings.

Many other passages show how the people can make no indelible impression on the blank indifference of the landscape: 'Men ploughed with wooden ploughs and yoked oxen, small on a boundless expanse, as if attacking immensity itself'. Often the narrator's perspective, like Giorgio's, is deliberately placed at a distance so that the people are diminished in importance. From the plain the stamp sheds and the houses of the mine appear 'like the nests of birds clustered on the ledges of a cliff': 'The zigzag paths resembled faint tracings scratched on the wall of a cyclopean blockhouse'. Similar effects to those in the scene on the plain watched by Giorgio occur when the aristocratic families are in flight to take sanctuary with the robber Hernandez. They pass a roadside rancho of woven rushes and a roof of grass which has been set on fire by accident:

Great masses of sparks mingled with black smoke flew over the road; the bamboos of the walls detonated in the fire with the sound of an irregular fusillade. And then the bright blaze sank suddenly, leaving only a red dusk crowded with aimless dark shadows drifting in contrary directions; the noise of voices seemed to die away with the flame; and the tumult of heads, arms, quarrelling, and imprecations passed on fleeing into the darkness. (p. 360)

Often in *Nostromo* Conrad gives this impression that behind visible

shapes hovers a ghost world, whose truth negates the conscious aims of
the characters. Here the movements of the people are in fact far from
aimless as they flee to save their lives. But the description transforms
them into shadows, not understanding their true purposes, and eventually drifting away into the darkness. There are many occasions when
suddenly the colourful events appear to one character as unreal or
dreamlike. As Decoud rides in the carriage after the troops of General
Barrios have embarked, he gazes on the mass of people trudging along
the road, all turning their heads in sombreros and rebozos, as a train
passes quickly out of sight behind Giorgio's house:

> And it was all like a fleeting vision, the shrieking ghost of a rail-
> way engine fleeing across the frame of the archway, behind the
> startled movement of the people streaming back from a military
> spectacle with silent footsteps on the dust of the road. (p. 172)

This impression of a ghost-world mocking the illusions of the characters is fixed in our minds by the opening chapter. There we are told the
story of the two wandering American sailors who, according to legend,
organized an expedition to search for treasure in the peninsula of
Azuera, but were never seen again. Their ghosts, now rich and hungry
and thirsty, are supposed still to mount guard over their treasure,
unable to tear themselves away. Their legend reflects most obviously
the way the silver mine casts its spell on Charles Gould and Nostromo.
The latter often compares himself to the American sailors, and as he
eventually assumes guard over the stolen silver, appears in a sense to
have merged his identity with theirs. Such ghosts reflect the inevitable
futility of the projects of man. After Nostromo has returned to Sulaco
leaving Decoud stranded with the silver, he meets Dr Monygham, the
eccentric sceptic whose pessimism has been tempered by romantic
feeling for Mrs Gould. As in the Custom House Dr Monygham
explains to Nostromo his scheme to bring back General Barrios to
Sulaco, behind them the dead body of Señor Hirsch hangs from the
roof, apparently listening attentively. He is a reminder of the absurd
horrors involved in the movements of history.

3

In *Conrad's Models of Mind*, Bruce Johnson points out that although
Conrad had always been concerned with the problems involved in the

creation of the self, nowhere before *Nostromo*, not even in *Lord Jim*, does he employ so direct a vocabulary for the discussion: 'The novel is full of phrases such as "self-discovery", "sense of individuality" ... "thinking, acting individuality", "lost personality", "doubt of his own individuality" and so on and on.' [4] The problem for the characters in *Nostromo* is how to create an identity which is not a false mask, which does not dissolve into a futile shadow. They need an 'idealized' concept of their own existence to keep the ghost-world at bay. Baines thinks the novel 'perhaps the most impressive monument to futility ever created' [5] because he believes all the characters fail in this process of self-identification. I agree that many do fail, but I believe there are exceptions. Conrad's attitude to 'idealization' is ambiguous, and he seems to be groping towards a concept of personal responsibility.

The character who most obviously fails is Nostromo. In a letter to Ernst Bendz, a Swedish professor who had written a study of his work, Conrad said: 'I will take the liberty to point out that Nostromo has never been intended for the hero of the Tale of the Seaboard. Silver is the pivot of the moral and material events, affecting the lives of everybody in the tale.' [6] He is one of a group of characters, Gould, Mrs Gould, Decoud and Dr Monygham in particular, around whom the central problems of self-identity revolve. In his Author's Note, Conrad explains that he needed for his thief 'a man of the People as free as possible from his class-conventions and all settled modes of thinking'. Nostromo 'does not aspire to be a leader in a personal game. He does not want to raise himself above the mass. He is content to feel himself a power—within the People.' Nostromo is rootless, unable to achieve the full life that Mrs Gould admires, one that contains 'the care of the past and of the future in every passing moment of the present'. This is why his vanity is so important to him. Brave, resourceful and handsome, he delights in his reputation with men and women. This is his claim *to exist*, to have established some form of recognizable personality, for Sulaco is not his home, and he has no connection with the land. He has justified his title to incorruptibility not in response to an inherited concept of duty, but as a means of establishing his own personality, an ideal of the self. He loves personal display, as in the incident where he allows the pretty Morenita to cut off his silver buttons. Decoud, with his usual acumen, perceives how 'this man was made incorruptible by his enormous vanity, that finest form of egoism which can take on the aspect of every virtue'. Nostromo is a man 'that seemed as though he would have preferred to die rather than deface the perfect form of his egoism'.

And so Nostromo, our man according to his nickname in Sulaco, is a person without a real existence or name. In spite of his glamorous outward show, his brightly-coloured clothes and silver accoutrements, he has no ultimate reality, as if he were only a ghost-reflection crossing the eyes of the Costaguanans. His essence, value, reality, consist in his personal reputation, and in nothing else. He is *nothing*, 'nothing to any one', as he himself realizes when talking to Dr Monygham under the gaze of the dead Señor Hirsch.

When after the lighter has sunk he is forced to practise concealment, Nostromo's old self dies, and he is reborn into a new identity. His change of name to Captain Fidanzo indicates that he is a different man. It is interesting to compare this rebirth with that of Lord Jim. Jim is mending a watch, the symbol of practical order, when he decides to jump out of the stockade. After sticking in the mud, he is reborn into the twilight world of romance, where at least he can temporarily achieve a new identity, even though he eventually fails. Nostromo's rebirth takes place when he awakes from his long sleep in the long grass of the old fort on the mainland:

> He stood knee deep amongst the whispering undulations of the green blades with the lost air of a man just born into the world. Handsome, robust, and supple, he threw back his head, flung his arms open, and stretched himself with a slow twist of the waist and a leisurely growling yawn of white teeth, as natural and free from evil in the moment of waking as a magnificent and unconscious wild beast. Then, in the suddenly steadied glance fixed upon nothing from under a thoughtful frown, appeared the man. (pp. 411–12)

He immediately recognizes that his old way of life is over. He feels betrayed, as he contemplates how the rich men have used him for their own purposes. It is 'like the end of things', as if the previous years had been 'vain and foolish, like a flattering dream come suddenly to an end'. The thought that he could no longer sit in the place of honour among the people in Sulaco, admired and fêted, 'made it appear to him as a town that had no existence':

> The confused and intimate impressions of universal dissolution which beset a subjective nature at any strong check to its ruling passion had a bitterness approaching that of death itself. (p. 417)

Like the landscapes and crowds, his identity has lost itself in a process of universal dissolution, in the death of all forms. In 'the downfall of all the realities that made his force', he thinks of Giorgio's wife, Teresa, whose dying wish for a priest he refused, and wonders if she is alive or dead:

> As if in answer to this thought, half of remorse and half of hope, with a soft flutter and oblique flight, a big owl, whose appalling cry: 'Ya-acabo! Ya-acabo!—it is finished; it is finished' announces calamity and death in the popular belief, drifted vaguely like a large dark ball across his path. (p. 418)

The owl's cry signifies the death not only of Teresa but also of the old Nostromo. He flits along the shore 'like a pursued shadow', a ghost indeed. In contrast to Lord Jim, he is not allowed a hope of redemption.

In this state of mind Dr Monygham is the worst person he could have met. Obsessed by his own scheme to defeat Sotillo, the rebel commander from Esmeralda who is desperately trying to capture the silver, Monygham shows no interest in Nostromo as a *person*. He too wants to use the Italian for his own ends, as an essential element in his deception of Sotillo, and does not care if Nostromo is killed in the enterprise. Nostromo has been absorbed by his own self-conceit; when this is taken away from him, he is no longer incorruptible. He is transformed into a thief, a slave of the treasure, 'as if an outcast soul, a quiet, brooding soul, finding that untenanted body in its way, had come in stealthily to take possession'. In his case the ghost world proves all-powerful. It is fitting that he should be finally shot in error by Giorgio as he returns in darkness, alone, out of the public eye, to take away more of the silver.

4

Nostromo's character appears to be determined by circumstances. The missing four silver ingots, used by Decoud to weigh down his body after he shot himself, make it impossible for Nostromo to tell the truth. Everyone would presume he was a thief. His state of consciousness is fixed by exterior events, and he drifts into love with Giselle because of a natural unthinking sexual response. In the novel all men at times seem to be free, and are believed by others to be free; but as with Nostromo there is much in the narrative to suggest that all human lives are trapped in determined historical processes.

Although as usual Conrad admires the brave men in the story, such as Giorgio and Captain Mitchell, these people are constantly shown as ironically deluded. Captain Mitchell is a kindly man, but pompous and a fool. His bravery is a form of stupidity: 'It was not so much firmness of soul as the lack of a certain kind of imagination—the kind whose undue development caused intense suffering to Señor Hirsch.' The bravery of these men seems without any abiding influence on the patterns of history. Giorgio, scornful of the populace 'as your austere republican so often is', has transformed Garibaldi and Liberty into his divinities. In the past he has fought as one of Garibaldi's immortal thousand in the conquest of Italy; now he keeps a coloured lithograph of his hero in a black frame on the white wall of the hotel. His simple devotion to 'a vast humanitarian ideal' has ended in loneliness in this alien land, where his wife's handsome face has turned yellow because the climate of Sulaco does not suit her. At the beginning of the novel, the family crouch in their inn listening to the frightening noises of the riot. When these have passed away, Giorgio unfastens the door, and 'the crude colours of the Garibaldi lithograph paled in the sunshine'. The political enthusiasms of Garibaldi have also faded, as if the lithograph enshrouds the ghost of a lost ideal. The fight for political reform, in which so many good men were killed, has been defeated. Giorgio lives in his memories, and his old-fashioned concept of honour proves dangerous when he kills Nostromo.

Don José Avellanos's patriotism is similarly treated ironically. He has an attractive personality; he is a poet, man of culture and statesman who has represented his country at several European Courts. His sufferings under the dictator Guzman Bento have proved his courage and resilience. He desires for Costaguana peace, prosperity and (as the end of the preface to *Fifty Years of Misrule* has it) 'an honourable place in the comity of nations'. He uses his influence to support Ribiera, and believes that, with the help of the Goulds, a new era of peace is about to dawn upon his beloved country. When he receives the news that Ribiera has been voted for five years the extraordinary powers needed to establish the peace, he is so overcome by emotion that he totters, and has to be supported by Mrs Gould. This reference to his physical weakness is introduced at this moment to hint that these hopes are those of a failing, old man. The references to his book, *Fifty Years of Misrule*, are always ironic, and its language is made high-flown and sentimental, unrelated to the brute facts of political conflict. During the riot, he is broken down by grief. After the smashing of the printing presses, the pages of his book float in the gutter or are blown in the wind. At the end we see him being carried away by his daughter, Antonia, to safety under the protection of the outlaw, Hernandez. Charles Gould looks down at 'Don José stretched out, hardly breathing, by the side of the erect Antonia, vanquished in a lifelong struggle with the powers of moral darkness, whose stagnant depths breed monstrous crimes and monstrous illusions'.

Don Juste Lopez is a less engaging character. Before the riot he is President of the Provincial Assembly. He has a fan-shaped beard, half of which is singed off during the riot. The result is that he loses nine-tenths of his outward dignity. He is an inept believer in parliamentary institutions, and when the victory of Montero becomes known, he favours compromise. He is described by Decoud in his letter with contempt. Decoud leaves the meeting of the Assembly as Lopez begins a solemn oration in which he tries to persuade himself of the 'clemency and justice and honesty, and purity of the brothers Montero'. The solemn effect of his speech is destroyed by the disaster to his beard. As he turned his head from side to side, Decoud writes, it was as if there had been two men inside his frock-coat, one nobly whiskered and solemn, the other untidy and scared. A ghost-face comments ironically on his false rhetoric. When Lopez visits Gould to persuade him to conciliate Perdito Montero, his voice is described contemptuously and typically as like the deep buzzing of some ponderous insect. Like Decoud, Conrad does not believe that parliamentary government can solve the problems created by material interests. Don Juste Lopez survives his discomfiture to become Chief of the State in the new Occidental Republic, but for this he deserves no credit. The mask of the politician does not satisfy the search for a true identity in any of the characters of the novel. In an article on Anatole France published just after he finished *Nostromo* Conrad wrote: 'Political institutions, whether contrived by the wisdom of the few or the ignorance of the many, are incapable of securing the happiness of mankind.'[7]

5

The determined historical processes are most clearly illustrated in the career of Charles Gould. Conrad detests the sentimentalizing of commercial power by a man such as the American captain of industry and finance, Holroyd, and shows how Gould ruins himself by allying himself with this fanatic. In his letters Conrad expressed his distrust of the rationalizations of American imperialism in Cuba and the Philippines: he believed that capitalism and imperialism destroy the individuality of people. The philosophy of progressive capitalism is explained by Gould to his wife in the early days of their love:

> 'What is wanted here is law, good faith, order, security. Any one can declaim about these things, but I pin my faith to material interests. Only let the material interests once get a firm footing, and they are bound to impose the conditions on which alone they can continue to exist. That's how your money-making is justified here in the face of lawlessness and disorder. It is justified because the security which it demands must be shared with an oppressed people. A better justice will come afterwards. That's your ray of hope.' (p. 84)

The failure of these ideals in the novel seems at times virtually total. When the Goulds first visit the mine, the narrator describes the waterfall and tree-ferns, a hanging garden above the rocks of the gorge, as 'a paradise of snakes'. The Goulds bring corruption into this natural wilderness. At first Mrs Gould is successful in establishing her hospitals and schools, and the mine provides peace and stability for the Indian workmen. But gradually other less fortunate influences are noticeable. The 'material apparatus of perfected civilization' obliterates the individuality of old towns under the stereotyped conveniences of modern life. The railway disturbs the picturesque simple lives of the people, replacing with its yards the land previously used for popular festivals. The miners begin to lose their identities in Village One, Village Two and Village Three, places like Nostromo, without an inherited name. By interfering in Costaguana politics, the mine is responsible for another revolution, that of Montero against Ribiera. At the end Antonia and Father Corbelan are plotting to annex the rest of Costaguana for the new Occidental Republic, and we know that bloodshed and horror will return. History is proved to be cyclical, as the broken time scheme implies, not in accord with Gould's dreams of a progressive capitalism. Dr Monygham is allowed the last word:

> 'There is no peace and no rest in the development of material interests. They have their law, and their justice. But it is founded

on expediency, and is inhuman; it is without rectitude, without the continuity and the force that can be found only in a moral principle.' (p. 511)

The novel might properly end with Mrs Gould, alone in a garden, betrayed by her husband's obsession with the mine, stammering out as if in the grip of a merciless nightmare: 'Material interests'.

This historical process has a metaphysical dimension. Charles Gould is trying to conquer matter, and to make its hard intransigence his servant. If he succeeds, he will prove consciousness is not a passing shadow, but capable of imposing its values on the material world. He is promoting an industrial civilization which with its railways, roads and mines will make Nature conform to a human idea. As he listens to the growling mutter of the mountain pouring its stream of treasure under the stamps, he is listening to his own desire, and he imagines the noise must reach to the uttermost limits of the province. For both the Goulds in the early years of their marriage, each passing of the escort with the silver under the balcony of their house is like another victory gained in the conquest of peace for Costaguana. The silver passes through Sulaco at dawn; in the whole sunlit range of empty balconies along the street 'only one white figure would be visible high up above the clear pavement—the wife of the Señor Administrador—leaning over to see the escort go by to the harbour, a mass of heavy, fair hair twisted up negligently on her little head, and a lot of lace about the neck of her muslin wrapper.' They are redeeming the land; this symbolic scene places her 'high up', as if floating away in innocence and purity from the corruption of Costaguana. It is a new dawn, a dream of human justice, order and love. For Emilia at this time, the silver becomes an embodiment of her aspirations: 'she endowed that lump of metal with a justificatory conception, as though it were not a mere fact, but something far-reaching and impalpable, like the true expression of an emotion or the emergence of a principle.'

The faith of the Goulds is treated with bitter irony. According to Royal Roussel, Gould cannot escape from the fundamental process in Conrad's world whereby the source of life continually negates and reabsorbs its own creation. He is possessed by the mine, by matter, as after death the body itself must turn to dust. His consciousness solidifies, petrifies, so that his inhuman coldness can no longer respond to the tenderness of his wife. In the battle between matter and mind, the former always wins. In the last sentence of the novel, the white cloud shining like a mass of solid silver hangs over the Placid Gulf, symbolizing that all the creations of men will eventually be absorbed back into the elemental components of Nature.

This pessimism is certainly the main impression we take away from a first reading; we may concur with Dr Monygham, who tells Emilia that the mine will eventually weigh upon the people as heavily as the barbarism, cruelty and misrule of previous years. Gould at the end seems to have been transformed into a ghost, like the American adventurers on Azuera. But some doubts remain. The paradise was *of snakes*, and we may remember that the Indians do achieve a happiness in their villages denied to them in their previous poverty-stricken existence. Although the total historical process may appear determined, a provisional freedom for short periods of time seems attainable, and by no means to be treated with disdain. Some of the Goulds' ideals are achieved, if only temporarily.

We may also wonder how far Gould's failure is a determined historical process, and how far it is the result of personal weakness. His submission to material interests is a developing process of irrationality. He becomes increasingly obsessed with the mine, until he is willing to blow it up to protect it from his enemies. At times this process seems an inevitable result of his mistaken confidence in the rational benefits of progressive capitalism, as well as of the war between mind and matter. But on other occasions we feel that Gould fails for psychological reasons, and that a different man would not have treated his wife so shamefully. Is there any universal reason why Gould's misplaced faith in capitalism should result in his apparent sexual frigidity? He is irrational in his attitude to the San Tomé mine largely because he is reacting emotionally to the career of his father. The tumult of words and passion poured out about the mine in his father's letters aroused in him a fascination:

> Mines had acquired for him a dramatic interest. He studied their peculiarities from a personal point of view, too, as one would study the varied characters of men. He visited them as one goes with curiosity to call upon remarkable persons. He visited mines in Germany, in Spain, in Cornwall. Abandoned workings had for him strong fascination. Their desolation appealed to him like the sight of human misery, whose causes are varied and profound. They might have been worthless, but also they might have been misunderstood. His future wife was the first, and perhaps the only

person to detect this secret mood which governed the profoundly sensible, almost voiceless attitude of this man towards the world of material things. (p. 59)

Presumably service of mines becomes a substitute for service of his father: he will slay the dragon that killed his father, and so prove his own manhood. His re-opening of the mine coincides with the first year of his marriage. His father died at the moment when he and Emilia were discovering their love, and so their devotion to the mine becomes, almost subconsciously for them, a way of repaying the father who never lived to hear of their engagement: 'A vague idea of rehabilitation had entered the plan of their life. That it was so vague as to elude the support of argument made it only the stronger.' Decoud argues that the eventual corruption of Charles results from this personal kind of engagement. He tells Emilia that Charles is an Englishman, and therefore must idealize every simple feeling, desire or achievement: 'He could not believe his own motives if he did not make them first a part of some fairy tale. The earth is not quite good enough for him, I fear.' In his letter to his sister, Decoud describes how Gould's sentimentalism attaches a strange idea of justice to his work at the mine: 'He holds to it as some men hold to the idea of love or revenge. Unless I am much mistaken in the man, it must remain inviolate or perish by an act of his will alone.' Like other idealists in Conrad's novels, he is dangerous to other men because he will not face facts. He has grown to hate the bribing and intriguing necessary from the beginning for the preservation of the mine, and so he has interfered directly in politics, and supported the Ribierist faction. He is not satisfied by a provisional commitment, by a temporary state of order. He wants to conquer the whole land, to impose his spiritual idea on everything. In this, he imitates Holroyd. These desires have eaten away the true being of Gould, so that he is too confident in his own rectitude:

> For all the uprightness of his character, he had something of an adventurer's easy morality which takes count of personal risk in the ethical appraising of his action. He was prepared, if need be, to blow up the whole San Tomé mountain sky high out of the territory of the Republic. This resolution expressed the tenacity of his character, the remorse of that subtle conjugal infidelity through which his wife was no longer the sole mistress of his thoughts, something of his father's imaginative weakness, and something,

too, of the spirit of a buccaneer throwing a lighted match into the magazine rather than surrender his ship. (pp. 365–6)

As he reflects on the riot, he is dominated by a fixed idea, and in the years that follow this brings untold suffering on his wife. The narrator's comment does not equivocate: 'A man haunted by a fixed idea is insane. He is dangerous even if that idea is an idea of justice, for may he not bring the heaven down pitilessly upon a loved head?'

Is it not possible, therefore, that some other man might have succeeded in developing the mine without becoming so inflexible? We cannot attribute all the misfortunes of Emilia to the malign influence of 'material interests'. Certainly they cannot be blamed for the Goulds' failure to produce a child, though the barrenness of the marriage appears symbolic. If the suffering of Emilia is in some degree a consequence of personal weaknesses in her husband, then a possibility emerges that men do have some qualified freedom to escape from the determined processes of history. Conrad's comment on Gould's need for action has been quoted as a total summary of the scepticism of the novel: 'Action is consolatory. It is the enemy of thought and the friend of flattering illusions. Only in the conduct of our action can we find the sense of mastery over the Fates.' But action does influence events in *Nostromo*, and bring a temporary peace, as Dr Monygham proves, when he courageously deceives Sotillo and so succeeds in altering the future history of Costaguana. Gould himself makes a great impact on the lives of many people. For several years they are given security, justice and order.

On some occasions, therefore, Gould appears morally responsible for his behaviour, and his actions change the course of history. At others he seems caught by inevitable historical and metaphysical processes. *Nostromo* is full of sadness at human suffering, but it does not convey a sense of unmitigated futility. There are possibilities available for meaningful action, at least in a limited context. There are also possibilities available for fidelity and passion.

6

Whereas Antonia Avellanos is depicted superficially, Mrs Gould is portrayed with a depth rare in Conrad's treatment of women. What she represents is a 'humanizing influence', and its lights cannot be entirely put out by the darkness of the Gulf:

She kept her old Spanish house (one of the finest specimens in Sulaco) open for the dispensation of the small graces of existence. She dispensed them with simplicity and charm because she was guided by an alert perception of values. She was highly gifted in the art of human intercourse which consists in delicate shades of self-forgetfulness and in the suggestion of universal comprehension. (p. 46)

She builds up a community, a living witness to human solidarity, which even seduces Decoud temporarily by its virtues. In her loneliness, her attitude to her husband's obsession is like that of a mother for the weakness of a son. On one occasion, she touches his cheek 'with a light touch, as if he were a little boy'. Her desolation is tragic, for her husband has betrayed the values of personal relations which are her own supreme possession. Conrad writes of 'her unselfishness and sympathy':

She could converse charmingly, but she was not talkative. The wisdom of the heart having no concern with the erection or demolition of theories any more than with the defence of prejudices, has no random words at its command. The words it pronounces have the value of acts of integrity, tolerance, and compassion. A woman's true tenderness, like the true virility of man, is expressed in action of a conquering kind. (p. 67)

While her husband fails to impose his ideal order on matter, she *does conquer*. Her care for people gathers around her the best men of Sulaco, charmed by her warm affection and habits of consideration. Don Pépé, Don José, Dr Monygham and Decoud find it easy to place confidence in her. While her husband grows increasingly obsessed with material interests, she develops her schools and hospitals. She resembles 'a good fairy', 'as if radiating a light of her own'. At the end she feels her magic is powerless, as Charles drifts further away from her. Yet we remember the sick and dying men she cared for in her courtyard during the riot. We remember her countless acts of consideration and tact. Although she ends the novel deserted and alone, she has created something with which to oppose the Void.

7

Decoud and Nostromo have some things in common, for both are adventurers without real ties with one specific country. When Father

Corbelan accuses Decoud of believing in nothing, 'neither in stick nor stone', Decoud replies that in this he is at one with the Capataz of the Cargadores. In his letter to his sister, he tells her that Nostromo 'like me, has come casually here to be drawn into the events for which his scepticism as well as mine seems to entertain a sort of passive contempt'.

When Nostromo becomes aware of his lack of true relationships, of his existence solely in terms of reputation, his identity is destroyed, and he is reborn into a zombie-like way of life. In contrast, Decoud is highly intelligent, and therefore continually aware that there is an element of pose in all the roles he assumes. This self-consciousness makes it impossible for him ever to commit himself entirely to human relationships, because he cannot rid himself of a self-mockery that watches his own antics cynically, as he plays out his part in the human drama. This double consciousness prevents him from ever achieving a fixed identity, for he cannot 'idealize' any one kind of purposeful action. In Ian Watt's words about Conrad himself, he cannot 'establish any real connexion between the alienation he felt and the commitment he sought'.[8] Because he cannot fix himself permanently in any one life style, his identity becomes like the clouds and the landscapes, something continually dissolving in a fluid manner from one moment to the next. His problem is summed up when he turns to the assembled throng in Mrs Gould's house, who are talking of Montero, and shouts into the room with all the strength of his lungs: 'Gran' bestia!' Is this just a piece of journalistic rhetoric as he himself supposes? Or is he being to some extent reborn into his true nature as a patriot? The doubtful status of this outcry is typical of his actions. When he falls in love, 'his familiar habit of ironic thought fell shattered against Antonia's gravity'. As patriot and lover, he does not know how far he is honest, how far he is a poseur. His thoughts, feelings and actions, as well as the opinions of other characters on him, accumulate into a pile of separate entities, but never coalesce into a vital organism.

This uncertainty makes Conrad's treatment of Decoud often seem contradictory. This is a problem that affects the whole novel. There is no Marlow through whose narration we see the events. The anonymous story-teller of *Nostromo* has no identity; we know that this person visited Sulaco on occasions, but we are not given any information about his character, not even his age. Yet he makes quite firm moral judgments on certain occasions, judgments which may not seem validated either by the events or by his choice of imagery. The fluid quality of Decoud's character, transmitted to us in this uncertain manner, seems to me in tune with the total imaginative impact of *Nostromo*. Decoud is the new man of the twentieth century, whose scepticism and alienation make him a 'dilettante of experience',[9] and about whom the reader is given no definitive judgment. Conrad leaves us in our 'vertiginous stance'.

Both Albert Guerard and F. R. Leavis argue that Conrad was too personally involved with Decoud, and that this is the cause of our uncertainties. Guerard feels that Conrad was very much attracted towards scepticism, and that his condemnations of Decoud, including the decision to have him commit suicide, signify Conrad's subconscious desire to separate out and demolish a facet of himself, to condemn his own neurotic self-contempt by proxy: there is 'a marked discrepancy between what Decoud does and says and is, and what the narrator or omniscient author says about him.'[10] Leavis thinks Decoud's consciousness dominates the novel: 'In fact, Decoud may be said to have had a considerable part in the writing of *Nostromo*; or one might say that *Nostromo* was written by a Decoud who wasn't a complacent dilettante, but was positively drawn towards those capable of "investing their activities with spiritual value"—Monygham, Giorgio Viola, Señor Avellanos, Charles Gould.'[11] My feeling is that just as Conrad will allow the reader no organizing image by which to understand Costaguana, so his treatment of Decoud is deliberately unclear. Decoud wavers between commitment and non-commitment, and we are not certain how to judge him. His honesty interferes with his ability to create satisfying human relations. When on the Great Isabel he is withdrawn from all contacts with people, in a silence unalleviated even by the song of birds, he feels, like Nostromo, that he is nothing, and must die.

Decoud's identity passes through three stages. He is introduced as an 'idle boulevardier', an 'exotic dandy', who has been living a worthless life in Paris. The anonymous narrator treats this period of his life with contempt. Decoud has assumed 'a Frenchified—but most unFrench—cosmopolitanism, in reality a barren indifferentism posing as intellectual superiority'. He imagines he is a Parisian to his fingertips, but he is in danger of remaining 'a sort of nondescript dilettante' all his life: 'He had pushed the habit of universal raillery to a point where it blinded him to the genuine impulses of his own nature.' When he first appears in company with Antonia, his stylish cravat, round hat and varnished shoes suggest an idea of French elegance, yet, we are told, he is otherwise the very type of a fair Spanish creole, the type never tanned by its native sunshine.

But what are Decoud's 'genuine' impulses? Is the French elegance a pose, or his Spanish birthright the key to his nature? In Sulaco, in the second stage of his development, Decoud's love for Antonia introduces him to genuine feelings which surprise him by their intensity. He prefers to believe that love is another form of illusion, but in company with Antonia his growing affection awakens in him a new sensibility: 'He remained silent for a minute, startled, as if overwhelmed by a sort of awed happiness, with the lines of the mocking smile still stiffened about his mouth, and incredulous surprise in his eyes.' His plan for the new Occidental Republic is not just a freak of fancy, for he is carried away by what, to some extent, must be rated a 'genuine' enthusiasm.

Decoud's sceptical intelligence cannot be written off as merely 'barren', for it enables him to reach a degree of understanding of the other characters beyond the scope of anyone else in the novel. His analysis of Gould's sentimentality seems definitive, and he perceives most clearly the nature of Nostromo's egotism. Such clarity of insight exemplifies an honesty of its own, and gives weight to his general observations on life. He himself has 'no faith in anything except the truth of his own sensations'. In his opinion, convictions are merely particular views of our personal advantage either practical or emotional: 'It seemed to him that every conviction, as soon as it became effective, turned into that form of dementia the gods send upon those they wish to destroy.' The career of Charles Gould appears to prove him right. The alternatives seem to be a barren, cold detachment, or a commitment, like that of Dr Monygham for Emilia, which may prove highly dangerous to other people. The 'fatal touch of contempt for himself to which his complex nature was subject' is a feature both of Decoud's honesty and of his inability to commit himself to a moral principle.

8

Decoud's fluid identity cannot survive the experience of sensory deprivation during his ride with Nostromo on the lighter across the Placid Gulf, and once more his identity changes. When the two men leave the jetty, it is as if they have jumped off the earth into a condition of chaos before creation. The blackness of night becomes one of Conrad's symbols for twentieth-century experience. It is comparable with E. M. Forster's Marabar Caves, where all utterance is reduced to a meaningless echo; but Conrad's Placid Gulf is more imaginative and profound. The atmosphere is created in the opening chapter:

> At night the body of clouds advancing higher up the sky smothers the whole quiet gulf below with an impenetrable darkness, in which the sound of the falling showers can be heard beginning and ceasing abruptly—now here, now there. Indeed, these cloudy nights are proverbial with the seamen along the whole west coast of a great continent. Sky, land, and sea disappear together out of the world when the Placido—as the saying is— goes to sleep under its black poncho. The few stars left below the frown of the vault shine feebly as into the mouth of a black cavern. In its vastness your ship floats unseen under your feet, her sails flutter invisible above your head. The eye of God Himself—they add with grim profanity—could not find out what work a man's hand is doing in there; and you would be free to call the devil to your aid with impunity if even his malice were not defeated by such a blind darkness. (pp. 6–7)

In this black cavern, the world of substances disappears. Neither God nor Devil have power here, and so on their lighter Nostromo and Decoud enter a condition of moral negation. Conrad's obsession with the journey into metaphysical blackness finds here its most compelling expression. The smothering quality of the clouds is reminiscent of the fog in *Heart of Darkness*, when Marlow feels buried in cotton wool. Decoud passes through an experience where he is deprived of all connections with the daylight world of people and places. His 'active sensations and feelings from as far back as he could remember seemed to him the maddest of dreams.' Even his passion for Antonia, into which he had worked himself up out of the depths of his scepticism, 'had lost all appearance of reality'. He is deprived of his sensations, on whose truth he had relied, and as a result he feels his identity i taken away from him.

The characteristic features of this strange imaginative experience can be seen in the following passage:

> The solitude could almost be felt. And when the breeze ceased, the blackness seemed to weigh upon Decoud like a stone.

> 'This is overpowering,' he muttered. 'Do we move at all, Capataz ?'
>
> 'Not so fast as a crawling beetle tangled in the grass', answered Nostromo, and his voice seemed deadened by the thick veil of obscurity that felt warm and hopeless all about them. There were long periods when he made no sound, invisible and inaudible as if he had mysteriously stepped out of the lighter. (pp. 262–3)

We almost feel the blackness, weighing down like a stone. We are made aware of the silence; Nostromo, like a ghost, seems to have stepped out of the lighter. Decoud is so crushed by the darkness that it is as if no free, meaningful action, no imposition of purpose on Nature, will ever again be possible. All human actions are powerless and frustrated, like those of a beetle caught on grass. These images of blackness, weight and entanglement suggest what is happening to Decoud's mind. In this situation Nostromo's voice seems 'deadened', as if all sharp distinctions are being obliterated. Decoud exists alone in a 'featureless' world where voices sound from the distance as in a dream, from an obscurity in which hope is illusion: 'No intelligence could penetrate the darkness of the Placid Gulf.'

After he has been left marooned with the silver on the Great Isabel, Decoud feels impotent before the uniform texture of the night. The smooth darkness, like a solid wall, oppresses him with a bizarre sense of unreality 'affecting the very ground upon which he walked'. The gulf negates all the forms of creation, all methods of apprehension, both sensuous and rational. In contrast to *Heart of Darkness*, the blackness is no longer actively hostile. What is frightening is its imperturbability: its complete rejection of human kinds of discernment.

The narrator tells us Decoud died from solitude, and want of faith in himself and others. Unable to make an ideal concept of the self, he has no identity strong enough to face this crisis. The affectations of irony and scepticism need the visible forms of society for their food; they exist as viable attitudes only when there is some object for them to contemn. Soon the fluidity of Decoud's personality seems to him to be dissolving into the landscape:

> After three days of waiting for the sight of some human face, Decoud caught himself entertaining a doubt of his own individuality. It had merged into the world of cloud and water, of natural forces and forms of nature. In our activity alone do we find the sustaining illusion of an independent existence as against

the whole scheme of things of which we form a helpless part. Decoud lost all belief in the reality of his action past and to come.' (p. 497)

The people in Sulaco seem to him 'unreal and terrible', like 'gibbering and obscene spectres': 'He beheld the universe as a succession of incomprehensible images.'

In other words, Decoud is close here to many statements about reality made by Marlow in *Heart of Darkness* and *Lord Jim*. But Marlow achieves some kind of suspension between comprehensibility and incomprehensibility, between action and detachment. In contrast, Decoud has never engaged in work that has become fully meaningful for him. Even in his passion for Antonia he has retained a sense that his actions are only a game. In his melancholy he is said to be vaguely conscious of 'a misdirected life given up to impulses whose memory left a bitter taste in his mouth', and this, the narrator tells us, 'was the first moral sentiment of his manhood'. This comment implies a set of values which oppose the pessimism that leads to his suicide. His decision to take his life reflects upon his previous lack of generosity and love, the characteristics of Emilia Gould. Her life may end in bitter disillusion, but at least, unlike Decoud, she never surrenders to the claims of moral negation.

Decoud's final attitude to the universe is expressed by an image of torture: 'the solitude appeared like a great void, and the silence of the gulf like a tense, thin cord to which he hung suspended by both hands, without fear, without surprise, without any sort of emotion whatever.' This position recalls that of Señor Hirsch, undergoing the horror of the estrapade. References to torture occur throughout the novel. For Decoud, the only sensible policy is to break the cord. He disappears into the waters of the gulf, 'swallowed up in the immense indifference of things'.

9

The ambiguous treatment of 'idealism', 'scepticism' and 'action' is reflected in the career of Dr Monygham. At first he is a cynic, a bitter eccentric, 'whose short hopeless laugh expressed somehow an immense mistrust of mankind'. His sufferings during Guzman Bento's dictatorship have left him with the worst possible view of human motives. He can never forget how he himself betrayed his friends under the torture imposed by Father Beron. Like Lord Jim, or Razumov in *Under Western Eyes*, he cannot eradicate this treachery from his consciousness. Because he has learnt the limits of his own endurance, he disbelieves in the honesty of everyone else. But his cynicism is a form of idealism. He has created 'an ideal conception of his disgrace':

> It was a conception which took no account of physiological facts or reasonable arguments; but it was not stupid for all that. It was simple. A rule of conduct resting mainly on severe rejections is necessarily simple. Dr Monygham's view of what it behoved him to do was severe; it was an ideal view, in so much that it was the imaginative exaggeration of a correct feeling. It was also, in its force, influence, and persistency, the view of an eminently loyal nature. (pp. 375–6)

This loyalty he has settled upon Emilia. The comments of the narrator are typically elusive and dark. We sympathize with Dr Monygham for his 'exaggeration of a correct feeling', and he, unlike Decoud, is not afraid to commit himself to a grand passion. But at the time of the riot this 'idealism' makes him as fanatical as Father Corbelan. Intoxicated by his plan to deceive Sotillo, he is perfectly indifferent to Decoud's fate, and oblivious to Nostromo's struggle to re-create his sense of identity. He is engrossed 'by a desperate adventure of his own', terrible in the pursuit of his idea. A simple man in essence, he believes his humiliation by Father Beron suits him for the role of traitor, and that he alone can persuade Sotillo to waste time seeking for the treasure. And so this arch-sceptic acts positively and energetically, and succeeds in saving his Emilia.

As the years go by, he is transformed by her humanizing influence, and he even stops dreaming of Father Beron. He becomes like a young adolescent in his adoration, and Conrad's ironic voice can still be heard. But he alone understands how much Emilia's life 'had been robbed of all the intimate felicities of daily affection which her tenderness needed as the human body needs air to breathe'. Should we admire him? Throughout *Nostromo* Conrad treats the idealization of the self as a necessary though possibly dangerous illusion. Certainly the symbolic negation of the Gulf, the images of human insignificance, cannot completely dissolve away Dr Monygham's integrity and devotion.

Chapter 5

The Secret Agent: The Irresponsible Piano

An empty bus
hurtles through the starry night.
Perhaps the driver is singing
and is happy because he sings.

GÜNTER GRASS, '*Happiness*'

I

When I think of *The Secret Agent*, I immediately remember that extraordinary piano. The characters of the novel, with a few important exceptions, are obese, indolent and passive. Verloc lies back recumbent on a sofa, and although he sees the shadow of his wife's arm with the clenched hand holding a carving knife, he cannot summon up enough energy to move. In contrast, inanimate objects have become peculiarly active, like the gurgling water-pipe which parodied Lord Jim's mental anguish.

The piano entertains the customers in the beer saloon in the basement of the renowned Silenus Restaurant. Comrade Ossipon is trying to find out from the Professor how much he knows about the bomb explosion that morning:

> An upright semi-grand piano near the door, flanked by two palms in pots, executed suddenly all by itself a valse tune with aggressive virtuosity. The din it raised was deafening. (p. 61)

It ceases as abruptly as it had started. Its next performance occurs when the Professor is describing his search for the perfect detonator, 'a variable and yet perfectly precise mechanism', which could kill everyone in the restaurant:

> The piano at the foot of the staircase clanged through a mazurka with brazen impetuosity, as though a vulgar and impudent ghost

were showing off. The keys sank and rose mysteriously. Then all became still. (p. 67)

And the piano provides a final accompaniment to the Professor's departure from the beer hall:

> The lonely piano, without as much as a music stool to help it, struck a few chords courageously, and beginning a selection of national airs, played him out at last to the tune of 'Blue Bells of Scotland'. The painfully detached notes grew faint behind his back while he went slowly upstairs, across the hall, and into the street. (p. 79)

The piano is aggressive, brazen and courageous, qualities lacking in Karl Yundt, Comrade Ossipon and Michaelis, the lazy, ineffective anarchists who discuss their plans in Verloc's shop. In *The Secret Agent*, the inanimate world's refusal to submit to the ordering devices of the human mind has become even more pronounced, and this is one reason why this might seem Conrad's most pessimistic novel. The piano, with its absurd exuberance, deafens the beer-drinkers, reduces the little professor's dreams of power to ridicule, as he retires to the tune of 'Blue Bells of Scotland'. Conrad described *The Secret Agent* as an attempt to treat a melodramatic theme ironically; the sensational events are set in a context suited to the drama of Ionesco or the poetry of Günter Grass. In Grass's 'The Sea Battle'

> An American aircraft carrier
> and a Gothic cathedral
> simultaneously sank each other
> in the middle of the Pacific.

That upright piano would have recognized this event as suited to its own world of dehumanized characters and humanized objects. It plays its own tunes, wildly, almost madly, while human beings disintegrate into the damp fog and stones and gutters of London.

The piano is not the only object with a separate identity alien to the characters. The bell of Verloc's shop is hopelessly cracked, but 'at the slightest provocation, it clattered behind the customer with impudent virulence'. The Assistant Commissioner first appears 'bent over a great table bestrewn with papers, as if worshipping an enormous double inkstand of bronze and crystal'. Speaking tubes resembling snakes are tied by the heads to the back of his wooden armchair so that 'their gaping mouths seemed ready to bite his elbows'. Mrs Verloc's two gas-burners, being defective, first whistle 'as if astonished', and then purr comfortably like a cat. In this strange universe, the conventional relations between humans and objects no longer pertain. Perhaps most bizarre is Mr Verloc's hat. Comrade Ossipon, still ignorant about the murder, is sent by Mrs Verloc to put out the light in the parlour which contains her husband's dead body:

> But the true sense of the scene he was beholding came to Ossipon through the contemplation of the hat. It seemed an extraordinary thing, an ominous object, a sign. Black, and rim upward, it lay on the floor before the couch as if prepared to receive the contributions of pence from people who would come presently to behold Mr Verloc in the fullness of his domestic ease reposing on a sofa. (p. 285)

As soon as he is dead, Mr Verloc becomes 'nothing', 'of no account in every respect'. The hat survives, mocking its owner by its apparent willingness to assist in a public show as at Madame Tussaud's. Hats in Conrad's fiction often act as symbols of identity, as in 'The Secret Sharer'. In this strange melodrama, Verloc's identity in death seems to have been rubbed out, while the hat lives on, as if humans only temporarily interrupt the antics of a world of malevolent objects. The hat, which should protect Verloc from the weather, demonstrates its alienation by jeering at his downfall. Like the piano, it seems to exist in complete freedom from the control or understanding of the people in the novel.

The book ends with a final gesture from the piano in the Silenus Restaurant, which 'played through a valse cheekily, then fell silent all at once, as if gone grumpy'. The Professor and Ossipon walk away, moving across an urban landscape which exists in aloof disdain of their passions and misfortunes.

2

The Secret Agent has been considered by many readers as the most grim of Conrad's novels, and not only because of the strange cavortings of inanimate objects. The action takes on the character of a parody of the conventional detective thriller. On the surface this is a story of a strange explosion at Greenwich Observatory whose mysteries are solved by the clever Assistant Commissioner, a born detective in the tradition of Sherlock Holmes. There are few of the dislocations of time so characteristic of the early pages of *Nostromo*. Suspense is aroused because we at first believe Verloc is dead, and only later do we discover that it was Stevie who dropped the bomb and so blew himself up. The problem is solved by the discovery of Stevie's name on the shred of collar picked up with his remains, and by the Assistant Commissioner's visit to Verloc's shop, in a suitable disguise.

But this linear development towards a solution of the mystery is rendered absurd by the existence of another kind of discovery. Verloc, Mrs Verloc and Ossipon experience a moment of self-understanding which plunges them into despair. After Stevie is blown to pieces, Mr Verloc's state of dismay suggests, in the words of the Assistant Commissioner, 'an impulsive man who, after committing suicide with the notion that it would end all his troubles, had discovered that it did nothing of the kind'. These three characters all proceed towards a condition of mind that seems appropriate to the other side of death. They discover the meaninglessness of their own self-created identity, and the shock drives them inevitably towards breakdown and suicide.

Verloc's life in London among the revolutionaries is depicted as a secret game, in which even the police participate. Its purpose is to preserve the status quo, to maintain a superficial law and order, and Verloc is really a typical domestic bourgeois. Yet this conventional shop-keeper sells pornography, and works as a secret agent for a foreign power. In a sense the purpose of the novel is anarchic, to expose the façade by which society carries on its day-to-day routines.

Before Vladimir orders him to blow up the Greenwich Observatory, Verloc has been loyal to an idea of social stability suited to his indolent temperament. As a secret agent he thinks of himself as the preserver of civilized security, achieving this end by betraying the plans of the anarchists. But he is himself like the revolutionaries in his distaste for work; we are told in the first pages of the story that 'he had an air of having wallowed, fully dressed, all day on an unmade bed'. It is typical of the novel to blur distinctions between one class of person and another, and to treat Verloc and his companions with contempt:

> . . . Mr Verloc, temperamentally identical with his associates, drew fine distinctions in his mind on the strength of insignificant differences. He drew them with a certain complacency, because

the instinct of conventional respectability was strong within him, being only overcome by his dislike of all kinds of recognized labour—a temperamental defect which he shared with a large proportion of revolutionary reformers of a given social state. For obviously one does not revolt against the advantages and opportunities of that state, but against the price which must be paid for the same in the coin of accepted morality, self-restraint and toil. The majority of revolutionists are the enemies of discipline and fatigue mostly. There are natures, too, to whose sense of justice the price exacted looms up monstrously enormous, odious, oppressive, worrying, humiliating, extortionate, intolerable. Those are the fanatics. The remaining portion of social rebels is accounted for by vanity, the mother of all noble and vile illusions, the companion of poets, reformers, charlatans, prophets, and incendiaries. (p. 53)

His interview with Vladimir shatters Verloc's complacency, and he begins to realize that his domestic peace depends on fragile supports. His insomnia suggests the breakdown of all the routines which have previously constituted his sense of reality. In spite of this new consciousness of personal agony, he struggles to re-create the illusion of security. Even after the explosion he takes it for granted that a return to his domestic comforts is still possible. As Winnie struggles to control her anguish at Stevie's death, his egotistic self-complacency utters words whose astonishing inappropriateness reflects the ironic tone of the whole novel: 'Do be reasonable, Winnie. What would it have been if you had lost me?' Into the murder blow, Mrs Verloc put all 'the simple ferocity of the age of caverns'. The illusion of their marriage is shattered by a return to destructive savagery.

Winnie's journey away from the secure world of domestic illusion derives from a cataclysmic experience from which there seems little hope of recovery. Before the explosion, she has played the role of a good wife, placid, obedient, willing to satisfy Verloc's sexual demands. Her philosophy consisted in not looking too closely into things, in 'not taking notice of the inside of facts'. But her wifely pretences hide a violent maternal passion for Stevie, exalted morbidly in her childhood by the oppression of their father. When she hears that Stevie is dead, she feels as if her identity has been stripped from her: 'The palms of her hands were pressed convulsively to her face, with the tips of the fingers contracted against the forehead, as though the skin had been a mask which she was ready to tear off violently'. Her husband's treachery changes her concept of reality, 'altering even the aspect of inanimate things'. As the whole meaning of her existence flows away into nothing she gazes appropriately at the white-washed wall of the kitchen, as if her personality has become similarly a blank. Poor Mr Verloc engages in a last moment of unconscious irony, when his sexual invitation to her brings the plunge of the carving knife into his breast. After the blow, she enjoys 'her complete irresponsibility and endless leisure, almost in the manner of a corpse'. She has destroyed not only Verloc but also her own identity. In *The Secret Agent* the pure act of anarchism is self-destruction.

The novel ends with Ossipon's breakdown. Confronted by the murder, 'he was incapable by now of judging what could be true, possible, or even probable on this astounding universe'. His betrayal of Winnie, and her suicide, so oppresses him he loses the will to live. The death or living death of Verloc, Winnie and Ossipon makes the Assistant Commissioner's investigations seem beside the point. He is struggling to survive in a social world whose pretensions seem absurd in relation to the torture undergone by these three, whose Fate it is to witness the destruction of their life-illusion.

3

When Verloc, Winnie and Ossipon confront the darkness, and are thus driven towards self-destruction, they are granted an illumination which appears to be that of the sardonic narrator himself. The voice of Conrad seems now at one with the chaos symbolized by blackness in previous novels. No Jewel or Marlow or Mrs Gould offers us a glimpse of saving truth to alleviate the prevailing gloom. The Assistant Commissioner sharpens his wits for the investigation not because of a passion for justice, but because he feels personally threatened, and his instinct for self-preservation is alerted. If Michaelis is arrested for complicity in Verloc's plan, the Assistant Commissioner will lose favour with the great lady who is the anarchist's patroness, and there will be domestic complications with his wife. He concentrates his mind to prevent this disaster, and so discovers the truth. All the characters, except the half-witted Stevie, are selfish in their motivation. Even the Professor's sense of moral outrage feeds on thwarted vanity, on personal impulses disguised into creeds. Often Conrad ironically labels his people by epithets of relationship. Mrs Verloc's mother is called so to the end, and we never learn her real name. We are constantly reminded that Stevie is Winnie's brother, and she has a moment of joy when her husband and Stevie go off down the street like father and son. But in fact social relationships have become empty forms; all the people are imprisoned in their own obsessions, and during the many interviews in the novel continually misunderstand each other. Conrad seems to have almost abandoned hope that humans might create a meaningful community. Poor Stevie's mangled remains in the morgue could be taken as a symbol of the total meaning of the novel, for London has been metamorphosed into a great cemetery, where humans exist in isolated fragments, without true connections, without honest relationships.

Marlow's function as narrator has now been taken over by an anonymous voice which presents the action in dramatic scenes in the fictional present. This narrator adopts a sardonic tone, an ironic superiority, which stems from no obvious moral stance. There is something unfocused, destructive, about this tortuous irony, which shows little compassion or generosity towards the misfortunes of the characters. This feature disturbs Irving Howe, whose own political idealism finds Conrad's pessimism objectionable:

> It is one thing for a novelist gradually to deprive his characters of their pretensions or illusions, another thing to deny them the mildest claims to dignity and redemption . . . The qualifications required by irony are present in abundance, but it is difficult to determine *what* is being qualified, which standard of behaviour is being singled out for attack or defence. So peevish an irony must have its source less in zeal or anger than in some deep distemper.[1]

Like Howe, both Guerard and Moser consider this irony to be reductive in its influence. The liberal or the Marxist discerns in *The Secret Agent* only a self-destructive hopelessness; while the Freudian or the Jungian finds no profound introspective analysis of character. Writers with these approaches tend to judge this a minor novel.[2]

I agree with F. R. Leavis and J. Hillis Miller in believing *The Secret Agent* to be among Conrad's outstanding achievements. This is not to deny the astonishingly chill quality of much of the irony. The characters are ruled by a mocking, derisory Fate, which ensures that their actions produce the opposite of what they intend. Mrs Verloc's mother deliberately sacrifices her own comfort so that her son-in-law will not consider the presence of two relatives in his house as a burden, and so turn against Stevie. Winnie herself encourages her husband to take an interest in the lad, and so both women bring about the death of the person to whom they are obsessively attached. The instances of such irony in the novel are legion. Poor Stevie's generosity is played upon by the poverty of the cab-driver and Mrs Neale, both of whom retire to the pub as soon as they obtain money. At the other extreme in society, the lady-patroness of Michaelis self-indulgently deludes herself with her dreams of altruism, unaware that attacks on capitalism have any relevance to her own inherited wealth. Conrad's scorn spills out over the hardened worldly faces that surround her, on the Assistant Commissioner's wife, for example, who is 'devoured by all sorts of small selfishnesses, small envies, small jealousies'.

What is most difficult to assess is the total ironic tone, which plays upon the people and events with a zany vitality all its own. Sometimes we seem to be in the area of the mock-heroic, with Ossipon as a failed Apollo, the Assistant Commissioner as Don Quixote, and the butcher boy, in the opening chapter, a charioteer in the Olympic Games. But this butcher boy's gusto is significant. We recall Winnie's first love, also a butcher boy, whose animal spirits contrast with Verloc's indolence. Perhaps there are people outside the death-in-life world of the Verlocs who still retain some zest and joy in life. The irony, with its sparkle and energy, suggests there might be, and that the narrator is one of them. There is a comic exuberance in the tone of writing, as Conrad creates this extraordinary world of fat humans and lively pianos.

4

These strange ironic effects can be seen in the references to cannibalism. Among his companions at Verloc's shop, Karl Yundt, the old terrorist without teeth, enjoys his denunciations of capitalism and is overheard by Stevie:

> 'Do you know how I would call the nature of the present economic conditions? I would call it cannibalistic. That's what it is! They are nourishing their greed on the quivering flesh and the warm blood of the people—nothing else.'
> Stevie swallowed the terrifying statement with an audible gulp, and at once, as though it had been swift poison, sank limply in a sitting posture on the steps of the kitchen door. (p. 51)

Yundt's melodramatic rhetoric seems obviously excessive, yet Stevie, innocent and half-witted, takes him seriously. And Yundt is ironically proved right, when poor Stevie's remains are gathered together at the morgue: 'a heap of rags, scorched and bloodstained, half concealing what might have been an accumulation of raw material for a cannibal feast'. We remember these cannibal references just before Mr Verloc is murdered, when he is overcome by a sensation of unappeasable hunger:

> The piece of roast beef, laid out in the likeness of funereal baked meats for Stevie's obsequies, offered itself largely to his notice. And Mr. Verloc again partook. He partook ravenously, without restraint and decency, cutting thick slices with the sharp carving knife, and swallowing them without bread. (p. 253)

It is as if he is eating Stevie's body.

In what way do these scenes relate together? A simple explanation would be that Yundt is right, and modern industrial society is indeed cannibalistic in its treatment of these prisoners in the vast city. The disasters of their lives are inevitable consequences of economic necessity. Avrom Fleishman argues:

> Physical disintegration begins in the tendency to reduce the human being to its component parts. Men are seen first as animals, then simply as fat, flesh, or meat. In this connection, the notion of cannibalism is introduced with telling effect. With the ultimate reduction of the human being to fragments of matter ('"He's all there. Every bit of him. It was a job"'), man is imaginatively— and literally—annihilated in *The Secret Agent*. Conrad is the English writer who saw, as Brecht did, that in modern life 'man feeds on others' . . .
>
> The imagery of cannibalism is in accord with anarchist doctrine . . . The novel proves it to be an accurate description of the workings of society. In this condition men are dismembered not only accidentally or metaphorically but systematically—as in the novel's report of the German recruits whose ears are torn off by their officers.[3]

This interpretation does not seem to me the whole truth. It presupposes a firm moral condemnation, but the quality of the language does not support this. As always, Conrad is closer to Kafka than to Brecht, and on each occasion when cannibalism is cited the irony introduces elements which do not fit in with an easy moral stance. Yundt is obviously enjoying his self-righteous indignation, and his own comfort contrasts with his horrifying visions. Stevie's mangled remains nauseate Inspector Heat, but suddenly Conrad suggests to us, with a strange aloofness, that they might have given pleasure to cannibals. What are we to do with this unexpected reflection? Mr Verloc's greedy swallowing down of the beef is strangely comic in its lack of restraint, as though he were a figure in a Jacobean melodrama. There is a touch of absurdity in the use of the carving knife as the instrument of revenge, as if the narrator is enjoying such sensational links. Conrad appears to be deriving some amusement from the idea of cannibalism, and this does not accord with a straightforward attitude of moral indignation.

In this manner the irony creates its own values, pushing away the characters to a distance, and protecting itself from involvement. This ironic manipulation of horror has something in common with Günter Grass's *The Tin Drum* or Joseph Heller's *Catch-22*. In a universe of inexplicable nightmare, the artist protects himself by the virtuosity of his wit. Ian Watt asks the crucial question about *The Secret Agent*: 'How is it that a tale so deeply depressing on the face of it, a tale in which every possible card is stacked against human freedom and happiness, should be, for some readers at least, tonic rather than depressive in its final effect?' [4] His answer is that Conrad negotiates the conflict between the ideal and the actual in his gloomy vision by means of comic style, and in this way the novel seems modern in the same way that Yeats, Eliot, Joyce are: 'All of them assume that it is the artist's voice alone which can impose some order on the vulgar folly of the modern world.' In *The Secret Agent*, 'the tension between what is seen and how it is presented betokens an admirable elasticity of spirit.'

Conrad was not finally satisfied with this retreat into style. In *Under Western Eyes* and subsequent novels he returns to the problems of social relationships, and examines once again how action can be meaningful. But in *The Secret Agent* he created a great masterpiece of the modern imagination.

5

In his Author's Preface, Conrad recalls that his early apprehension of the novel had as background 'the vision of an enormous town', 'a monstrous town more populous than some continents and in its man-made might as if indifferent to heaven's frowns and smiles: a cruel devourer of the world's light'. Conrad's depiction of London is obviously influenced by Dickens. Both writers capture the spirit of London by grotesque tricks of style, though Dickens has a confidence in human benevolence which works against the darker side of his imagination. In *The Secret Agent*, the house, 1 Chesham Square, which has strayed at least sixty yards from Chesham Square itself, is a typical Dickensian fantasy, but fits in well with the wayward behaviour of inanimate objects in other parts of the novel.

Mr Verloc begins the story walking westward to the Embassy through the diffused light cast by a peculiarly bloodshot London sun. In this atmosphere of powdered old gold, neither wall, nor tree, nor beast, nor man cast a shadow. Hillis Miller writes:

> The diffused light makes everything look alien. Instead of seeing houses, walls, carriages and people as distinct objects, the spectator also sees the identical gleams which the diffused light casts on each indiscriminately. It may be, in fact, that nothing exists except these gleams, since one evidence of the solidity of objects, the fact that they interrupt the light and cast shadows, is missing. No thing or person has a shadow, and it is as if they did not exist as massive forms, but had been dissolved into scintillations of light. To see things in this way is to understand how little of what is seen derives from objects themselves, and how much is a reflection of the pervasive light which makes things visible. The spectator sees that the world is composed of splotches and blobs and gleams, gleams which his intelligence distorts by fitting them into its pre-existent concepts.[5]

Such effects convey a sense of human insubstantiality. Verloc is 'steady like a rock—a soft kind of rock'; the qualification draws attention to his vulnerability in contrast with the houses, with 'the majesty of inorganic nature, of matter that never dies'. Then there is that odd policeman, who looks 'a stranger to every emotion, as if he, too, were part of inorganic nature, surging apparently out of a lamp-post'. In this example Conrad retains the 'as if', and does not, as on occasions with the mechanical piano, flagrantly break the relation between his patterns of words and usual concepts of reality. But we sense that things are more permanent than people. Carriages go bowling by, 'with here and there a victoria with the skin of some wild beast inside and a woman's face and hat emerging above the folded hood'. The skin, mentioned first, seems to be engulfing the woman, as if the dead are eating the living. There is a hint too of the hidden savagery behind civilized appearances. This kind of surreal landscape, where policemen surge out of lamp-posts and skins of wild beasts ride in victorias, reflects the confusion of society itself. The novel equates anarchists with bourgeois, policemen with criminals, men with beasts and fishes, perversely mocking the usual rational distinctions. The city is a place of blind cruelty and violent disorder, actively resistant to human attempts to impose meaning. Even the children squabble and run 'with a shrill, joyless, rowdy clamour'.

The Verloc domesticities are enclosed in a sunless house, and the novel continually contrasts the security of indoors with the dangers of walking the streets. After he has been instructed to blow up Greenwich Observatory, Verloc prepares for bed:

> Then after slipping his braces off his shoulders he pulled up violently the venetian blind, and leaned his forehead against the cold window-pane—a fragile film of glass stretched between him and the enormity of cold, black, wet, muddy, inhospitable accumulation of bricks, slates, and stones, things in themselves unlovely and unfriendly to man.
>
> Mr. Verloc felt the latent unfriendliness of all out of doors with a force approaching to positive bodily anguish. There is no occupation that fails a man more completely than that of a secret agent of police. It's like your horse suddenly falling dead under you in the midst of an uninhabited and thirsty plain. The comparison occurred to Mr. Verloc because he had sat astride various army horses in his time, and had now the sensation of an incipient fall. The prospect was as black as the window-pane against which he was leaning his forehead. And suddenly the face of Mr. Vladimir, clean-shaved and witty, appeared enhaloed in the glow of its rosy complexion like a sort of pink seal impressed on the fatal darkness.
>
> This luminous and mutilated vision was so ghastly physically that Mr. Verloc started away from the window, letting down the venetian blind with a great rattle. Discomposed and speechless with the apprehension of more such visions, he beheld his wife re-enter the room and get into bed in a calm, businesslike manner which made him feel hopelessly lonely in the world. (pp. 56–7)

Verloc is separated from chaos by only a fragile film of glass. As in a mirror, he sees the face of Vladimir—a 'luminous and mutilated vision', from whose reality he can no longer escape. Normal divisions of time and space no longer compose together for him a secure framework of existence. During nights of insomnia he enters a limbo of consciousness. The darkness has spoken to him and revealed itself in the lineaments of Vladimir—the 'Hyperborean swine'. From this point of view, the business-like efficiency of Winnie is part of a world with which he has lost all connection.

Michaelis's prison is described as a huge morgue, and London itself, the world of outdoors, seems to be suffering from a slow process of decomposition. The street where the Professor confronts Inspector Heat has on one side low brick houses, empty shells awaiting demolition. Later on the same day, the Assistant Commissioner gazes out at the rain, where 'the flickering, blurred flames of gas-lamps seemed to be dissolving in a watery atmosphere'. The lofty pretensions of mankind appear to him in a similar state of dissolution. Mrs Verloc's suicide by drowning becomes a kind of consummation to which the whole of London seems inevitably moving. Like Verloc, the Assistant Commissioner looks out from a secure room on the darkness outside, 'as vast as a sea'. When he eventually begins his journeys, 'his descent into the street was like the descent into a slimy aquarium from which the water had been run off.' He is enveloped by the murky, gloomy dampness, a queer 'foreign fish' not so different from those which preoccupy the mind of his master, Sir Ethelred. In this atmosphere he enjoys a sense of loneliness, of 'evil freedom', as 'he seemed to lose some more of his identity'. Verloc fears this loneliness, and is too timid to venture deliberately beyond the pane of glass. The Assistant Commissioner is a brave man, but when he leaves behind the warm rooms and the safe conventions, he is free to do anything. The imaginative effect of these episodes suggests a Swiftian pair of alternatives. We either live secure in illusion, protected by the police and social hypocrisies; or we walk out into the streets where chaos encompasses us, where our social identity slips away leaving us free to commit pure acts of destruction. Mrs Verloc also experiences a moment of freedom when she realizes she is no longer bound to Verloc, and in that instant of clarity plunges the carving knife into his breast. Later she walks out into the streets, and immediately becomes a lost soul: 'The entrance into the open air had a foretaste of drowning; a slimy dampness enveloped her, entered her nostrils, clung to her hair.' She realizes she is completely isolated: 'She was alone in London: and the whole town of marvels and mud, with its maze of streets and its mass of lights, was sunk in a hopeless night, rested at the bottom of a black abyss from which no unaided woman could hope to scramble out.' It is a moment of recognition. When she eventually jumps into the sea, she is only entering a condition of nothingness into which London itself is hopelessly sinking, and which the novel has already imaginatively realized for us.

On a number of important occasions, characters are described walking across London. As Mr Verloc lies sleepless, the passers-by seem to be pacing out eternity, from gas-lamp to gas-lamp in a night without end. The walkers seen by the Assistant Commissioner vanish, as if out of existence. The novel ends with Ossipon and the Professor walking, Ossipon towards a life of inevitable degradation, the Professor, like a pest in a streetful of men. The final irony is that our apparent freedom to walk, to move our bodies across the alien land-scape, can never alter the inevitable processes of dissolution. Man-made objects dissolve into their primary elements; men themselves possess only the freedom to kill and to die.

6

The three slim characters, the Assistant Commissioner, Stevie and the Professor, might seem to be endowed with qualities not entirely engulfed in the abyss of London, but the ironic tone adopted towards them is wayward and ambiguous. We have already seen the mixture of praise and mockery in the descriptions of the Assistant Commissioner. Stevie is admirable, morbid, ridiculous, by turns. The best side of him is shown after the cab-ride during which he has been regaled with the misfortunes of the driver, who explains that he must treat his horse cruelly to make money for his starving family. Stevie cannot tolerate such injustices. He is the only character in the novel who is honest— 'delicately honest', in Conrad's words. Whereas Winnie trusts in face values and domestic hypocrisies, Stevie always tries 'to go to the bottom of the matter'. He is 'frank and as open as the day himself'. His emotional ideal of justice is the trait on which Verloc plays to persuade him to assist in the Greenwich adventure. He says little, but as he reflects on the cab-driver's story, he sums up in isolated words much of the feeling in the novel:

> ... he came to a stop with an angry splutter: 'Shame!' Stevie was no master of phrases, and perhaps for that very reason his thoughts lacked clearness and precision. But he felt with greater

completeness and some profundity. That little word contained all his sense of indignation and horror at one sort of wretchedness having to feed upon the anguish of the other—at the poor cabman beating the poor horse in the name, as it were, of his poor kids at home. And Stevie knew what it was to be beaten. He knew it from experience. It was a bad world. Bad! Bad! (p. 171)

This honesty contrasts forcibly with the hypocritical use of words by the other characters. Mr Verloc's extraordinary public voice can make a policeman jump when he is fifty yards away, but he keeps dark from his wife the truth about his work as a secret agent. Michaelis has lost the habit of consecutive thinking, and writes his book in delighted self-absorption, his words floating in the air without ever touching reality. His communications with his patroness are like 'the efforts at moral intercourse between the inhabitants of remote planets'. Stevie speaks simple truth: 'Bad world for poor people.'

Because of this simple honesty, Stevie has sometimes been compared with Prince Myshkin in Dostoevsky's *The Idiot*, but this seems to me wrong. The Prince's epileptic fits are associated with moments of almost mystical insight, so that he becomes a kind of divine fool, in the tradition of Don Quixote. In contrast, there is something depressing and terrifying in Stevie's half-witted idealism. He is easily duped by the cab-driver, as well as by Mrs Neale. He morbidly combines passionate compassion for suffering with outbursts of destructive violence. When he reads about the German officer tearing half-off the ear of a recruit, he shouts and stamps and sobs, and Winnie has to take the carving knife from him: 'He would have stuck that officer like a pig if he had seen him then', she tells her husband. Ossipon's classification of Stevie as a degenerate conveys a half truth.

On occasions the narrator seems to be enjoying the farcical elements in this morbidity. How else are we to explain the bizarre episode when, his feelings wrought up to a high pitch by tales of injustice told him by the office boys, Stevie lets off catherine wheels, squibs and fierce rockets on the staircase of his employer: 'An awful panic spread through the whole building. Wild-eyed, choking clerks stampeded through the passages full of smoke, silk hats and elderly business men could be seen rolling independently down the stairs.' The narrator contemplates the scene with an hilarious enjoyment of this ridiculous misfortune. This incident betrays something of the quirky humour that later compares Stevie's mangled remains to a cannibal feast.

Stevie occupies his spare time in drawing circles with compass and pencil on a piece of paper: 'circles, circles, circles; innumerable circles, concentric, eccentric; a coruscating whirl of circles that by their tangled multitude of repeated curves, uniformity of form, and confusion of intersecting lines suggested a rendering of cosmic chaos, the symbolism of a mad art attempting the inconceivable.' Stevie is the one true anarchist, attempting on these blank pages (a parody of Conrad's own fiction, in a way) to create an art to encompass chaos and eternity. The circles represent a harmony of form, an ideal justice which Stevie would like to create in society; but the obsessed scribbling, the final sense of cosmic disorder, suggests the impossibility of the task. He takes refuge in destructive acts, for only the annihilation of society can rid the world of its cruelties. The bomb plan enables him, or so he thinks, to put his ideals into practice, and the paper and pencil given him for the drawing of circles now lie blank and idle on the kitchen table. The accident proves ironically the message of the whole novel, that the only true anarchist act involves self-destruction.

In *The Sense of an Ending*, Frank Kermode argues that we need fictions to make sense of our contradictory world, but we err if we transform them into myths. In our love affair with reality, the mind may rearrange the world to suit its longing for forms, may take refuge in style as opposed to the chaos of experience; but if we try to impose these models on life we become dangerously immoral. When an artist such as Ezra Pound tries to imprint his vision on society, in his case by supporting Mussolini, the result is increased suffering and cruelty:

> What is ... wrong and dangerous is the belief, gratefully learnt by fascism from the innocent pragmatists, that fictions are to be justified or verified by their practical effects. Thus the world is changed to conform with a fiction, as by the murder of Jews. The effect is to insult reality, and to regress to myth.[6]

The ethical neutrality implied in Kermode's book was a position whose attractions Conrad fiercely resisted; in this he has much in common with other modern writers such as Yeats and Eliot. But he comes closest to these stoical assumptions in *The Secret Agent*. Stevie, the idealist and mad artist, creates a pure symbolism of circles and confused intersecting lines. When he tries to interfere with the muddles and tragedies of life his efforts result only in grotesque misfortune. The threat of fascism is reflected in the career of the Professor, and to this I shall turn in a moment. Stevie's mangled remains represent the condition to which society is moving; interference by the artist can only accelerate the process, and logically involves an anarchic act of self-destruction. The truth seen by the narrator is that human forms of identity are self-created illusion, and knowledge of their real death-in-life condition destroys Verloc, Winnie and Ossipon. The narrator escapes by entertaining himself in ironic detachment from the tragic spectacle. Later Conrad felt queasy about this stance, or lack of stance, and in his Preface denied that he intended to commit a gratuitous outrage on the feelings of mankind, professing to have no secret scorn for natural sensibilities. But in *The Secret Agent* he can no longer contain the explosive force of his nihilism. This is why political reformers such as Irving Howe recoil from the novel. Stevie's drawings and his self-destruction parody Conrad's own problems as an artist. The Swiftian choices for the artist are suicide or the consolations of style.

Like Stevie, the Professor at times seems to be admired by the narrator for his single-minded fanaticism. He certainly wins his argument with Inspector Heat, whose comfortable domestic virtues are disgusted by this puny, unhealthy specimen. The Professor clutches the detonator which will destroy himself and everyone near him if he is arrested; at least he dares to commit an act of self-destruction. Heat prefers thieves because he can identify with their pursuit of property; he cannot understand the Professor's zeal for destruction. But in the end we know, and the Professor himself knows, he is destined to fail. Like Kurtz, his revulsion from the mass of humanity causes him to preach a policy of extermination. He declares to Ossipon:

'Do you understand, Ossipon? The source of all evil! They are our sinister masters—the weak, the flabby, the silly, the cowardly, the faint of heart, and the slavish of mind. They have power. They are the multitude. Theirs is the kingdom of the earth. Exterminate, exterminate! That is the only way of progress. It is! Follow me, Ossipon. First the great multitude of the weak must go, then the only relatively strong. You see? First the blind, then the deaf and the dumb, then the halt and the lame—and so on. Every taint, every vice, every prejudice, every convention must meet its doom.' (p. 303)

His words are prophetic of fascism and Hitler's Germany. But Conrad suggests that the Professor's fascism in a sense is superficial, for he can never really trouble what he thinks of as 'the odious multitude of mankind'. In his heart he fears their great numbers, the hugeness of the amorphous masses who will never submit to his ideas of order and justice. In contrast to Yeats, T. S. Eliot, D. H. Lawrence and other moderns, Conrad was never in any way attracted to fascism. His own temptation was suicidal nihilism, and it is this that he resists in *The Secret Agent* by means of ironic style.

7

The drift towards death in *The Secret Agent* is well depicted in the strange cab-ride of Mrs Verloc's mother to her final resting-place in the charity home. Some critics have judged this episode too much a caricature, but I agree with Hugh Walpole that this ride is perhaps the most beautiful, touching and moving thing in the whole of Conrad.[7]

The conveyance in which Stevie, Winnie and their mother must travel 'would have illustrated the proverb that "truth can be more cruel than caricature", if such a proverb existed. Crawling behind an infirm horse, a metropolitan hackney carriage drew up on wobbly wheels and with a maimed driver on the box.' The emaciated horse carries a little stiff tail, which seems 'to have been fitted in for a heartless joke, and at the other end the thin, flat neck, like a plank covered with old horse-hide, drooped to the ground under the weight of an enormous bony head'. Accompanied by this macabre horse and driver, the journey in the 'Cab of Death' takes on a grotesque mythic quality. Incarcerated in a dark, low box on wheels, symbol of the coffin, the three passengers seem to have moved out of normal definitions of time and space. The cab moves so slowly, 'time itself seemed to stand still': 'In the narrow streets the progress of the journey was made sensible to those within by the near fronts of the houses gliding past slowly and shakily, with a great rattle and jingling of glass, as if about to collapse behind the cab.' The houses, the objects we pass on our journey through life, take their shape and significance only from our subjective consciousness. When we are not there, they collapse into nothing. As the cab jolts along 'the effect was of being shaken in a stationary apparatus like a medieval device for the punishment of crime'. So, surrounded by grotesque absurdities, through a landscape of darkness and misery, Mrs Verloc's mother wilfully chooses a kind of living death, and so unwittingly brings about the blowing up of her half-witted Stevie.

But this scene throws us just one crumb of possible comfort. As the carriage leaves, the cabman 'made as if to hoist himself on the box, but at the last moment, from some obscure motive, perhaps merely from disgust with carriage exercise, desisted. He approached instead the motionless partner of his labours, and stooping to seize the bridle, lifted up the big, weary head to the height of his shoulder with one effort of his right arm, like a feat of strength: '"Come on," he whispered, secretly.'

Although the narrator suggests otherwise, we may hope Stevie's complaints had touched the driver's compassion, that the young man did not die without influencing one person for good.

Chapter 6

Under Western Eyes: The Deaf Man

> One is faced with a simple choice: either one must run with the
> pack (when in Rome, do as the Romans do); or one becomes a
> neurotic.
>
> ROBERT MUSIL, *The Man Without Qualities*

I

'Nobody is exhibited as a monster here', wrote Conrad in his Author's
Note to *Under Western Eyes* (1911). In this novel he seems to be
renouncing the detached, non-committal stance of *The Secret Agent*,
which has its share of monsters. After his continued fluctuations
between belief in social values and sardonic, destructive withdrawal, he
now turns back to commitment. Tekla, the Good Samaritan, finds her
true identity in self-sacrifice. Natalia Haldin exemplifies devotion and
trust. The centre moral act of the story is Razumov's confession of
guilt, after a nightmare in which he realizes his balance of mind depends
on truthful relations with other people. Instead of the ironic vision of
The Secret Agent, Conrad appears to be developing towards the ideas
of fellowship and community at the heart of later novels such as
Chance, Victory, The Arrow of Gold and *The Rover*.

In his Author's Note, Conrad even suggests that Peter Ivanovitch,
Madame de S. and Nikita, the terrorist, are not monsters, and he
asserts that all these revolutionaries are typical products of their
background:

> The most terrifying reflection (I am speaking now for myself) is
> that all these people are not the product of the exceptional but of
> the general—of the normality of their place, and time, and race.
> The ferocity and imbecility of an autocratic rule rejecting all
> legality and in fact basing itself upon complete moral anarchism

provokes the no less imbecile and atrocious answer of a purely Utopian revolutionism encompassing destruction by the first means to hand, in the strange conviction that a fundamental change of hearts must follow the downfall of any given human institutions. (pp. ix–x)

This expresses Conrad's usual conservative view of revolution: it also attributes the horrors of Russian political life to a special kind of social conditioning, and in the novel these are deliberately contrasted with the safe but uninteresting environment of Geneva and England. To the Western eyes of the narrator, the old English teacher of languages, the Russians appear caught in a maelstrom of passion and violence beyond his comprehension. According to Conrad, the oppressors and the oppressed are all Russians together; their misfortune is to live in a country given up to tyrannical lawlessness, and this is the cause of their suffering. Their situation constitutes a special case, and should not be taken as representative of the human condition.

As usual, Conrad's Author's Note is too simple. The treatment of Western Europe as a secure retreat seems odd when we recall the macabre comedy of *The Secret Agent*, with the gruesome depiction of the deaths of the Verlocs, and the descriptions of the 'monstrous town' of London. The nihilism implicit in *The Secret Agent* cannot so easily be put aside, and there is still clear evidence of this in *Under Western Eyes*. The clumsy manipulation of the English narrator suggests that Conrad is unsure about his own point of view, and on occasions there is a return to the sardonic tone of earlier writings. Most important of all, the treatment of Razumov's confession is ambiguous. In the concluding chapters we may discern a repressed nihilism which reacts imaginatively to Razumov's deafness rather than to Tekla's sacrifice. There are signs of a regression to simpler attitudes of mind, of tiredness in the writing, and there are none of the strange analogies which throw the reader off balance in *The Secret Agent*.

Conrad is rather like the Lady of Shalott. In *The Secret Agent* he chooses a safe island of ironic withdrawal, of aesthetic distance, viewing the world through the mirror of art. When he looks away from these reflections to involve himself with life he places himself under a curse. After she has looked at the brilliant Sir Lancelot, the Lady of Shalott must immediately die. In Conrad's later works, commitment to human relationships is inevitably associated with an act of self-immolation.

2

Conrad's use of the English teacher as narrator is a most unsatisfactory device. This is partly a technical weakness. His presence during the confession scene between Razumov and Natalia is embarrassing, as if he were a voyeur peeping in at this scene of torment. We may echo Razumov's complaint: 'How did this old man come here?' His insistence on his lack of imagination appears ridiculous, for he recounts his tale with compelling force. The pretence that he is simply recording his memories wears thin, and we may wonder where this supposedly smug and impotent onlooker found his grasp of language and astute powers of artistic selection. He is himself a participant during important scenes, and this double role, as uncomprehending bystander and imaginative narrator, muddles his effects, particularly when he is describing his impressions of Razumov in Geneva.

This uncertainty of narrative tone affects the moral issues raised by *Under Western Eyes*. In an excellent study of this novel,[1] Tony Tanner points out the double irony in having this modest, decent, tolerant liberal recount the irrational manifestations of Razumov's guilt. The teacher of languages may persuade us of the undesirability and remoteness of his Russian material, but the depth of feeling in Razumov and Natalia may convince us of the inadequacy of the narrator's complacent virtues. Certainly the novel is not an anti-Russian polemic, and we may feel that the Russians, like Lord Jim or Decoud, achieve a kind of superiority by their submission to the truths of extreme experience. They have looked into the abyss of which, according to the narrator, the Swiss are stupidly ignorant.

But Conrad's control over this double irony is unsure. The narrator's boring insistence that his Russians are incomprehensible to Western Europeans is contradicted by his own clear portrayal of their suffering, and by the invitation to the Western reader to become vicariously involved, which is the *raison d'être* of the novel. The continual belittling of the Swiss contrasts forcibly with the sympathetic treatment of Razumov's anguish, and we naturally associate ourselves with this point of view. In the public garden where Razumov walks with Natalia, the narrator makes this comment on the local inhabitants:

> ... I observed a solitary Swiss couple, whose fate was made secure from the cradle to the grave by the perfected mechanism of democratic institutions in a republic that could almost be held in

the palm of one's hand. The man, colourlessly uncouth, was drinking beer out of a glittering glass; the woman, rustic and placid, leaning back in the rough chair, gazed idly around. (p. 175)

A similar contempt is expressed in the scenes on the little island where, under a bronze effigy of Rousseau, Razumov commits to paper his story of suffering and betrayal: 'There was something of naïve, odious and inane simplicity about that unfrequented tiny crumb of earth named after Jean Jacques Rousseau.' Conrad is satirizing the romantic optimism of the author of the *Social Contract*; but in these scenes in the park and on the island the condemnation of the Swiss gets out of hand. The contempt for Geneva, presumably Conrad's own feeling, appears awkwardly in the words of the placid teacher of languages. The attack on Swiss mediocrity seems to come not so much from the narrator's point of view as from an aristocratic revulsion from common humanity. The novel partially fails because it is difficult to sort out the several attitudes of the narrator, Conrad and Razumov, and we may suspect that this confusion derives from Conrad's inability to reconcile the warring elements in his own values. His desire for a clear, sure framework of moral standards is working in opposition to his fundamental imaginative response to life, and the result is confusion and simplification.

A cold contempt for certain specimens of humanity is expressed appropriately enough in the scenes at Château Borel. Peter Ivanovitch, who is modelled on Bakunin, *is* a monster, and a worthy sequel to the revolutionaries in *The Secret Agent*. His big soft hand, his featureless bearded face, hidden behind dark glasses, his obscene affair with Madame de S., all produce an effect of nausea. What is his sexual relation with his painted, bedizened, dead-faced, glassy-eyed Egeria? She is a ghoul, and Razumov is reminded by her painted face of a grinning skull. The suffering imposed on Tekla by Peter Ivanovitch and this 'galvanized corpse out of some Hoffman's tale' is monstrously evil. Nikita, too, is a sinister grotesque. His squeaky voice contrasts absurdly with his fat bulk; it pierces the ear ridiculously, like the falsetto of a circus clown beginning an elaborate joke: 'The abrupt squeaks of the fat man seemed to proceed from that thing like a balloon he carried under his overcoat.' He is supposed to have killed more gendarmes and police agents than any revolutionist living. These creatures of Château Borel emerge from a distorted world, on which Conrad's imagination broods, and whose terrors he minimizes in his Author's Note.

An implicit despair expresses itself in more general terms when Razumov visits the low eating-house in search of Ziemianitch, the driver of a team of three horses, who is supposed to carry off Haldin to safety. Like Mrs Neale in *The Secret Agent*, the people in the eating-house are stripped of their humanity. The company includes 'a horrible nondescript, shaggy being with a black face like the muzzle of a bear' and 'a wet and bedraggled creature, a sort of sexless and shivering scarecrow', washing glasses over a wooden tub by the light of a tallow dip. The place is like an underground asylum for rats: 'The house was an enormous slum, a hive of human vermin, a monumental abode of misery towering on the verge of starvation and despair.' Razumov's journey through the snow to this eating-house takes him away from his isolated room into contact with suffering humanity; but it is typical of Conrad that the scene is depicted like a bizarre voyage to an underworld, towards areas of experience perhaps better forgotten. Razumov finds Ziemianitch dead drunk in a cavernous stable 'like a neglected subterranean byre'. The eating-house keeper holds up a lantern: 'The intense black spokes of shadow swung about in the circle of light.' This weird setting, with the shadows of evil falling across the light of rationality, continually returns to Razumov's tormented consciousness after he has betrayed Haldin. In his frustration he belabours Ziemianitch with the handle of a stablefork. His fury is ascribed by Conrad to the blind rage of self-preservation; but the scene also suggests the impotent anger of the intellectual confronted by the irrationality of the common man. Haldin, with his sentimental trust in people, thinks of Ziemianitch as 'a bright soul, a hardy soul'. The reality is a drunken peasant deserted by his woman. Razumov feels done for, caught between the stupefied Ziemianitch, incapable of action, and the dream-intoxication of Haldin, incapable of perceiving the reason of things and the true character of men. The scepticism about humanity implicit in this situation is that of Conrad himself.

This pessimism ought to be balanced by the nobility of Tekla and Natalia, but these characters fail to come alive. Tekla is the more satisfactorily presented, but Conrad turns her into a figure of grotesque pathos. Her self-sacrifice places her in subjection to the sadism and miserliness of Peter Ivanovitch. She has devoted her energies to the service of dangerous and perverted revolutionaries. Even her assistance to the stricken Razumov seems touched by a strain of masochism, a need to sublimate her feeling of personal inadequacy by self-effacing devotion to others.

Natalia has been admired by many readers of the novel, but in my view Conrad is evasive in his treatment of her. She believes trustingly in a future era of concord and justice, yet she is incapable, as far as we can tell, of forgiving Razumov. At the end the narrator looks with sad irony at her sentimental faith that love and harmony will spring 'like a heavenly flower from the soil of man's earth, soaked in blood, torn by struggles, watered with tears'. We are asked to mix admiration for her qualities of trust with the knowledge that she comprehends little of the realities of evil, in spite of her contact with Razumov. She's supposed to be intelligent, but her political beliefs are those of simple naïveté.

Her sexual nature also seems a little obscure. She has a dark complexion, with red lips and a full figure. The teacher of languages falls in love with her, as far as he is capable, but he is too impotent to make any positive approach. He suggests she is delightfully feminine, but oddly he on two occasions finds manly qualities in her. He tells us: 'The grip of her strong, shapely hand had a seductive frankness, a sort of exquisite virility.' Her voice, slightly harsh, fascinates by 'its masculine and bird-like quality'. Conrad is unsure what kind of person she is, and his taste for the dominating type of women infiltrates itself into the narrator's comments. She is supposed to respond warmly to Razumov, but little of this is shown to the reader. Instead she remains featureless, and in this resembles the statuesque Antonia Avellanos. Her goodness and truth lack the force to counteract the atmosphere of nightmare engendered by Razumov and the revolutionaries.

3

In Russia Razumov has led an isolated, withdrawn life, adopting a pose of non-commitment. He is a disowned bastard, a man without political or family ties: 'He was as lonely in the world as a man swimming in the deep sea.' This sentence recalls Stein's analysis of the destructive element in *Lord Jim*. Razumov exists in that state of alienation which Conrad felt to be a crucial testing time. Like Jim in Patusan, or Nostromo after the lighter is sunk, he must create his own identity. He cannot rely on the forms and relations provided by an inherited involvement in the community.

As a student Razumov has tried to locate himself in society by the disciplines of work. Intelligent and self-aware, he has conceived for himself a linear kind of self-development, proceeding via the silver medal for the prize essay to the role of celebrated professor. The narrator comments:

> . . . a celebrated professor was a somebody. Distinction would convert the label Razumov into an honoured name. There was nothing strange in the student Razumov's wish for distinction. A man's real life is that accorded to him in the thoughts of other men by reason of respect or natural love. (pp. 13–14)

Razumov's progress in the novel is towards a more profound understanding of this 'real life' in the thoughts of other men. But before Haldin's arrival Razumov maintains his balance of mind, in a period of mental and political unrest, by keeping an instinctive hold on normal, practical everyday life. He submerges himself in the familiar, using the trivialities of daily existence as an armour for the soul: 'The exceptional could not prevail against the material contacts which make one day resemble another.' He trusts in institutions, because they seem to him 'rational and indestructible'. They express 'a force of harmony', attractive to him because it opposes both the anarchy of the revolutionaries and the unregulated void of his alienated life. He is proud of the lucidity of his mind, and hopes to create his own future by the free use of the intelligence.

This rational existence is destroyed by the sudden appearance of Haldin, demanding help after he has assassinated the Minister-President. Haldin seems to Razumov like an emissary of the Fates, or as a ghost which he is powerless to exorcize. Haldin represents the forces of irrationality and absurdity which so often in Conrad surge up from unexpected depths to confound the man of imagination. Tony Tanner compares this incident to the extraordinary arrival of Jones, Ricardo and Pedro at Heyst's island paradise; or we may recall Gentleman Brown's destructive influence on Jim's dream of Patusan.

Razumov employs a variety of expedients to cope with this eruption of the irrational. He first appeals to his father, choosing the institutions of law and order with which he has always associated himself. He decides to give Haldin up to the authorities, and in his heart knows he has from the beginning determined to do this. He justifies this decision to himself by appealing to rational political argument. He believes in the organic growth of institutions, which anarchism can only destroy, like a disease. And so he scrawls on a square sheet of paper:

History not Theory.
Patriotism not Internationalism.
Evolution not Revolution.
Direction not Destruction.
Unity not Disruption. (p. 66)

It is the credo of his intellectual freedom. From such a conservative idea of society it is rational and just to betray Haldin.

Razumov soon discovers the inadequacy of this philosophy to satisfy his emotional needs. The reality behind the ideal of autocracy has already taken shape in the figure of General T——, to whom his father, Prince K——, conducts him to tell his story. The General stares at him from blue, unbelieving eyes; Razumov loathes him, and can never forget the eyes which seemed to start out of the General's head. He is shocked by this 'grotesque' aspect, by the evil he discerns in this 'goggle-eyed imbecile'. From this moment he no longer can keep his mind sane by appeal to the familiar, by involvement in daily routine. The clock on the General's mantelpiece makes no sound; the silence of the room is like the silence of the grave. Razumov emerges from this encounter reborn into a world of irrational absurdities, beyond the control of his political philosophy. He begins to see life as 'a comedy of errors', as if 'the devil himself were playing a game with all of them in turn'.

Haldin's appearance demonstrates to Razumov that his pose of non-commitment is impractical; human beings will keep bumping into him, shoving forward their claims on his moral allegiance. He is forced to acknowledge that his prized freedom of mind lies at the mercy of the irrationality which governs others. From the moment Haldin invades his room he is given an identity not under his own control. Haldin expects loyal support. His fellow students take for granted he is a revolutionary. The authorities impose on him the role of secret agent. He is no longer his own man.

Back in his room after he has sent off Haldin to his death, he is shocked to find that his watch has stopped: 'Razumov looked wildly about as if for some means of seizing upon time which seemed to have escaped him altogether.' Memories of the General bring on positive nausea. His act of betrayal is accompanied by a breakdown of the normal functions of the senses. Tanner compares this condition of mind to that evoked in Sartre's *Nausea*, in which matter without meaning becomes monstrous. Without inner truth, his senses run amok, and turn the world into a form of delirium. In Tanner's words, 'the usual significances have drained out of the objects of the pheno-menological world.'[2] After his room is searched, he feels that his old identity, created out of discipline and routine, is destroyed for ever. His neat piles of paper and notes have been shuffled up and heaped together in the middle of the table:

> This disorder affected him profoundly, unreasonably. He sat down and stared. He had a distinct sensation of his very existence being undermined in some mysterious manner, of his moral supports falling away from him one by one. He even experienced a slight physical giddiness and made a movement as if to reach out for something to steady himself with. (pp. 76-7)

He acknowledges to himself that his attempt to guide his conduct by reasonable convictions, to exert his intelligence and develop his faculties, is no protection against the 'destructive horror' Haldin has let loose into his life. Immediately after this incident, he falls into a state of peculiar irresolution:

> This irresolution bore upon the question whether he should con-tinue to live—neither more nor less. But its nature was very far removed from the hesitation of a man contemplating suicide. The idea of laying violent hands upon his body did not occur to Razumov. The unrelated organism bearing that label, walking, breathing, wearing these clothes, was of no importance to any one, unless maybe to the landlady. The true Razumov had his being in the willed, in the determined future—in that future menaced by the lawlessness of autocracy—for autocracy knows no law—and the lawlessness of revolution. The feeling that his moral personality was at the mercy of these lawless forces was so strong that he asked himself seriously if it were worth while to go on accomplishing the mental functions of that existence which seemed no longer his own. (pp. 77-8)

Eventually he falls ill, in a kind of low fever which 'all at once removed him to a great distance from the perplexing actualities, from his very room even. He never lost consciousness; he only seemed to himself to be existing languidly somewhere very far away from everything that had ever happened to him.'

When we meet him in Geneva, he has recovered from this inertia, but he now finds his concept of reality has entirely changed. Inanimate objects, human beings, the very air itself have lost their previous significance. He attempts to exist in a state of angry, mocking aloofness. Conrad's brilliant exposé of this detachment reflects a complete turn-about from the implicit narrative tone of *The Secret Agent*. In Russia before his departure Razumov treats the poverty-stricken revolutionary student with amused contempt, recording how his nose nipped bright red by the sharp air looked like a false nose of painted cardboard between the sallow cheeks. He treats the student as a clown, a fantastic person in an absurd world whose claims he can reject. The moral danger of this withdrawal is seen in the malicious pleasure with which he deceives the hare-brained Kostia. Kostia is made to steal from his father to help Razumov escape; Razumov throws the money away out of the window of his railway carriage. By this act he demonstrates his sense that moral obligations are preposterous, a game of make-believe.

In Geneva his personality falls apart under the strain imposed by his new pose of detachment. He engages in verbal duels with Peter Ivanovitch and Sophia Antonovna in which he tries to preserve his freedom by manipulation of other people. He can remain aloof only if he resists their efforts to understand him, but such continual hypocrisy offends his natural sensibility. Like Macbeth, his crime disturbs the natural functions of the body. He cannot sleep, and lies unwinking in the dark, angrily passive in the toils of disastrous thoughts. His voice becomes practically extinct, dried up in his throat. In his conversations, he cannot control himself, and he must talk about his suspicions. He observes the operations of his body with amazement, and often seems to be watching his own physical dislocation from a great distance. After his first visit to the painted Egeria, 'he felt, bizarre as it may seem, as though another self, an independent sharer of his mind, had been able to view his whole person very distinctly indeed'. Tanner comments: 'This sort of incipient schizophrenia experienced by people under stress is a recurring theme in Conrad, but never had the danger and stress been as great as for his character Razumov to whom absolute self-mastery and lucid integration are necessary for survival.'[3]

The pose of ironic detachment, of aesthetic contemplation of the meaninglessness of values, proves a kind of suicidal schizophrenia. On his little island, beneath the statue of Rousseau, his identity flickers, fades, appears close to extinction. He sits motionless, 'without thought and sight and hearing, almost without life'.

The breakdown of Razumov proves the truth of the narrator's comment: 'No human being could bear a steady view of moral solitude without going mad.' The wish to retire, simply to retire, involves a death of one's essence as a human being. The famous words which conclude Razumov's interview with Councillor Mikulin reverberate through the novel:

> 'To retire', he repeated.
> 'Where to?' asked Councillor Mikulin softly. (p. 99)

4

From the beginning of the novel we are not allowed to forget that Razumov betrays Haldin largely through fear for his own skin, an instinct of self-preservation which makes his decision inevitable. When, returning from his visit to the drunken Ziemianitch, he hears the words, 'O thou vile wretch!' shouted hoarsely by a driver as two sledges collide, it seems an echo from the depths of his own moral nature. The reality behind his violent disgust for his assumed roles in Geneva is that he is ashamed of his betrayal, that he knows he is responsible. The claim Haldin makes on him is fundamentally nothing to do with matters of politics or revolution. Haldin asks for protection and help, and Razumov, in spite of all his self-justifications, knows he has rejected a simple human appeal. His betrayal is like the Ancient Mariner's killing of the albatross, an abandonment of the ties that bind man and nature, man and man. It is an archetypal sin, like the murder of a guest or a friend. Peter Ivanovitch compares Razumov to Brutus, and the analogy is more apt than he realizes.

Immediately after Haldin departs towards capture and death, Razumov feels like a man undergoing torture, and he longs to admit his guilt. His mind hovers on the borders of delirium: 'He heard himself suddenly saying, "I confess", as a person might do on the rack.' References to torture occur again during his interview with Councillor Mikulin. In his condition of incipient schizophrenia, Razumov observes himself in a dream-like state as if he were participating in a scene from the Inquisition. He watches his own brain, suffering on the rack: 'a long, pale figure drawn asunder horizontally with terrific force in the darkness of a vault, whose face he failed to see.' It seems likely that Conrad himself had experienced such moments of torment. The key to the dream lies in the lines: 'The solitude of the racked victim was particularly horrible to behold. The mysterious impossibility to see the face . . . inspired a sort of terror.' The *solitude* seems a main cause of the suffering. Conrad appears to be using Razumov's act of betrayal to explore the consequences of alienation for his own psychology. He vicariously participates in his hero's racked consciousness, and concludes that his own self-induced isolation involves inevitable mental breakdown. His sense of guilt is not, as Jocelyn Baines argues, a result of his desertion of Poland, but an imaginative awareness, typical of other writers such as Henry James or T. S. Eliot, that his modern sensibility cuts him off from communion with his fellow beings. For Razumov, to see the face in the dream would be to recognize his own self, and so acknowledge the true consequence of his betrayal. He has assumed the role of a Judas.

His split personality can be healed only by confession. After his beating of Ziemianitch, he embraces for a whole minute a vision of rushing back to his lodgings and flinging himself on his knees before Haldin: he would 'pour out a full confession in passionate words that would stir the whole being of that man to its innermost depths; that would end in embraces and tears; in an incredible fellowship of souls—such as the world had never seen'. Although this sentimental idyll cannot permanently drive away his fear, he discovers that such longings for fellowship may not be suppressed. He wants to confess to Mikulin, though he is not sure to what: 'To be understood appeared extremely fascinating.' He enjoys his conversations with Mikulin because he is the only person on earth he can talk to, taking the Haldin adventure for granted. In Geneva he tries to restrain a compulsive need to speak of his experiences; he is resisting a natural human longing to communicate. Deprived of honest speech, he turns to writing, and in spite of risk commits his thoughts and memories to paper. His journal takes the form of a confession to Natalia, an area of truth in contrast to the lies that he must utter while in her presence. The English teacher of languages thinks that the activity of writing proved for Razumov a formula of peace: 'There must be a wonderful soothing power in mere words since so many men have used them for self-communion.' Razumov must communicate, if only with an imaginary Natalia. He is like the modern artist, who, when his contacts with society are broken, turns for relief to the consolation of words. In a sense Razumov's writing mimes the activities of the early Eliot or Plath or Lowell or

Beckett; yet Conrad now insists that this alienation from society should be seen in terms of guilt and betrayal. 'Is it possible that I have a conventional conscience?', Razumov asks himself, as he watches his own shrinking away from hypocrisy. The answer is yes; he is the victim of remorse. In *Under Western Eyes* the conventional moral conscience proves to be a natural phenomenon, an essential part of a human being. Razumov's schizophrenia results from his failure in his response to another human being. In his later work, Conrad finds the answer to his own (and by implication the modern artist's) suicidal despair in a renewal of ordinary human relationships.

This linking of moral goodness with a concept of the natural is introduced on a number of occasions. After visiting Château Borel, Razumov expels his breath with force 'to get rid of the last vestiges of the air he had been breathing inside'. It is as if the moral corruption of Peter Ivanovitch and his Egeria taints the very air itself. Immediately afterwards he is forced into colloquy by Sophia Antonovna, one of the few revolutionaries Conrad treats with respect (she too has 'a manly handgrasp'). Razumov feels that the choking fumes of falsehood had taken him by the throat, 'without the hope of ever renewing his strength by a breath of fresh air'. Sophia recommends a glass of cold water, and it is as if she is reminding him of the virtues in simple, natural behaviour. His haunted figure seems deprived of natural life, of sleep, of food, of air. After his admission of guilt to Natalia, he walks back to his lodgings through the rain. The owner says to him:

> 'You've got very wet.'
> 'Yes, I am washed clean', muttered Razumov, who was dripping from head to foot . . . (p. 357)

He departs to make his confession in a thunderstorm, the thick fall of rain enveloping him like a luminous veil in the play of lightning.

This moment of redemption recalls Dostoevsky, although the treatment of rebirth in Conrad is always ambiguous, slightly muffled in its message of hope. But we can acknowledge that, in contrast to *Nostromo*, *Under Western Eyes* does present a linear development of plot. Razumov proceeds from betrayal to guilt to purification. Natalia reveals to him his emotional needs as a human being: 'It was as though he were coming to himself in the awakened consciousness of that marvellous harmony of feature, of lines, of glances, of voice, which made of the girl before him a being so rare, outside, and, as it were, above the common notion of beauty.' In his journal he records the truth she has taught him:

> You were appointed to undo the evil by making me betray myself back into truth and peace. You! And you have done it in the same way, too, in which he ruined me: by forcing upon me your confidence. (p. 358)

He is disgusted by his fantasy that he might marry her without telling her of his guilt. With Mrs Haldin he perceives that the son's ghost lives on in its influence on the mother, while he himself has chosen non-life, non-relationship. The nature of human life is to betray us into love, to demand truth in our relationships. And so as he departs to confess, a single clap of thunder sounds 'like a gun fired for a warning of his escape from the prison of lies'.

In the moment of confession Razumov admits that from Haldin's arrival in his room he has never been able to extinguish his sense that they are for ever involved, related together. Although he tries to forget, he cannot exorcize the ghost. As he returns from his encounter with Ziemianitch, he suffers an hallucination that Haldin, solid, distinct, real, clad in brown close-fitting coat and long boots, is lying on his back before him in the snow. He walks across the body, deliberately opposing his conscious will to this irrational phenomenon. But the phantom is not so easily defeated. It appears again in his rooms, with extraordinary completeness of detail. The words and events of that evening 'must have been graven as if with a steel tool on Mr Razumov's brain'. He discovers that the mind cannot control the objective world outside the senses, cannot remain independent. Like Wordsworth, he learns that subject and object, the mind and what it perceives, are inextricably bound together, and that sanity, moral health, depend on a true relationship between the inner and the outer life. Haldin departs running on tip-toe from Razumov's room down the deep black shaft of the staircase, which has a tiny gaslight at the bottom: 'It was a light, swift, pattering sound, which sank away from him into the depths: a fleeting shadow passed over the glimmer—a wink of the tiny flame.' It is as if he has descended into a region of consciousness whose existence had previously been ignored by Razumov's rational ways of life.

So, as he sets off to make his confession to the assembled revolutionaries, he waits until the exact moment of Haldin's departure, the stroke of midnight, and then runs swiftly downstairs. He mimes Haldin's descent into the regions of emotion and morality. In this curious ritual, he identifies himself with Haldin, by his imitation testifying to an involvement which his whole being has been unable to deny. It is a symbolic event for Conrad too. In spite of his tendency towards nihilism, his novel-writing satisfies his need to keep open communications with his fellow men. His imagination satisfies itself by an act of vicarious participation.

5

Sophia Antonovna admires Razumov's courage in his decision to confess. He has realized he could not suppress his sense of ignominy. 'There's character in such a discovery,' she tells the narrator. But he is not allowed to begin a new life of creative endeavour. In a violent scene, Nikita bursts his ear-drums; the stricken Razumov steps under a tram, and is so badly hurt he can never recover. His confession, his act of commitment, becomes a kind of suicide. As he himself knows, he must confess *and perish*. He lives on in a condition of deafness which suggests imaginatively the condition of many other Conrad characters. In spite of his attempt to communicate, he is cut off from his fellows. They speak but he cannot hear; the world moves on soundlessly, and natural relationships are no longer fully possible for him.

This soundless world is imaginatively created at the beginning of the novel, and suggests the kind of ultimate truth, the knowledge of the void, which sends Decoud to his death. Sounds are muffled by the snow as Razumov sets off to seek out Ziemiantich: 'Along the roadway sledges glided phantom-like and jingling through a fluttering whiteness on the black face of the night.' Passers-by loom up black in the snowflakes close by, then vanish all at once, without footfalls. Outside his solitary room, he already exists like a deaf man, in a silent, cold landscape without meaning. He is attracted by the passive anonymity that Russia's immense size offers him:

> Razumov stamped his foot—and under the soft carpet of snow felt the hard ground of Russia, inanimate, cold, inert, like a sullen and tragic mother hiding her face under a winding-sheet—his native soil!—his very own—without a fireside, without a heart . . .
>
> Razumov received an almost physical impression of endless space and of countless millions.
>
> He responded to it with the readiness of a Russian who is born

to an inheritance of space and numbers. Under the sumptuous immensity of the sky, the snow covered the endless forests, the frozen rivers, the plains of an immense country, obliterating the landmarks, the accidents of the ground, levelling everything under its uniform whiteness, like a monstrous blank page awaiting the record of an inconceivable history. It covered the passive land with its lives of countless people like Ziemianitch and its handful of agitators like this Haldin—murdering foolishly.
It was a sort of sacred inertia. (pp. 32–3)

He then associates this vision with the necessity for autocracy. The strong leader will represent the land, will give the masses a sense of direction and purpose. Yet this immensity is uniformly white, a monstrous blank page, as if the people are obliterated into insignificance by the hugeness of the land. The faith in the great autocrat seems a kind of self-obliteration. Razumov blends imaginatively into the endless spaces and countless millions, losing that individuality which is so vulnerable but which is his only unique quality. This spirit of negation Conrad tries to repudiate. After the betrayal, Razumov dreams 'of walking through drifts of snow in a Russia where he was as completely alone as any betrayed autocrat could be; an immense, wintry Russia which, somehow, his view could embrace in all its enormous expanse as if it were a map.' The vision of autocracy and Russia does not cure his loneliness; his betrayal of Haldin is a betrayal of himself: 'His existence was a great cold blank, something like the enormous plain of the whole of Russia levelled with snow and fading gradually on all sides into shadows and mists.'

Yet his confession condemns him to just such a blankness. He lives on crippled, ill, getting weaker every day, in a little two-roomed wooden house, hiding within the high plank-fence of a yard overgrown with nettles. Confession may heal his split personality, but only by deafness, by no longer hearing the voices of the comic, grotesque world around him. Symbolically it is as if Conrad recognizes that commitment to people, to love, meant for him a kind of deafness, a withdrawal like a snail into its shell. The voices of absurdity, to which he responded imaginatively in *Lord Jim*, need to be silenced for the sake of mental balance. Like Razumov, he lives on after the writing of this novel, comforted by the Tekla-like devotion of his wife, yet increasingly deaf to the problems of modernism which so tore him apart during the period of his greatest imaginative achievements.

Chapter 7

Outcasts in *Chance* and *Victory*

'No one but you could gain admittance through this door, since this door was intended only for you. I am now going to shut it.'

KAFKA, *The Trial*

I

On his first voyage as second mate on Captain Anthony's ship, the *Ferndale*, the young Mr Powell is alone on the poop, at about ten o'clock at night, with the weather gloomy and threatening. A dead head wind is blowing, and the *Ferndale* under reduced sail is stretching close-hauled across the track of the homeward-bound ships, which are running before the wind towards England.

Among the white, breaking seas, under the black sky, Mr Powell makes out the lights of an approaching ship which seems to be heading straight at the *Ferndale*. He tries to call up the Captain, but forgets the strange sleeping arrangements, whereby the Captain has taken his quarters on the port side, and given his own room to his wife and her father, the swindler de Barral. As a result Powell's shouts alert both Flora Anthony as well as the Captain, and she emerges from her cabin in time to help to light the flare which saves the ship from a terrifying collision:

'The strange ship, a darker shape in the night, did not seem to be moving onwards but only to grow more distinct right abeam, staring at the *Ferndale* with one green and one red eye which swayed and tossed as if they belonged to the restless head of some invisible monster ambushed in the night amongst the waves. A moment, long like eternity, elapsed, and, suddenly, the monster which seemed to take to itself the shape of a mountain shut its green eye without as much as a preparatory wink.

'Mr. Powell drew a free breath. "All right now", said Captain Anthony in a quiet undertone. He gave the blazing flare to Powell and walked aft to watch the passing of that menace of destruction coming blindly with its parti-coloured stare out of a blind night on the wings of a sweeping wind. Her very form could be distinguished now black and elongated amongst the hissing patches of foam bursting along her path.

'As is always the case with a ship running before wind and sea she did not seem to an onlooker to move very fast; but to be progressing indolently in long, leisurely bounds and pauses in the midst of the overtaking waves. It was only when actually passing the stern within easy hail of the *Ferndale* that her headlong speed became apparent to the eye. With the red light shut off and soaring like an immense shadow on the crest of a wave she was lost to view in one great, forward swing, melting into the lightless space.' (p. 319)

The vivid force of this scene contrasts with the slackness of style typical of many other sections of the novel. Conrad's imagination responds to the dangers of the sea; his intimate knowledge of shipboard life brings this incident alive in a manner never achieved in other descriptions in the novel, such as the country cottage scenes where Marlow meets the civil servant Fyne and his lesbian wife.

The strange ship hurls itself towards the *Ferndale* like some 'monster' of the waves. Its 'menace of destruction' emerges out of 'a blind night', and eventually is lost to view, 'melting into the lightless space'. I am reminded of the silent black squall that threatens the *Patna* in *Lord Jim*, eating up the sky, swallowing the stars. The ship, the microcosm of society, is suddenly threatened by an infernal agent from the other side of life, from the blackness of chaos. When Powell's first attempt to strike the blue light on the rail misfires, he undergoes, like Jim, 'a paralysis of thought, of voice, of limbs'. His mind conjures up a picture of the enormous flare and uproar if the dynamite in the *Ferndale* explodes, and his power to act only returns when he receives a clear order from Captain Anthony. This incident might persuade us to consider Jim's terror more leniently, for Powell is a reliable, steadfast seaman.

As we have seen on several occasions before, Conrad's imagination takes fire at moments like these, when innocence is suddenly threatened by some diabolical power representative of universal meaninglessness.

Eventually the Captain and Flora enjoy some years of married bliss together, which Conrad typically passes over in a few sentences, but the monster catches up with them in the end. In thick fog the *Ferndale* is cut in half in a collision, and Captain Anthony is drowned. Mr Powell comments: 'Good men go out as if there was no use for them in the world.'

2

Both *Chance* (1913) and *Victory* (1915) deal with outcasts who try to form a paradise outside the conventions of society. Anthony ran away to sea to escape from the tyranny of his father, the sentimental, romantic poet, Caerleon Anthony, and made for himself a secure refuge in his profession as a seaman. Flora has to carry the burden of a father who is a criminal, and relatives without any generous sympathies towards her misfortune. When at first these two decide to live together on the *Ferndale*, Marlow depicts them as a new Adam and Eve: 'Those two were outside all conventions. They would be as untrammelled in a sense as the first man and the first woman.'

But both these novels are more successful in depicting moral isolation than in realizing a viable alternative. In *Victory*, as we shall see, Heyst is a most interesting and sympathetic recluse, but his love for Lena is treated in a confused, unsatisfactory manner. In *Chance*, the strange ship, like a monster, bears down on the Anthonys with a menacing strength that makes their love seem flimsy and unreal. In both novels the heroes are defeated by wayward chance, Anthony by the collision and Heyst by the extraordinary bad luck of Jones's arrival in Samburan. In *Chance*, appropriately titled, Marlow comments *ad nauseam* on the arbitrary workings of fate. Against this background Conrad attempts to capture in words the feelings of his lovers, but his style goes smudgy and incoherent as soon as these characters seek to escape from alienation.

Presumably *Chance* became a best seller and established Conrad's financial position because it includes a love affair in strange conditions, a strong narrative line, a varied group of characters, some of Dickensian origin, and a happy ending. Yet the story touches upon much that is actively unpleasant. There are several examples of sexual aberration and neurosis. Flora, the main character, endures when only fifteen years old a horrifying assault on her balance of mind as a result of her governess's sexual jealousy. This sudden invasion of her innocence parallels, in its general effect, the unexpected menace of the 'monster' ship that threatens the *Ferndale*.

While the widower de Barral is apparently making his fortune through his Thrift and Independence Aid Association, his daughter Flora is looked after by a high-toned governess aged nearly forty, who bullies the father into establishing them in a splendidly furnished house in the most expensive part of Brighton. Sexually frustrated, the governess harbours a taste 'for patronizing young men of sorts—of a certain sort'. When she is informed of de Barral's impending financial ruin, she turns violently against the innocent Flora. She is sexually enraged because no longer will she have sufficient money to pay her latest inamorato, named Charley, for his favours.

Flora is to endure two moments of awakened consciousness during the novel, one into knowledge of evil, the other into love of Captain Anthony. The former has the far greater imaginative impact. The governess's resentment for Flora's youth and charm erupts into an uncontrollable urge to destroy the young girl. The emanation of evil in her eyes frightens Flora, stirs in her 'that faculty of unreasoning explosive terror lying locked up at the bottom of all human hearts and of the hearts of animals as well'. The governess's venom as she reveals that de Barral is a criminal destroys Flora's confidence in her selfhood, shatters her concept of her own identity. Her panic throws her into the kind of 'abyss' which Conrad's previous heroes have usually experienced at some climax of violence at sea. Her imagination goes off 'in a wild bound to meet the unknown'. She turns cold with terror, and for two years afterwards her face remained bloodless and white like a ghost. Although touched with melodrama, this scene of sexual violence is unforgettably disturbing. It is as if animal passions, both of lust and fear, had suddenly welled up from underneath the superficial crust of civilization. After this awakening, Flora has to suffer various schemes to reintegrate her into society, ending with the attempt of the German husband to seduce her. Inevitably she succumbs to a mental weariness, to a deadening feeling that nothing concerns her any longer. She is only prevented from committing suicide by the lucky accident of Marlow's presence at the foot of the cliff, and finally by Captain Anthony's infatuation. Her lack of self-confidence makes her too passive when Anthony, with foolish altruism, arranges for them not to consummate the marriage. He thinks she is marrying him because she wants to be rescued from her disastrous social situation, and only the climactic moment when her father tries to poison him reveals to him the truth of her love.

The governess's outburst is the cause of all the complexities of the story. Its evil is paralleled by other incidents and characters. When Flora goes off with Anthony, his sister, Mrs Fyne, is worked up by a lesbian fury at this supposed betrayal of her guardianship. Marlow shows some affection for Fyne the husband, an honest, dull man, but Mrs Fyne and her daughters are usually treated with contempt. The children are malicious and arrogant, nursing a secret scorn for all the world. Marlow tries to be tolerant towards the mother, but he cannot suppress his dislike for her 'smooth-cheeked face of masculine shape'. He depicts her labours for women's rights, her desire to transform every female into an 'unscrupulous sexual nuisance', as a distasteful aberration.

De Barral and his respectable cousin are squalid and inhuman. The mean selfishness of the cousin lacerates Flora's feelings, confronts her with 'a view of the utmost baseness to which common human nature can descend'. De Barral himself is a tragi-comic figure whose colour-less personality is as incapable of an attitude as a bed-post. His bank-ruptcy exposes to public knowledge his grotesque, incredible plans, and like a sinister farce, the court-room witnesses bursts of laughter in a setting of the mute anguish of the deceived creditors. After his release from prison, de Barral is insane in his self-absorption. He is a Dicken-sian figure (the comparison is specifically mentioned by Conrad himself) whose melodramatic attempt to poison his son-in-law and his own suicide read too much like a sensational novelette. He lurks about like a ghost set on frustrating the sexual embrace of Anthony and Flora. The Freudian interpretation is difficult to resist. Anthony must bring about the death of the girl's father, before he can overcome his innate fastidiousness, and claim Flora for himself.

Animal passion erupts in an unexpected manner to destroy Flora's self-possession; all the characters seem to exist under a similar threat of violence. In the opening chapter, young Powell travels down to London docks late at night, to be held up at the locked gates:

> Some human shapes appearing mysteriously, as if they had sprung up from the dark ground, shunned the edge of the faint light thrown down by the gateway lamps. These figures were wary in their movements and perfectly silent of foot, like beasts of prey slinking about a camp fire. (p. 25)

He is lucky not to be attacked by this 'mob of ugly spectres'. This is one of several scenes in which London is depicted as bestial and evil. The atmosphere during de Barral's trial is 'stifling' and 'poisonous'. On the occasion when Marlow and Flora talk together outside the Eastern Hotel, where Fyne is objecting to Captain Anthony about the proposed marriage, a sombre stream of humanity flows past them 'whose joys, struggles, thoughts, sorrows and their very hopes were miserable, glamourless, and of no account in the world'. The voices of Marlow and Flora have to compete with 'the odious uproar of that wide roadway thronged with heavy carts'. The noise is wearisome, passionless, crushing. In this context Anthony comes to Flora like a knight of chivalric romance to carry her away from the waste land, and to restore her wounded soul by the healing balm of a secure, innocent life at sea.

3

All these events are presented to us through Marlow's indirect mode of narration, but in *Chance* the device proves cumbersome and at times absurd. He tells the story to the anonymous author of the novel, but the interruptions of this featureless personage are invariably superficial, and only draw attention to Marlow's extraordinary misogyny. Marlow is not an eye witness to most of the events; indeed, often the anonymous narrator is telling us what Marlow told him about what somebody else recounted to Marlow about the private feeling of a fourth participant in the novel. In other Conrad stories we respond to the richness of multiple perspectives. Here there is often no reason for the third-hand narrative, and the total effect is to leave the action blurred. Marlow himself is sometimes dull. His diatribes against women, which draw forth protests from the anonymous narrator, are tedious, and sanctimoniously on the side of males: 'There is not between women that fund of at least conditional loyalty which men depend on in their dealings with each other.' Marlow appears to have lost some of the respect for human nature which characterizes his namesake in *Lord Jim* and *Heart of Darkness*. His misogyny is simply unpleasant. At times he cannot repress an amused contempt for the other characters. While discussing with the Fynes the inexplicable disappearance of Flora and the possibility of suicide, he suddenly becomes 'mentally aware of three trained dogs dancing on their hind legs', because he thinks they are all becoming too solemn. Such aberrations suggest that he does not sympathize with the suffering of his companions, and his whole narrative totters uneasily between jest and earnest. We feel a sense of bewilderment, as if Conrad himself is not sure what tone of voice is appropriate for Flora's misfortunes. Marlow 'had a narrow, veiled glance, the neutral bearing and the secret irritability which go together with a predisposition to congestion of the liver.' The anonymous narrator's opinion of him is inconsistent. On some occasions he finds him malicious. On others he suggests that the cynicism is a cover for Marlow's sympathy for the human need for illusions. In my estimation, the Marlow of previous narratives is a person with whom I would gladly participate in a convivial dinner-party. In contrast, if the Marlow of *Chance* offered me his company, I would seek an excuse for a quick exit. It is fortunate that the narrative is often directed to us through the ingenuous enthusiasm of Powell, whose instinctive enjoyment of life gives vigour to the writing.

The many unpleasant characters ought to be counterbalanced by the integrity of Captain Anthony. Unfortunately, like Heyst, Anthony's behaviour in his passion is not above criticism. His chivalrous offer to rescue Flora stems from his own need for affection, from his own repressed sexual desires: 'Such men are easily moved. At the least encouragement they go forward with the eagerness, with the recklessness of starvation.' Flora is frightened by his excessive joy because she has need of him: 'the rapacious smile that would come and go on his lips as if he were gloating over her misery'. His own situation as outcast, without parents to console and comfort, makes him long for rescue. By transference, he is sexually aroused by the desire to perform an act of rescue for somebody else. Because she has been ill-used, she becomes inexplicably attractive to him: 'It was not pity alone, I take it. It was something more spontaneous, perverse and exciting. It gave him the feeling that if only he could get hold of her, no woman would belong to him so completely as this woman.' She finds his 'ferocity' terrifying. Conrad depicts the psychology of Anthony with an understanding presumably derived from his own experiences as a motherless child. But the dialogue between the lovers is hackneyed, and it is not clear why Flora finds him so attractive. The suggestion is made that she likes to be dominated, but in the sections of the novel that deal with her love she becomes somewhat ethereal and insubstantial.

Anthony's passion proves to be too fastidious. Once he suspects that Flora does not care for him he withdraws into his quixotic scheme to marry her but leave her virgin. It is the perversity of his emotions that we remember rather than their eventual consummation. In *The Limits of Metaphor*, Guetti argues that Captain Anthony's example proves the impossibility of the human longing to order experience. His pursuit of Flora is an attempt to possess something unequivocally, and by so doing to render it and all experience meaningful. Flora represents his own loneliness. By isolating her on his ship he tries to ensure that he controls her both physically and imaginatively. So he cherishes his illusion—'Something as incredible as the fulfilment of an amazing and startling dream in which he could take the world in his arms—all the suffering world—not to possess its pathetic fairness but to console and cherish its sorrow.' But his paradise is inhabited by a snake, de Barral, and the lovers suffer a period of debilitating frustration. When at last they are safe in each other's arms, the narrative hurries on quickly to the scene of Anthony's drowning.

I find *Chance* enigmatic and evasive. Marlow does his good turn, and helps Powell to marry Flora. But Flora has become a pasteboard figure, and at the conclusion the new lovers fade away into a sentimental dream. We remember more clearly Flora's despair when she learns that Anthony does not intend to consummate the marriage:

> 'He conducted her through the dangers of the quay-side. Her sight was dim. A moving truck was like a mountain gliding by. Men passed by as if in a mist; and the buildings, the sheds, the unexpected open spaces, the ships, had strange, distorted, dangerous shapes. She said to herself that it was good not to be bothered with what all these things meant in the scheme of creation (if indeed anything had a meaning), or were just piled-up matter without any sense. She felt how she had always been unrelated to this world. She was hanging on to it merely by that one arm grasped firmly just above the elbow. It was a captivity. So be it.'
> (p. 337)

Conrad understands completely the outcast's lack of relationship with the visible universe.

<h2 style="text-align:center">4</h2>

Writers about Conrad diverge widely in their estimates of *Victory*. The case for the opposition is powerfully argued by Albert Guerard. He considers *Victory* to be second-rate, popular romantic fiction: 'The rudimentary but exciting adventure story, the romantic pose of world-weary detachment, the simple yet vague erotic fantasy of the island shared with a grateful uneducated girl—all these are naturally pleasing materials to the adolescent mind.' [1] He finds the prose of many parts of *Victory* flat and unenergized, while on other occasions the descriptions of passion are desperately over-written.

In contrast, F. R. Leavis, while acknowledging that the novel is of a decidedly lesser order than *Nostromo*, still claims for it a classical standing. He most perceptively analyses the character of Axel Heyst, who is wholly sympathetic in his scepticism while Decoud is not. Leavis admires the melodramatic boldness with which Conrad treats the villains, and finds them convincing in a Dickensian manner: 'a Dickens qualified by a quite un-Dickensian maturity: they exist in strict subservience to Conrad's quite un-Dickensian theme and to their function, which is to precipitate Heyst's predicament to an issue in a conclusive action.' [2] Leavis believes the significance of this 'conclusive action' is clear. Lena's sacrifice symbolizes the triumph of love. By his suicide Heyst confesses to the inadequacy of his scepticism, and to his tragic failure to trust in life: 'It is an ironical victory for life, but unequivocally a victory.'

In my view, *Victory* includes some of the best and worst of Conrad's writing. The best is seen in the depiction of Heyst, whose philosophy of stoical non-involvement is shown in typical Conradian fashion as temptingly attractive and yet ultimately suicidal. The worst is reflected in the crude melodrama of the stage villains, Jones, Ricardo and Pedro, the spectre, the cat and the ape; and in the mushy sentimentality which surrounds Lena, the girl from the obnoxious Zangiacomo's travelling orchestra, with whom Heyst falls in love.

I agree, therefore, with Guerard in his criticism of the melodramatic and turgid elements in the style, but feel that Leavis is right to find in Heyst a fascinatingly complex portrait. But Leavis misunderstands the nature of Conrad's genius. The virtues and defects of Leavis's method of approach can be seen in the following sentence: 'The characteristic Conradian sensibility is that of the creator of Heyst; that of the writer so intimately experienced in the strains and starvations of the isolated consciousness, and so deeply aware of the sense in which reality is social, something established and sustained in a kind of collaboration ("I have lived too long within myself," says Heyst, "watching the mere shadows and shades of life").' [3] Leavis is right about the typical Conradian sensibility, but his definition of reality as social simplifies the central ambiguities both in this novel and in Conrad's work as a whole. Conrad is unsure about the nature of social reality, and in his fiction dramatizes conflicting points of view. Like Decoud, Heyst is a fluid character, whose Good Samaritan actions to help Morrison and Lena reveal unexpected potentialities for good and evil in himself which he cannot understand or control. The narrator's tone towards these adventures falters between approval for Lena and a merging with Heyst's habitual sceptical condemnation of all human action. There is a feeling of meaninglessness which Lena's charms cannot exorcize. The conclusion in particular is confused. Leavis is wrong to say the victory is 'unequivocal'. We cannot be so sure, as we respond to the mixture of melodrama, sentimentality and acute psychological observation in the last chapters.

5

Heyst inherits his scepticism from his father. His mother died while he was still a baby, and the father's influence is dangerously rational and negative. After leaving school at the age of eighteen, Heyst lived with him for three years. Heyst Senior is a man of considerable intellect who adopts a Schopenhauer-like philosophy of withdrawal from the folly of human passions, actions, involvement. Heyst admits to Lena that he was easily persuaded by these stoical doctrines, and learnt to agree with his father that 'man on this earth is an unforeseen accident which does not stand close investigation'. He determines to wander about the world as an 'independent spectator':

> Three years of such companionship at that plastic and impressionable age were bound to leave in the boy a profound mistrust of life. The young man learned to reflect, which is a destructive process, a reckoning of the cost. It is not the clear-sighted who lead the world. Great achievements are accomplished in a blessed, warm mental fog, which the pitiless cold blasts of the father's analysis had blown away from the son.
> 'I'll drift,' Heyst had said to himself deliberately.
> He did not mean intellectually or sentimentally or morally. He meant to drift altogether and literally, body and soul, like a detached leaf drifting in the wind-currents under the immovable trees of a forest glade; to drift without ever catching on to anything.
> 'This shall be my defence against life,' he had said to himself

> with a sort of inward consciousness that for the son of his father
> there was no other worthy alternative. (pp. 91–2)

When he settles on his island retreat at Samburan, his living-room is
filled with his father's books, and there is a portrait of his father which
looks severely into space as the son compromises his independence by
making love to Lena. Underneath this framed profile, Heyst is accustomed to study his father's writings composing his face, as if under the
author's eye, into the withdrawn self his father admired. Conrad's
treatment of Heyst Senior is both critical and sympathetic: his portrait
is 'exiled and at home, out of place and masterful'. His philosophy
witnesses to a kind of integrity which is both arid and praiseworthy.
As the sadistic Ricardo invades Heyst's sanctuary, the portrait's aloof
coldness seems for this moment a possibly justifiable stance.

At first Heyst drifts amongst the islands around Java and New
Guinea, enigmatical and disregarded like an insignificant ghost. His
identity becomes a void, as he loses the habit of asserting himself, and
adopts a pose of polite, considerate withdrawal. But the men he
encounters will not leave this enigma alone. They fasten names onto
him—'Enchanted Heyst', when he succumbs to the magic of the
islands; 'Hard Facts', when he absorbs himself in Morrison's foolhardy
scheme to mine for coal at Samburan; 'Heyst the Enemy', when he
proposes to develop and so transform the peaceful islands for the
Tropical Belt Coal Company; 'Hermit', when he retires to meditate
alone on his little island. Society intrudes by insisting on definitions,
and Heyst cannot resist this process. The hotel-keeper, Schomberg,
maliciously tells his clientele that Heyst has squeezed his partner
Morrison dry and then sent him home to die. This is accepted because
Heyst has created no explicable identity to counteract such poisonous
gossip. 'Heyst the Spider' becomes his latest nickname. When later he
hears of this calumny from Lena, he is disproportionately enraged
because it proves the impracticality of his negative philosophy. As long
as he is alive, society will impose a relationship, will fix on him a name.
Language imposes social relationships by which he is affected, however
distorted by illusion they may be.

Heyst has determined to be loyal to himself rather than to the community. His first betrayal of this ideal occurs when he accidentally finds
Morrison in desperate need of a small loan to extricate his brig from the
Portuguese authorities. Morrison is a kind-hearted man who supplies
the natives with food for which he is rarely paid. Like Davidson, who

appears later, he is a person of delicate feelings, with a true humanitarian impulse. These sailors represent an ideal of service to the community in direct contrast to Heyst's negative philosophy. Both are treated as slightly foolish and quixotic, but their goodness is a kind of strength Heyst cannot ignore. Ironically, he acts towards Morrison in a Christ-like role, as he pays the debt and so provides the answer to Morrison's prayer to God in his distress. Heyst himself cannot resist claims on his charity, and so proves his father's angry scepticism is alien to his temperament: 'No decent feeling was ever scorned by Heyst.' When Morrison insists that his good fortune in the magnificent coal-mining venture should be shared by Heyst, the 'hermit' cannot resist this claim on his allegiance. Morrison returns to England to promote the enterprise; but unfortunately on a visit to Dorsetshire to see his people he 'caught a bad cold, and died with extraordinary precipitation in the bosom of his appalled family'. For a moment the irony recalls the tone of *The Secret Agent*. The phrase 'with extraordinary precipitation' suggests a mocking aloofness from the absurdities of life worthy of Heyst Senior.

Heyst feels guilty as if someone might reproach him with the death of Morrison. This proves how ill-prepared he is to cope with real problems. He tries to expiate his guilt by working for the Tropical Belt Coal Company: 'He was very concrete, very visible now.' But with its liquidation he becomes 'invisible', and it is some time before the gossipers in Schomberg's hotel discover that he is living alone on Samburan, surrounded by the debris of the forlorn coal project.

6

On his island-paradise Heyst is attempting to become an invisible man, to break all social ties, to resist the relationships and identities thrust on him by the community. He has withdrawn from history into the insularity of pure self. Conrad is deliberately creating a fictional situation whereby he can examine the extreme alternative to social commitment. Heyst is enchanted by the islands because of their magic stillness, because of their attractive silence: 'The very voices of their people are soft and subdued, as if afraid to break some protecting spell.' His retreat is like Prospero's island, a magical refuge from a corrupt civilization. His servant, Wang, vanishes and materializes as if like Ariel he can transcend the laws of physics. It is Captain Davidson who eventually discovers Heyst's retreat; on one occasion as Davidson departs Heyst himself symbolically disappears into the landscape:

> ... Davidson went on board his ship, swung her out, and as he was steaming away he watched from the bridge Heyst walking shoreward along the wharf. He marched into the long grass and vanished—all but the top of his white cork helmet, which seemed to swim in a green sea. Then that too disappeared, as if it had sunk into the living depths of the tropical vegetation, which is more jealous of men's conquests than the ocean, and which was about to close over the last vestiges of the liquidated Tropical Belt Coal Company—A. Heyst, manager in the East. (p. 29)

He has withdrawn into a natural paradise, merging his identity with the flow of Nature, and not surprisingly this passage hints that to annihilate oneself in a green shade, in Conradian terms, may be a kind of suicide. His most frequent visitors are the shadows of clouds, relieving the monotony of the inanimate, brooding sunshine of the tropics. Wang, his servant, chooses to stay with Heyst in Samburan because this undisturbed existence suits his oriental preference for security and invulnerability.

Nirvana has its attractions, but from the opening sentences of the story it is treated with irony: Heyst 'was out of everybody's way, as if he were perched on the highest peak of the Himalayas, and in a sense as conspicuous'. His eccentricity has drawn upon him the interest of everyone in the surrounding area. His scepticism has not prevented him from succumbing to the illusion that he might find sanctuary, but even on his island he cannot escape from the wagging tongues. His paradise is perched above the coal-fields, and the black jetty, the deserted bungalows, the tall heap of unsold coal at the wharf, all reflect a sense of hidden corruption and desolation. The gigantic and funereal blackboard sign of the Tropical Belt Company emerges from the wild growth of bushes like an inscription stuck above a grave. Indeed, by becoming an invisible man Heyst has buried his living self. His nearest neighbour 'was an indolent volcano which smoked faintly all day with its head just above the northern horizon, and at night levelled at him, from amongst the clear stars, a dull red glow, expanding and collapsing spasmodically like the end of a gigantic cigar puffed at intermittently in the dark.' Heyst is a smoker, and he joins the volcano each evening in making the same kind of intermittent glow. The absurd companion-ship withdraws the narrator from identification with Heyst's ideal of sanctuary, and delicately mocks his isolation. Heyst recalls to Lena how once, when the volcano shot up ashes during a thunderstorm, the island received a mud-shower. His tranquillity will eventually be threatened by Nature itself, by the inevitable processes of decay. Lena hates the blazing sunshine, 'all aquiver with the effort to set the earth on fire, to burn it to ashes'. She hates the great stillness, the panoramic view of the sea to which Heyst leads her through the forest: 'That empty space was to her the abomination of desolation.' She understands instinctively that Heyst's paradise is a void, a pure nothing, a replica of the meaninglessness which will assume sway when the earth is removed from the universe. At the climax, as he leaves her for what is to prove the last time, Nature declares itself irreducibly alien. There was 'something cruel in the absolute dumbness of the night'.

> The sense of the heavy, brooding silence in the outside world seemed to enter and fill the room—the oppressive infinity of it, without breath, without light. It was as if the heart of hearts had ceased to beat and the end of all things had come. (p. 373)

Heyst's plan to carry off Lena to his sanctuary, so they may become invisible together, ends inevitably with this moment of apocalypse. He has proved himself as romantic as his namesake, Axel Auërsperg in Villiers de l'Isle-Adam's *Axël*. When the villains arrive, Mr Jones appropriately remarks: 'I am the world itself, come to pay you a visit.' Heyst can withdraw neither from the cruelties of Nature nor from involvement with the world of men.

7

After he has determined to retire from society on Samburan, Heyst cannot resist a sense of loneliness. He asks Davidson to take him to Sourabaya to fetch his letters, thereby proving that his detachment from the world is not complete. During his stay, he meets Lena, and rescues her from the nauseating attentions of Schomberg by whisking her off to his island.

Heyst's love affair is unsatisfactorily presented because Lena is so vaguely realized. But Heyst's own thoughts and feelings, as he betrays all his father's precepts, justify Baines's claim that Heyst is the most complex character Conrad ever created. His decision to rescue Lena is quixotic, but it reveals a darker side to his nature, as he himself gradually becomes aware. The physical attraction is considerable, and

on the island the lovers are obviously enjoying a full sexual relationship. Unfortunately Conrad is unsuccessful in dealing with physical
intimacy, and stands off from such happenings; but he does convey
adequately the seduction of Heyst's imagination:

> Those dreamy spectators of the world's agitation are terrible once
> the desire to act gets hold of them. They lower their heads and
> charge a wall with an amazing serenity which nothing but an
> indisciplined imagination can give. (p. 77)

He possesses no defence against his own compassion. His ability to
think clearly, to see 'life outside the flattering optical delusion of everlasting hope, of conventional self-deceptions, of an ever-expected
happiness', is troubled by an awakening of tenderness. He accustoms his
mind to contemplation of his purpose, in order that by being faced
steadily it should appear praiseworthy and wise. 'For the use of reason
is to justify the obscure desires that move our conduct, impulses,
passions, prejudices, and follies, and also our fears.' So speaks the
anonymous narrator, whose scepticism would have met with the
approval of Heyst Senior.

When the lovers reach Samburan, and particularly after the arrival
of Jones, Ricardo and Pedro, Heyst is surprised to find his emotional
life is subject to evil impulses. He is bitterly hurt by Schomberg's
calumnies, as we have seen. He laughs scornfully:

> 'I never heard you laugh till today,' she observed. 'This is the
> second time.'
>
> He scrambled to his feet and towered above her.
>
> 'That's because, when one's heart has been broken into in the
> way you have broken into mine, all sorts of weaknesses are free
> to enter—shame, anger, stupid indignations, stupid fears—
> stupid laughter, too.' (p. 210)

Soon afterwards he loses control of himself, disgusted at the real
world he has so long evaded, and experiences a nervous reaction from
tenderness: 'All at once, without transition, he detested her.' This
mood passes in a moment, but he feels a growing resentment against
life itself, which has ensnared him. As he engages himself with social
life after his period of invisibility, he is offered a variety of roles. He is
not sure how to act, and the only thing absolutely certain is that he
cannot remain as tolerant and polite as he managed to be in his pose of
hermit-like withdrawal. He is drawn into conflict, but his fastidious

habits render him defenceless. He is symbolically deprived of his revolver, which is stolen by Wang, and so cannot fight against Jones and his henchmen. Above all, his over-delicate feelings prevent him from abandoning himself to his spontaneous, natural affection for Lena. 'You should try to love me!' she tells him, but he only can do this unreservedly when she is dead.

The other outcasts, particularly Lena and Jones, function to some extent as reflections of Heyst's warring attitudes, and the action becomes a kind of extension of his consciousness. Some critics, such as Richard E. Butler in 'Jungian and Oriental Symbolism in Joseph Conrad's *Victory*', see this archetypal quality of the action as an element in the novel's success; there is, Butler writes, 'an uncanny, frustrating, suggestive strangeness about the language which leads the reader to look beyond the surface.' [4] I agree that this gives some interest to Conrad's treatment of the other outcasts, but feel that the narrative claims a quality of realism for the archetypal events and characters which at times seems absurd.

The villains are dispatched to the island by Schomberg on the presumption that Heyst possesses a secret hoard of money. Wang first spots their boat, but when Heyst arrives at the jetty he can see no sign of the men. He presumes Wang has suffered some strange hallucination, but then discovers the boat under the jetty. He peers down at the extraordinary crew, Jones, Ricardo and Pedro: 'It was more like those myths, current in Polynesia, of amazing strangers, who arrive at an island, gods or demons, bringing good or evil to the innocence of the inhabitants—gifts of unknown things, words never heard before.' These images of irrational violence arise from the depths of Heyst's unconscious to confront him at the very moment that he has just hubristically declared: 'Nothing can break in on us here.' Even when he has withdrawn from society into the isolation of Samburan, he has not left behind the corrupting elements in his own personality.

Jones represents the evil pride of intellect, the obverse side of Heyst Senior's character, and he is symbolically dressed like the father in a blue dressing gown. He is linked repeatedly, far too repeatedly, to images of death: he is a skeleton, a corpse, a menace from beyond the grave, a spectre on leave from Hades. His voice matches his sunken eyes, sounding 'distant, uninterested, as though he were speaking from the bottom of a well'. He has a homosexual disgust for women, and suffers from fits of neurotic boredom, when he loses his will to live. He is wearied by the monotony of life, and assumes 'the privileged detachment of a cultivated mind, of an elevated personality'. In other words, he embodies the dangerous features of Heyst's scepticism, the death-like indifference, the withdrawal from human sympathies. He tells Heyst that he is a sort of fate, the retribution that waits its time. In a sense this is true, for Heyst's insularity in pure self might end in such a state of inertia. Heyst's disgust with life renders him defenceless, impotent. He realizes that he dare not kill another human being, dare not assert his right to protect Lena. When towards the end he confronts Jones, he is overwhelmed by weariness at the grotesque spectacle before him:

> At this moment, by simply shouldering Mr. Jones, he could have thrown him down and put himself by a couple of leaps, beyond the certain aim of the revolver; but he did not even think of that. His very will seemed dead of weariness. He moved automatically, his head low, like a prisoner captured by the evil power of a masquerading skeleton out of a grave. (p. 390)

His failure to act makes him partly responsible for Lena's death. When he learns that she and Ricardo are alone together in his house, he immediately doubts her loyalty. And next he thinks that he himself who is experiencing such evil jealousy has no business to go on living. The weakness of Heyst lies in what Conrad calls his 'indisciplined imagination'. He has not been disciplined by contacts with actual social problems. He has not learnt when to trust and when to act with purpose. After he finds out how much Lena loved him he can only say to Davidson: 'Woe to the man whose heart has not learned while young to hope, to love—and to put its trust in life!' He commits suicide by burning down his house: 'fire purifies everything', Davidson pronounces enigmatically.

And so we come to the question of Lena's so-called victory. Her two names, Alma and Lena, suggest both richness of life and Mary Magdalene, the prostitute on whom Christ took pity. She represents passion, the chaos of the emotions, feminine intuition, sex. Ricardo is the obverse of her character, with his uncontrolled sadism, but his behaviour is so ridiculous that his presence only harms the novel. He speaks some of the worst dialogue Conrad ever perpetrated: 'I went tired this morning, since I came in here and started talking to you—as tired as if I had been pouring my life-blood here on these planks for you to dabble your white feet in.' Lena defeats him by persuading him to give her his knife. We may offer sexual interpretations for this. She is the *femme fatale*, rendering her lover impotent. But the scene is so absurd that it is impossible to take its meanings seriously. She believes that 'her tremendous victory' is that by disarming him she has captured 'the very sting of death in the service of love'. Presumably this event should symbolize that love conquers death, but the cliché loses its force with the irony of Heyst's consequent suicide.

Lena's attitude to Heyst is distinctly odd. She realizes she cannot understand him, and fears to betray her inadequacies: 'She felt in her innermost depths an irresistible desire to give herself up to him more completely, by some act of absolute sacrifice.' She lives most intensely, is reborn into a new sense of her own reality, when she discovers that she can protect Heyst from Ricardo, that she can become the defender of the man who physically is so much stronger. The narrator tells us that her new confidence, her new selfhood, derives 'from pride, from love, from necessity, and also because of a woman's vanity in self-sacrifice'.

> A great vagueness enveloped her impressions, but all her energy was concentrated on the struggle that she wanted to take upon herself, in a great exaltation of love and self-sacrifice, which is woman's sublime faculty; altogether on herself, every bit of it, leaving him nothing, not even the knowledge of what she did, if that were possible. She would have liked to lock him up by some stratagem. Had she known of some means to put him to sleep for days she would have used incantations or philtres without misgivings. He seemed to her too good for such contacts, and not sufficiently equipped. This last feeling had nothing to do with the material fact of the revolver being stolen. She could hardly appreciate that fact at its full value. (p. 317)

Like Thomas Moser, in his book *Joseph Conrad: Achievement and Decline*, we may suspect that Conrad's misogyny is subconsciously influencing him here. Lena's sacrifice is analysed as an expression of egoism, of her desire to dominate. She wants Heyst defenceless, and likes him to be completely in her power. So she disobeys his instructions to escape, and seems happy to die convinced of her victory over death.

The end of the penultimate chapter is confusing: 'The flush of rapture flooding her whole being broke out in a smile of innocent, girlish happiness; and with that divine radiance on her lips she breathed her last, triumphant, seeking for his glance in the shades of death.' In a sense she is triumphant for indeed Heyst loves her. But such bad writing makes Leavis's admiration of this 'unequivocal' victory seem beside the point. We can only justify this language if we see it as heavily ironic, but words such as 'flush', 'divine radiance', and 'shades of death' suggest that Conrad has lost himself in sentimentality.

The real tragedy takes place just before this:

> Heyst bent low over her, cursing his fastidious soul, which even at that moment kept the true cry of love from his lips in its infernal mistrust of all life. He dared not touch her, and she had no longer the strength to throw her arms about his neck.
>
> 'Who else could have done this for you?' she whispered gloriously.
>
> 'No one in the world,' he answered her in a murmur of unconcealed despair. (p. 406)

Heyst's scepticism has prevented him from committing himself to life. He now realizes that with Lena's death he loses everything. But the imaginative impact of the final catastrophe does not support Leavis's optimism. In his passion for Lena, Heyst discovers a greater sense of his own reality than he had ever known before, but this awakened consciousness leads him inevitably to death. As we have seen before in Conrad, the turning towards love becomes an act of self-immolation. He places himself in the power of irrational emotions; he submits himself to chance and the fates.

In *Chance* and *Victory*, Conrad makes a determined effort to dramatize in fiction an escape from the isolation of the self. But in both novels the positive values are blurred, and the style reflects the sentimentalities typical of his last period. The 'monster' ship which threatened the *Ferndale* symbolizes 'The horror! The horror!' which still retains its hold on Conrad's imagination.

Chapter 8

Mirrors in 'The Secret Sharer' and *The Shadow-Line*

Now I am a lake. A woman bends over me,
Searching my reaches for what she really is.
Then she turns to those liars, the candles or the moon,
I see her back, and reflect it faithfully.
She rewards me with tears and an agitation of hands.
I am important to her. She comes and goes.
Each morning it is her face that replaces the darkness.
In me she has drowned a young girl, and in me an old woman
Rises toward her day after day, like a terrible fish.

SYLVIA PLATH, 'Mirror'

I

To peer too long into a mirror may prove disconcerting. We may recognize aspects of our personality we prefer to forget, and we may become uncomfortably aware that our identity is composed of numerous secret selves. If we stare hard enough we may wonder whether the reflection is completely under our control, and suspect that it might begin to form grimaces and attitudes of its own.

The fear of reflected images, common among primitive peoples, is described at length in Robert Rogers's *The Double in Literature*.[1] There is a widespread belief that shadows, reflections, and portraits of the body are the same as souls, or are at least vitally linked with the well-being of the body. The folk custom of covering mirrors or turning them to the wall after someone has died in a house is based on the idea that the soul reflected in the mirror may be seized by the ghost of the departed. It is thought especially dangerous for sick people to see themselves in a mirror. Even today people can suffer from catoptricophobia—fear of mirrors and reflections—and the superstition that breaking a mirror brings bad luck is a sign that these primitive feelings still run deep. The same fears are often occasioned by pictures. There are still places in Africa, even in a comparatively civilized community such as Khartoum, where it is unwise to take photographs in the street. It is assumed that the photographic image is an extension of the self, and that the camera may thus steal a man's soul from his body. The best-known example of the use of this motif in literature is presumably Oscar Wilde's *The Picture of Dorian Gray*.

A novelist who writes about heroes like himself is creating just such mirror-reflections; indeed it has even been suggested that fictional characters may all be projections of the author, all images of potential selves. Flaubert wrote: 'Madame Bovary, c'est moi'; and it has been argued that Dostoevsky's brothers Karamazov are all different facets of the novelist. Freud has commented on the tendency of modern writers to split up their ego by self-observation into many component egos, and in this way to personify the conflicting trends in their own mental life in many heroes.

Henry James, E. M. Forster, James Joyce, D. H. Lawrence and Virginia Woolf are among the many twentieth-century writers who use fiction to explore their own mirror-images. I am thinking of obvious examples, such as 'The Beast in the Jungle', *The Longest Journey*, *Portrait of the Artist*, *Sons and Lovers* or *The Waves*. The writing of such fictions may help the artist to master anxiety, or exorcize psychological conflicts, to achieve maturity through self-recognition. But the mirror may reveal more than the author intends. We may discern a morbid preoccupation in the writer with his own essence, and a submission to dangerous elements in his make-up. In the case of D. H. Lawrence there is the vicarious participation in sadistic killing in *The Plumed Serpent*. In *Sons and Lovers* the treatment of Miriam and Mrs Morel reflects double standards. Behind the supposed events, explanations and evaluations, as recounted by the narrator, the reader discerns that Paul's fixation on his mother accounts for more of his problems than the author consciously realizes. Lawrence's own psychological condition looks out from behind the story like some irrepressible ghost.

Conrad's 'The Secret Sharer' (1910) is one of the greatest examples in fiction of the use of the mirror-image. The device enables him to explore the conflicts in his personality between seaman and artist, loyalty and betrayal, sanity and insanity. The story brilliantly exemplifies the problems of the modern imagination as I have tried to define them in this book. In 'The Secret Sharer' he draws on his memories of his first command on the *Otago*, when he, like the captain-narrator, felt a stranger on his ship. He thus creates an image of himself in the captain, who is then confronted with a second mirror-reflection in Leggatt, the criminal doppelgänger who appeals for help after he has killed a man on board his own ship. Through the two mirrors, both in some way reflections of Conrad, both in some way reflections of each other, he identifies and examines a number of possible roles. Leggatt is both a real flesh-and-blood seaman as well as some kind of alter ego for the captain, and Conrad handles most delicately this double function. But the clue to interpretation of the story is that the mirror-reflections are multiple in meaning rather than simply dual. The story's imaginative success, as I hope to show, is that the dramatic situation bewilders and disturbs the reader, leaving him unsure where he should approve and where disapprove. As the two mirrors, captain and criminal, confront each other, their roles resist clear definition. As soon as we think we have grasped the true meaning of the symbolism, we are startled by some contradictory effect. The story expresses Conrad's sense of the variety of identities available to each intelligent individual. The captain is supposedly being initiated into maturity and responsibility, but we may wonder at certain moments whether the narrator, presumably telling his story years later, is a sane man. The mirror images are used to express rather than resolve the tensions in Conrad's personality, and he refuses to provide the reader with definitive judgments about the value of the identities on offer.

The story was published in 1912 in the volume *'Twixt Land and Sea* together with 'A Smile of Fortune' and 'Freya of the Seven Isles'. In a letter to Garnett, Conrad confessed how much he admired 'The Secret Sharer', how much it satisfied him:

> I dare say Freya is pretty rotten. On the other hand the Secret Sharer, between you and me, is *it*. Eh? Every word fits and there's not a single uncertain note. Luck my boy. Pure luck. I knew you would spot the thing at sight. But I repeat: mere luck.[2]

As the two young men, narrator and Leggatt, put their heads together in whispered colloquies, both dressed in identical sleeping suits, the image unsettles the reader, like some secret dream from the depths of the unconscious. Conrad was right to think he had found a highly stimulating idea from which his imagination could extract a wealth of effects. But he too might have wondered whether the mirrors revealed more than he intended. In this story, as in *Under Western Eyes*, he seems to use fiction as a kind of exorcism. He creates a drama in which the captain by a supposedly heroic act rids himself of the dark side of his consciousness. The meaning of the end is not so easy to figure out as some writers on Conrad have suggested. I feel that as Leggatt swims away into the darkness it is as if Conrad is saying farewell to some essential element in his artistic identity. The reflection in the mirror bears the soul away.

2

Both Freudian and Jungian interpretations throw some light on the symbolism of 'The Secret Sharer'. Robert Rogers gives a clear account of the Freudian approach. The captain on a ship has almost unlimited authority, and is easily associated with the psychological father. Leggatt's crime against discipline aboard ship thus becomes a symbol of the primal crime of the son: rebellion against authority. The captain-narrator associates himself with the crime because he feels guilty and inadequate at this moment when he is assuming the responsibility of his first command: 'In Eriksonian terms, the story portrays the new-made captain as undergoing an "identity crisis", an identity crisis which in Freudian terms harks back to the earlier oedipal crisis.' [3] He is anxious whether he has the ability to fulfil his new role, and so fears he is a usurper. The tension between subconscious guilt and a confident sense of responsibility is symbolized in Leggatt's story. His crime is against the established laws of discipline, yet committed in the interests of maintaining order among a crew berserk with fear, and with the purpose of saving the ship: 'Leggatt has, *in extremis*, usurped the role of his commander in both a maritime and a psychological sense.' [4] By helping the outlaw, the captain proves himself competent and resolute, and he eventually succeeds in getting rid of his scapegoat double. This justifies the happy ending, for he is now secure in his professional role, and no longer feels anxiety and guilt.

The Jungian interpretation is argued most cogently by Albert Guerard. According to this approach, the story, like *Heart of Darkness*, concerns an insecure and morally isolated man who meets and commits himself to a man even more isolated. In whispered, unrepeatable conversations, he holds communication with his secret self, and this represents a symbolic descent into the unconscious. The real moral dilemma for the captain-narrator is that he must recognize in Leggatt his own potential criminality, his own lower or more primitive self, and so through a new self-awareness initiate himself into true manhood. Integration of the personality occurs when the unconscious has been known, trafficked with and in some sense liberated. In Jungian psychology, as in dreams, the captain's floppy hat represents the personality, which can be transferred symbolically to another. The captain's gift of his hat to Leggatt demonstrates that he now accepts the unconscious self; this generosity saves the ship, and symbolically his own psychic health, when the hat is used as a marker to determine whether the ship has gathered sternway.

Jocelyn Baines treats these symbolic interpretations with some exasperation. In his view, the story is intensely dramatic, but, on the psychological and moral level, rather slight. He specifically attacks Guerard's arguments, and asks how the Jungian interpretation can make any sense of the last sentence, in which Leggatt departs 'a free man, a proud swimmer striking out for a new destiny'. This is no way for a symbol of the unconscious to behave. Baines argues that there is no indication in the story, explicit or implicit, that the captain sees any of his difficulties in Leggatt, or that he performs any self-examination. Nor is there any moral dilemma. There is no evidence in the plot that the captain would have failed as a seaman if Leggatt had not appeared. He realizes his own mistake in abandoning routine to take the anchor watch, and asks himself whether it is ever wise to interfere with the established routine of duties even from the kindest of motives. This occurs before he finds Leggatt at the bottom of the ship's ladder.

In *A Reader's Guide to Joseph Conrad*, Frederick R. Karl [5] adopts a similar no-nonsense approach. Like Baines, he attacks those who find some kind of cosmic significance in the story: 'The surface in this case *is* the story, and the surface is the arrival of the Captain at a degree of maturity in which he gains self-respect and confidence.' Karl argues that 'The Secret Sharer' deals principally and simply with the theme of growing up that Conrad dealt with in so many other stories and novels. The captain does not betray the outlaw (as Razumov does), and by arranging his escape proves his own manhood. The story is one of Conrad's best, a microcosm of his major themes, 'but for all its suggestiveness, it is, paradoxically, one of his most straightforward and obvious works. Its narrative is a model of clarity, like those uncomplicated narratives "Youth" and *The Shadow-Line*.' [6] According to

Karl, the story is psychologically shallow, and the theme of the alter ego is laboured to excess.

Baines and Karl have a case which needs answering. Neither the Freudian nor the Jungian interpretations can provide a complete explanation for every important detail of the story. Leggatt possesses several characteristics which unfit him for the role of symbol of the unconscious. He is a sane, determined man who, when immersed in the destructive element of the sea, swims purposefully towards the distant light of the captain's ship; he would never commit suicide. The Freudian analysis fits quite well, but takes attention away from the actual cause of the tension in the captain's mind. He almost breaks down because of the strain imposed by the very real problem of keeping Leggatt's presence hidden from the crew. It is difficult to accept that this is a symbol of his secret oedipal guilt, when he has every reason to fear exposure. Discovery might mean death for Leggatt, and the captain himself might have to stand trial for assisting a murderer to escape. Such rational explanation of his anxiety seems more to the point than a supposed sub-conscious identification with Leggatt's crime.

Yet Baines and Karl ignore many features of the story which do not fit in with their simple interpretations. Guerard is particularly success-ful in describing the symbolic reverberations of the landscape, the apparition of the headless swimmer, the business with the hat, or the blackness of Koh-ring. Although we may reject any *one* symbolic interpretation as incomplete, the method of narration suggests hidden meanings, and Freudian or Jungian ideas are inevitably aroused in the reader's mind. Also, the reading that sees this as only a forceful dramatic tale ignores several extraordinary incidents. Neither Leggatt nor the captain is a straightforward character. The various accounts of the murder include elements that suggest that Leggatt is not just an honest Conway boy who killed a man in a fit of justified temper. The captain's behaviour is at times so astonishing that we must look for sources additional to the strain of secrecy. And so we come to the great crux of the narrative, which neither Baines nor Karl considers. Why does the captain sail his ship so near to the black hill of Koh-ring? The obvious reply is that he wishes to give Leggatt every chance to swim safely ashore; but Leggatt has proved himself an excellent swimmer, and so there is no necessity for the ship to shave the land so dangerously close. The captain admits that his heart was in his mouth, and under any other circumstances he would not have held on a moment longer. The crew are convinced they are doomed. The plain fact is that for moral or psychological reasons the captain endangers his ship and the lives of his men unnecessarily, and they are only saved by the lucky accident that the floppy hat, dropped in his escape by Leggatt, serves as a marker in the water. Is this irresponsible piece of daring a sign of maturity, of his competence to assume the role of captain of the ship? It could be said he behaves like a madman. Why? Baines and Karl are clearly wrong to think there is anything simple about this story.

3

The story begins with a description of landscape whose delicate symbolism is not easy to define:

> On my right hand there were lines of fishing-stakes resembling a mysterious system of half-submerged bamboo fences, incomprehensible in its division of the domain of tropical fishes, and crazy of aspect as if abandoned for ever by some nomad tribe of fishermen now gone to the other end of the ocean; for there was no sign of human habitation as far as the eye could reach. To the left a group of barren islets, suggesting ruins of stone walls, towers, and blockhouses, had its foundations set in a blue sea that itself looked solid, so still and stable did it lie below my feet; even the track of light from the westering sun shone smoothly, without that animated glitter which tells of an imperceptible ripple. And when I turned my head to take a parting glance at the tug which had just left us anchored outside the bar, I saw the straight line of the flat shore joined to the stable sea, edge to edge, with a perfect and unmarked closeness, in one levelled floor half brown, half blue under the enormous dome of the sky. Corresponding in their insignificance to the islets of the sea, two small clumps of trees, one on each side of the only fault in the impeccable joint, marked the mouth of the river Meinam we had just left on the first preparatory stage of our homeward journey; and, far back on the inland level, a larger and loftier mass, the grove surrounding the great Paknam pagoda, was the only thing on which the eye could rest from the vain task of exploring the monotonous sweep of the horizon. Here and there gleams as of a few scattered

pieces of silver marked the windings of the great river; and on the nearest of them, just within the bar, the tug steaming right into the land became lost to my sight, hull and funnel and masts, as though the impassive earth had swallowed her up without an effort, without a tremor. My eye followed the light cloud of her smoke, now here, now there, above the plain, according to the devious curves of the stream, but always fainter and farther away, till I lost it at last behind the mitre-shaped hill of the great pagoda. And then I was left alone with my ship, anchored at the head of the Gulf of Siam. (pp. 91–2 in *'Twixt Land and Sea*)

The fishing stakes are 'mysterious', 'incomprehensible' and 'crazy', suggesting perhaps man's failure to impose his patterns of work on nature. The islets, like ruins, have their foundations in a blue sea whose 'solid', 'stable' quality we know to be an illusion. There is already a hint of menace, of man's isolation in a dangerous and inexplicable universe. Land, sea and sky merge together in a moment of stillness, a kind of dream-landscape, typical in Conrad as the hero approaches his test. The objects he perceives appear beyond his control, for there will be no consolations for his lonely mind in the monotonous sweep of Nature. The tug seems to have been swallowed up by the impassive earth, as all man-made things will eventually return to the non-human neutrality of the primal forms of matter. In *Joseph Conrad: The Imaged Style*, Wilfred S. Dowden [7] argues that the insignificant twin clumps of trees suggest the dyadic aspects of the captain's personality, and that the pagoda represents the higher ground of self-knowledge. Conrad's symbolic landscapes rarely convey such precise connotations. Indeed, it is the *lack* of significance which is being stressed. As the captain's eye watches the smoke of the tug gradually disappearing along the river, the scene suggests how little the eye can know, understand or control. The main impression is of insubstantiality. Later in the story the hill of Koh-ring and the stars above appear to move while the ship stands still; human reference points have no absolute validity. The ordeal takes place in a 'phantom' sea, a 'sleepy gulf', as if the captain and Leggatt inhabit an area of consciousness on the borders of dreams. This insubstantiality of the physical universe is for Conrad a simple fact which has to be accepted. The captain's quest for self-identification will not be helped by his perceptions of exterior objects. He must seek to find himself in his subjective consciousness, where sense-impressions never entirely lose the aspect of hallucination.

The captain admits he lacks self-confidence. The crew have been together for eighteen months; he is a stranger and, except for the second mate, the youngest. We begin to wonder what sort of man he is when he tells us: 'I was somewhat of a stranger to myself.' After his foolish decision to take the anchor watch, he enjoys introspective ruminations under the stars. He has not integrated himself into his appointed role, has not merged his separate identity into the functions demanded of a captain. We may sympathize with this imaginative side to his temperament, and conclude that this suggests he is superior to a conventional captain such as MacWhirr. But in the opening paragraphs he shows his inexperience of life. He rejoices in the great security of the sea as compared with the unrest of the land, in his choice of an un-tempted life presenting no disquieting problems, 'invested with an elementary moral beauty by the absolute straightforwardness of its appeal and by the singleness of its purpose'. Events are to prove that the sea can make confusing claims, and we may recall Jim's similar feeling of security just before the *Patna* collision.

Leggatt's self-confidence contrasts with the self-questioning, Hamlet-like behaviour of the captain. He first appears in the water at the bottom of the ladder like a headless corpse. It is the captain's fault that the ladder has been left overboard, as if he had subconsciously willed that Leggatt should come from the depths of the sea. In the phosphorescent flash caused by summer lightning on the water, Leggatt appears like a denizen from another world. What the captain draws up from the sleeping waters corresponds with his own dream of an ideal personality, or at first appears to do so. Leggatt is active, energetic and self-possessed, and has proved himself in dangerous extremities. Throughout the ensuing days the captain must confront this ideal image in living reality, must try to keep up to Leggatt's standards by successfully organizing the rescue. He must establish that his own head could properly be worn by Leggatt's body, that he has the right to recognize himself in his brave alter ego. But in this con-frontation between extrovert and introvert, the ideal and the actual, the captain is torn apart by inherent ambiguities and tensions in both roles. On the one hand his own active imagination induces a collapse of self-control, and a submission to neurotic strain. On the other, Leggatt's courageous service to the ship apparently involves a primitive, savage determination to survive.

After Leggatt has come on board and is hiding in the captain's cabin, many of the narrator's actions can be explained as legitimate devices to hide the outlaw from the crew. But soon the reader who has been vicariously identifying with the captain starts to feel uneasy and embarrassed. The captain's response to the crisis suggests extreme neuroticism. On the first morning, when he can eat nothing at breakfast, he already has to confess 'the dual working of my mind distracted me almost to the point of insanity'. The mental experience of being in two places at once affects him physically, 'as if the mood of secrecy had penetrated my soul'. He so far forgets himself that having occasion to ask the mate, who is standing by his side, to take a compass bearing on the Pagoda, he reaches up to his ear in whispers. A little later he startles the helmsman by moving to look at the compass with a stealthy gait as if he were in a sick room. He admits he had crept 'quietly as near insanity as any man who has not actually gone over the border'. Such lack of self-control hardly justifies those commentators who deduce that through the ordeal he proves his manhood. His reaction to the test is extraordinary, quite different from that of a brave man tackling a dangerous adventure. On one occasion he says of Leggatt: 'But there was nothing sickly in his eyes or in his expression. He was not a bit like me, really.' This is a surprising admission from the narrator. It implies that the captain has something sickly in his temperament; his antics with the mate and helmsman suggest confrontation with his alter ego shocks his soul to its very depth.

Leggatt claims the murder was justified. In a letter to Galsworthy, Conrad expressed shock that anyone should consider Leggat to be a murderous ruffian. Baines describes how Conrad deliberately toned down the details of the crime which he took from an actual incident on the *Cutty Sark*. The mate of the *Cutty Sark* was a despotic character with a sinister reputation, who killed an incompetent negro with a blow of a capstan bar. In contrast, Leggatt seems a model officer, whose bravery when he set the reefed foresail saved the ship. He strangled the insubordinate member of the crew in a fit of blind rage, dazed and eventually unconscious of what he was doing under the force of the huge wave that came over the side. The captain-narrator ascribes the murder to a justifiable sense of desperation: 'The same strung-up force which had given twenty-four men a chance, at least, for their lives, had, in a sort of recoil, crushed an unworthy mutinous existence.' At sea it is arguable that any act, even murder, committed to the end of keeping the ship afloat is moral. Leggatt has proved adequate where the true captain, Archbold, failed, and Archbold tries to cover up his weakness, his immorality in terms of the sea, by committing Leggatt to be hanged by the law of the land. Leggatt correctly judges that twelve respectable tradesmen in England will never comprehend the violent extremities necessitated by the morality of the sea.

And yet Leggatt's crime is not presented as just a fit of temper, and there are certain peculiar aspects to this outburst of violence. Leggatt behaves like a man possessed. He takes the insolent seaman by the throat, and goes on shaking him like a rat. When the great wave comes overboard, ten minutes are supposed to elapse before the two men are found together jammed behind the forebits. Leggatt tells the narrator: 'It's clear that I meant business, because I was holding him by the throat still when they picked us up. He was black in the face.' The crew are at first unable to prise Leggatt's fingers loose from around his victim's neck, and it is some time before he recovers consciousness. It is as if at this moment of heroic trial and endeavour his will has been abandoned to primitive, destructive urges. For a moment we may recall Kurtz, the apostle of the Savage God. Both Captain Archbold and his crew react to the killing as an event of unnatural horror, as though these ordinary, unexceptional seamen had been granted a glimpse of another dimension of being. Leggatt compares the crash of the wave to the sky falling on his head. The sea had gone mad: 'I suppose the end of the world will be something like that.' Like Kurtz, Leggatt is a man whose courage has carried him outside civilized restraints, to confront a moment of ultimate truth beyond the ken of normal social conventions.

Leggatt's case suggests that human survival depends on energetic self-assertion, and that men of his exceptional calibre may find themselves taken over by the desire for criminal violence. He admits that if he had tried to break out of his cabin when he was imprisoned on the *Sephora* he might have been forced to kill again. He explains that after his door had been left unlocked, and he had swum away from the ship, he was determined not to be dragged back 'fighting like a wild beast'. He is compared to Cain, and however much we sympathize with him, we must acknowledge that he is a man who would always kill to save himself from death. When the captain narrator himself is forced to act, and to make the crew comply with his orders to turn the ship about, he shakes the mate's arm violently, and goes on shaking it, rather as Leggatt shakes the seaman he kills. This story conveys no simple faith in the values of the good seaman. As in *Heart of Darkness*, the man of action submits himself to the ambiguous claims of the destructive element.

And so we come to the climax of the story, the captain's decision to sail his ship dangerously and unnecessarily close to the shore of Koh-ring. As usual in Conrad, we are given hints and possibilities rather than one clear motive. The captain sympathizes with Leggatt's isolation after the murder, and by the rash act of sailing close to the shore tries to give him a convincing demonstration of moral support. As Leggatt swims away he will appreciate the reason for this gesture, and this will console him later as he wanders barefoot under the alien sun. Is this what the captain means when he reiterates that 'it was now a matter of conscience to shave the land as close as possible'? But was such an extraordinary risk essential merely to encourage Leggatt with an expression of sympathy? If we take this as a sign of the captain's commitment to a fellow human being, then we must also accept that he endangers the lives of his crew in the process.

We must deduce that the captain sails close to Koh-ring because of some psychological necessity in his own being. He needs to prove his manhood by this act of self-assertion. He wants to behave in a daring and apparently irrational manner because of deep subjective needs he himself never seems properly to understand. Two contradictory attitudes are possible to this decision. We might argue that the captain identifies himself with Leggatt as an exceptional man who has courageously demonstrated that greatness involves the breaking of the social conventions, the law of the land. The captain proves to himself that he is not a rigid automaton, blindly obeying the seaman's code, but that he too in exceptional circumstances will take exceptional measures, wherever they may lead. But does this argument mean that action outside social conventions involves a submission to violence and irrationality? Is not the captain proving himself a dangerous lunatic who should never be given charge of a ship again? What evidence is there that he will never behave so foolishly a second time? And if we approve of his daring act, then do we agree that he would be right to repeat it on a comparable occasion? Anyone who holds that argument should be asked if he would like to travel as a passenger with the captain-narrator on the bridge.

As usual, this ambiguous treatment of heroic action reflects the tension in Conrad's own mind between loyal service to the seaman's code and a sense that his artistic nature and beliefs involve repudiation of social conventions. This imaginative obsession determines the symbolism of Koh-ring. The hill hangs over the crew 'like a towering fragment of the everlasting night'. The ship glides towards this enormous mass of blackness like 'a bark of the dead floating in slowly under the very gate of Erebus'. Once again Conrad depicts the journey towards the moment of truth, of self-recognition, as a voyage into the country of the dead. Just as in the opening description the tug appears swallowed up by the land, so the captain feels his ship is about to be 'swallowed up' by the shadow of Koh-ring. He confronts fearlessly the ultimate extinction of the subjective consciousness, the annihilation of human forms. By sailing as close as possible to the blackness, he proves that, unlike Lord Jim, he will never be rendered impotent by the vision of an ultimate meaninglessness. After this initiation, the man of imagination is fit to rule as captain. He forgets the secret stranger as he attends to the business of taking his ship away from danger: 'Already the ship was drawing ahead. And I was alone with her. Nothing! no one in the world should stand now between us, throwing a shadow on the way of silent knowledge and mute affection, the perfect communion of a seaman with his first command.'

And yet there is a sense of loss. The captain has enjoyed a special relationship with Leggatt which now is ended (and there is no need to support this argument by finding hints of homosexuality). The Freudian interpretation is that the ship is feminine, and the captain can now accept a mature sexual role, having purged the guilty shadow of the father. But Leggatt's status as hero and criminal, and his disappearance towards Koh-ring, the country of the dead, arouse other responses in the reader's imagination. The daring act of sailing the ship too close to shore seems to act like an exorcism for the captain. Leggatt has involved him in experiences which have brought him close to insanity, and which have demonstrated that his secret imaginative life might throw him completely off balance. He rids himself of this area of experience by depositing Leggatt at the very gate of Erebus. Is it possible that the efficient captain of the future will have forfeited the imaginative side of his nature which made him exceptional?

The last line rings out with apparent confidence, yet only adds to our uncertainties. Our last glimpse of Leggatt is of a man lowering himself in the water to take his punishment: 'a free man, a proud swimmer striking out for a new destiny'. Is the captain in future to live a life confined and circumscribed by the seaman's code? Should we in contrast prefer to admire the free man who in isolation, carrying his knowledge of guilt, makes a new destiny outside the security of civilization? Is it perhaps true that this story meant so much to Conrad because it enacted his own need to exorcize his mirror-image, to jettison those fantasies of alienation and suicidal loneliness which were disturbing his own balance of mind?

4

Written just after the outbreak of war in 1914, *The Shadow-Line* (1917) is rightly considered Conrad's last masterpiece. He had been in Poland when the war started, and only just escaped internment. *The Shadow-Line* was begun on his return, and completed by the end of March, 1915. The book, which appeared two years later, is dedicated to his son, Borys, who was serving at the front, and also to all the other young men who at that time had passed the shadow-line dividing youth from maturity, through the demands of duty, self-discipline and devotion to an ideal.

The story, therefore, describes another case of moral initiation, and like 'The Secret Sharer' it is based on personal reminiscences of Conrad's first command. It is written with a vivid directness at times reminiscent of *Typhoon*, and there are none of the embarrassing sentimentalities typical of his later work. Many commentators consider this story a minor achievement, a throw-back to the narrative felicities of his early period, without the ambiguities and multiple connotations of his greatest writings. Albert Guerard, with some justification, argues that the first two chapters are seriously defective, perhaps because they are so dependent on literal recall: Conrad is simply remembering his own problems in getting his first command, the *Otago*, away from Bangkok in 1888. A good deal of *The Shadow-Line* is taken from fact, and characters such as the dead captain and chief mate are closely modelled on actual people. The story has a straightforward linear development, with the voyage from Bangkok to Singapore symbolizing the captain-initiate's journey to maturity.

As might be expected, 'The Secret Sharer' and *The Shadow-Line* present quite different attitudes to the ordeal of initiation. 'The Secret Sharer', typical of Conrad's modernism, is a story of questioning and uncertainty about the grounds of being and action. *The Shadow-Line* ends with the test satisfactorily completed, and the captain successfully over the shadow-line. This line is not a clear dividing place, like a twenty-first birthday, but that transitional period when we abandon the illusory dreams of youth, and settle down to cope with our own mediocrity. At this time we are forced to acknowledge that we will never become Prime Minister or Poet Laureate, that our options are reduced in number, that we must accept second best. But although *The Shadow-Line* is comparatively straightforward, Conrad uses the events in a manner more subtle than that in superficial later works such as *The Rover*. *The Shadow-Line* is a true product of Conrad's imaginative search into the nature of his own identity. It offers solutions to the problems analysed in his great period, solutions which are not sentimentalized, and which are conveyed with moderation and balance. This story proves that admiration for human comradeship is not inevitably linked with failures in his art. After the breakdown of 1910, Conrad's new sense of commitment produced in *The Shadow-Line* a viable attitude towards life with which he could oppose his suicidal melancholia. Unfortunately in most of his writings after 1910 it is as if he has lopped away a vital part of his imaginative sensibility. *The Shadow-Line* is the exception.

5

The story begins when the narrator has just thrown up his comfortable berth as chief mate on an Eastern ship. He does not know why he has made this decision, and feels exasperated by friendly attempts by his companions to understand. His sickness is indifference, a breakdown of his sense of purpose akin to many similar experiences in Conrad's own life. The narrator tells us: 'I had never in my life felt more detached from all earthly goings on.' The decision is sudden, and its neurotic origin is revealed when he admits he is close to bursting into tears. He talks of 'this stale, unprofitable world of my discontent', and his condition corresponds to that of Hamlet. He is tempted by a feeling that everything is absurd, and that life is a waste of days. He is menaced by emptiness, by a spiritual drowsiness that numbs his will to live. The epigraph to the story is taken from Baudelaire's sonnet, 'La Musique': 'D'autres fois, calme plat, grand miroir De mon désespoir'. Music carries Baudelaire like a sea toward 'Ma pâle étoile'; but the poem ends with the words quoted by Conrad, a reverberating image of an inescapable lethargy.

Ian Watt excuses the slow-moving narrative of the opening two chapters by arguing that they are a necessary element in the total structure.[8] On his way from the docks to the Officers' Home the narrator is indifferent alike to the glare of the sun and the pleasure of the shade. When the friendly Captain Giles meets him there, and hints that a command may be waiting for him, his irritating refusal to take any notice is a sign of this state of indifference. The derelicts in the Officers' Home—the steward, who might commit suicide, Hamilton, the snobbish good-for-nothing, the drunken officer from the Rajah's yacht—witness to the state to which the narrator himself may regress. The comic absurdity of his conversations with Giles reflects the meaningless society into which he is drifting.

I both agree and disagree with Watt. A sense of lassitude is conveyed, and this contrasts with the coming ordeal. But Guerard is right to suggest that words are wasted here. Compared with 'The Secret Sharer', there are many paragraphs not strictly needed for the story. For example, the details concerning the Arab owner of the narrator's previous ship satisfy curiosity about conditions of service at this period, but hold little thematic relevance for the plot. Much as I admire *The Shadow-Line*, there are signs here of imaginative slackness.

The story takes life from the moment the narrator assumes his first command. As soon as he hears that a captain has died, and he is offered the position, his restless feeling of life-emptiness loses its evil influence. This proves he is a true seaman, and that in this way he assumes his proper identity. In the ship's saloon he sits down in the captain's chair at the head of the table, and looks at his face in a wide looking-glass in an ormolu frame. He realizes that he is taking his place in a line of men whom he did not know, of whom he had never heard, but who were fashioned by the same influences, who, in training, in conception of duty, were part of a continuous dynasty. It is as if 'a sort of composite soul, the soul of command' had joined itself to his own being: 'It struck me that this quietly staring man whom I was watching, both as if he were myself and somebody else, was not exactly a lonely figure.' It is one answer to Conrad's searchings into the mirror-reflections of his soul. He assumes a richer identity by accepting a social role; the previous incumbents stand behind him, healing the wound of loneliness.

It could be argued that this scene is ironic. When the narrator is trying to cope with fever among the crew at sea, he discovers the dead captain to be a villain who sold the quinine in the medicine-chest, and filled the bottles with useless powder. Yet, as Watt points out, Conrad is not attacking the seaman's code, but widening its terms of reference. The tradition of the past is not handed on unpurged of man's selfishness and weakness. The last captain has betrayed his calling, and it is against the forces of darkness he represents that the narrator must contend. In so doing he joins all men who struggle against anarchy, who try to maintain standards of human solidarity. He is allying him-self to a dynastic inheritance comparable to that assumed by Borys Conrad when he became an officer in the first World War. In this way, his identity takes on extra strength; he *does* escape from isolation.

The eccentricities of the previous captain, although to some extent based on Conrad's memories, fit well into the thematic patterns. He is about sixty-five, hard-faced, obstinate and uncommunicative. He used to keep the ship loafing at sea for inscrutable reasons, and then shut himself up in his cabin, and play on the violin for hours. This taciturn sailor is both artist and lover. In Haiphong he gets himself mixed up with a woman, and Mr Burns, the chief-mate, is left with a photograph:

> In due course I, too, saw that amazing human document (I even threw it overboard later). There he sat with his hands reposing on his knees, bald, squat, grey, bristly, recalling a wild boar some-how; and by his side towered an awful, mature, white female with rapacious nostrils and a cheaply ill-omened stare in her enormous eyes. She was disguised in some semi-oriental, vulgar, fancy costume. She resembled a low-class medium or one of those women who tell fortunes by cards for half-a-crown. And yet she was striking. A professional sorceress from the slums. It was incomprehensible. There was something awful in the thought that she was the last reflection of the world of passion for the fierce soul which seemed to look at one out of the sardonically savage face of that old seaman. However, I noticed that she was holding some musical instrument—guitar or mandoline—in her hand. Perhaps that was the secret of her sortilege. (p. 59)

It is not too much of an exaggeration to see in this photograph Conrad's farewell to Kurtz and the Savage God. The old seaman, with fierce savagery, has thrown over civilized conventions and abandoned him-self to the laws of Dionysus; but the picture now is debased, corrupt, without the fascination of Kurtz's wild mistress. When his affair is over, he determines to destroy himself and his crew. According to Mr Burns, the old man made up his mind to cut adrift from everything, and to go wandering about the world until he lost the ship with all hands. Before he dies, he throws his violin overboard, a final rejection of the consolations of art. It can be argued, from a Freudian view, that the dead captain symbolizes a powerful father image; or from a Jungian stance that his criminal desire to destroy himself repre-sents the dark side of the consciousness. The narrator must overcome and supplant this ghost who seems to hover around the crew like an evil spirit. But the connotations are richer than this. As artist and lover, the old seaman rejected the codes of society. In this fierce soul Conrad recalls his own fascination with the destructive element, with irrational sexual passion. In contrast, the narrator is the new Conradian hero, forming his identity in a relationship of fellow feeling with his crew.

When the narrator takes over the ship, he supplants Mr Burns, the chief mate, who had hoped to be offered the command. Mr Burns, with most of the crew, falls sick, and it is the captain's duty to nurse them back to health. Mr Burns is convinced that the dead captain is waiting for them in latitude 8° 20′, right in their way at the entrance of the Gulf, where he was buried. In his Author's Note, Conrad insists that the story was not intended to touch on the supernatural. Mr Burns suffers from delusion, and we are never supposed to think otherwise. Watt argues that Burns's madness signifies the corruption of the legitimate power of the past over the present. The narrator feels the inexpugnable strength of his common sense being insidiously menaced by this gruesome, insane fantasy. This superstitious awe, which indicates that Burns is unfit to assume command, awakens echoes in the narrator's mind as he succumbs to his own sense of unworthiness. According to Watt, the narrator shakes off this melodramatic hysteria, and survives his ordeal by attending to the disciplines of seamanship. Like Marlow in *Heart of Darkness*, his steering is a symbol of mankind's claim to the direction of its own fate.

I am not totally satisfied by Watt's interpretation. The ship is becalmed in a manner that seems perverse and devilish. Burns comes on deck and adjures the crew to act boldly, not to go whispering and tip-toeing about, for only in this way can the evil spell of the dead captain be broken. He then laughs loudly: 'a provoking, mocking peal, with a hair-raising, screeching over-note of defiance'. A hard gust of wind then blows freshly, sweeping clear the sooty sky, breaking through the indolent silence of the sea: 'The barrier of awful stillness which had encompassed us for so many days as though we had been accursed was broken.' Burns falls into a sound sleep, and wakes up sane. The ship carries them rapidly towards safety and Singapore. Although we need not attribute this climax to Burns's purging of the ghost, his screeching does happen at the appropriate time, and appears to have done the trick. In aesthetic terms, Burns's hysterical outburst acts as the catalyst that breaks down the period of enforced inertia. There is a sense that the event is a freak, a mysterious curiosity, and this takes away something from the *moral* implications of the climax. In narrating this event, and indeed in all the descriptions of darkness, Conrad finds it difficult to achieve a proper balance between the literal and the symbolic. Burns's mad shrieks are irrelevant on the rational level, and do nothing to save the ship. But on the psychological level his laughter acts as a necessary purging after a time of constraint and frustration. We are not surprised that this is followed by the gust of wind, which fills the sails, and breaks the curse. Because this moment of exorcism has no legitimate physical influence on the climax, *The Shadow-Line* seems to me a little unsatisfactory, without the symbolic complexities of the previous stories I have examined.

6

Apart from this flaw, the novel successfully depicts the captain's moral development. At the beginning his concept of reality is still under the influence of youthful romantic dreams, and this is partly why he throws up his satisfactory ordinary job. We have already seen how Conrad suggests to the reader that this self-illusion can end in depravity and breakdown. There are a number of significant little details that reveal the young man's ignorance of human nature. He is shocked when the Steward of the Officers' Home surreptitiously tries to prevent him from hearing about the vacant command so that he can procure it for Hamilton, who is sponging on him. It was the first instance, the narrator tells us, of harm being attempted against him, or at least the first he ever found out, and he is surprised and indignant. After he has crossed the shadow line, he has learnt that such malevolence is by no means unusual. The captain who transports him to Bangkok to join his new ship is the first really unsympathetic man he has ever come in contact with. His education is certainly far from complete. At first sight of his command, a high-class vessel, harmonious in the line of her fine body, in the proportioned tallness of her spars, his feeling of life-emptiness immediately loses its bitter plausibility; its evil influence dissolves 'in a flow of joyous emotion'. He is still too idealistic, like the narrator of 'The Secret Sharer', who begins his initiation complacently satisfied by the security of the seaman's profession. The captain in *The Shadow-Line* experiences a feeling of deep physical satisfaction at the sight of his ship, as if his ideal had embodied itself in an entirely appropriate form.

The test reveals the truth to him about man and Nature, and the question is how will he respond? The climate rapidly breaks down the crew's health, and he is forced to recognize that Nature is his enemy. The climate acts 'with the swiftness of an invisible monster ambushed in the air, in the water, in the mud of the river bank'. Even when he is out at sea, this tropical fever stretches its 'claw' after them, and the wind behaves with what can only be 'purposeful malevolence'. He confronts the knowledge which turned Lord Jim's knees to jelly, and paralysed his will.

Immediately he leaves the shore, the captain finds himself on one of those strange journeys into the darkness of apocalypse which so fascinated Conrad's imagination. Indeed, it is difficult to read *The Shadow-Line* without feeling that it recalls too precisely the symbolism of the *Patna* accident or the Placid Gulf. In the darkness the ship 'might have been a planet, vertiginously on its appointed path in a space of infinite silence'; the captain wonders if he is losing his sense of balance for ever. He is Everyman alone on his journey through an absurd universe. It is 'impossible to distinguish land from water in the enigmatical tranquillity of the immense forces of the world.' The land loses its substance, 'as if cut out of black paper and seeming to float on the water as light as cork'. Once again human distinctions, by which we try to define our activities, are blurred in this moment of apocalypse. The captain fights against loneliness by keeping a diary, like Razumov finding some kind of psychological relief in this form of art. He writes: 'There is something going on in the sky like a decomposition, like a corruption of the air, which remains as still as ever.' In this impenetrable darkness, the atmosphere seems to have turned to soot, as he awaits the end of all things:

> When the time came the blackness would overwhelm silently the bit of starlight falling upon the ship, and the end of all things would come without a sigh, stir, or murmur of any kind, and all our hearts would cease to beat like run-down clocks.
> It was impossible to shake off that sense of finality. The quietness that came over me was like a foretaste of annihilation. It gave me a sort of comfort, as though my soul had become suddenly reconciled to an eternity of blind stillness. (p. 108)

The darkness is like that before creation; all forms are 'blotted out in the dreadful smoothness of that absolute night'.

The Conradian hero must accept knowledge of annihilation, the ultimate apocalypse. He must not allow this moment of recognition to break his will, nor must he evade its significance by escape into the fantasies of romance. He must survive even when his imagination is most intensely affected by Nature's images of negation: 'To look round the ship was to look into a bottomless black pit. The eye lost itself in inconceivable depths.'

At first the captain proves unequal to his task. In a grotesque scene, he thinks that Burns, who is clipping off the thick growth of his red beard, is trying to commit suicide. His suspicion suggests to the reader that the idea of suicide is already present in his mind, and later he is jealous because Burns will presumably soon die: 'Enviable man! So near extinction . . .' The intense loneliness acts like poison on his brain, and he suffers from a morbid vision of the ship as a floating grave. His form of sickness is 'indifference', and he now must prove that he can overcome the temptation which led him to throw up his job at the beginning of the story: 'The creeping paralysis of a hopeless outlook.'

This indifference, symbolized by the immobility of the ship, comes partly from his awareness of human insignificance. It also derives from his secret sense of guilt. He feels responsible because he failed to check the quinine bottles. In his diary he confesses that in the past he had always suffered from a strange sense of insecurity. He suspected he might be no good.

The crew never reproach him, and this helps him to regain his self-confidence. In particular, Ransome, the cook, who suffers from heart disease, acts towards him in a Christ-like role. As the weather becomes more threatening, it is Ransome who prompts the captain to overcome his indifference, and to return on deck. In this crisis his seaman's instinct survives whole in spite of his moral dissolution. Remorse must wait, for he has to steer. Back in port he talks with Captain Giles about initiation. He has learnt not to hope too much, and not to expect too much, particularly from himself: 'The truth is', Giles explains, 'that one must not make too much of anything in life, good or bad.' A man must stand up to his bad luck, to his mistakes, to his conscience. The captain has proved himself such a man, has crossed his shadow-line, and he immediately sets off again in his ship, with a new crew.

Ransome's conduct exemplifies the ideal towards which all Conrad's self-questionings have tended. The cook 'positively had grace', and his devotion pays the ransom that frees the captain from his sense of unworthiness and indifference. But the moral implications are Conradian rather than Christian. Ransome has learnt to live with death, with an ever-present knowledge of his imminent extinction. The captain wonders whether Ransome's immunity from the tropical fever is 'perhaps because, carrying a deadly enemy in his breast, he had schooled himself into a systematic control of feelings and movements'. At the crisis he reports to the captain on the poop, stepping out of darkness into visibility suddenly, as if just created, and after giving reassurance about the state of the ship vanishes again into ultimate blackness. His behaviour is like the gleams of light in *Heart of Darkness*, a promise that salvation is possible, that meaningful action has not been rendered finally absurd.

And so Ransome is *savagely* determined to live. He refuses to continue the journey with the captain, for life is a boon to him, and he dare not risk further ordeals. He lives in the knowledge that the individual spirit is not free, that it is conditioned and limited by circumstance. Salvation is through work, through honest service of traditional social roles, through humble acceptance of personal limitations and the ultimate annihilation of death. 'Live at half-speed', the captain mutters disconsolately to Captain Giles. That is what Conrad himself was doing during the later years of his imaginative life.

Chapter 9

Conclusion

> Many a man has heard or read and believes that the earth goes round the sun; one small blob of mud among several others, spinning ridiculously with a waggling motion like a top about to fall. This is the Copernican system, and the man believes in the system without often knowing as much about it as its name. But while watching a sunset he sheds his belief; he sees the sun as a small and useful object, the servant of his needs and the witness of his ascending effort, sinking slowly behind a range of mountains, and then he holds the system of Ptolemy. (pp. 73–4)
>
> CONRAD, *Notes on Life and Letters*

I

In my first chapter I argued that there is no clear development of ideas throughout Conrad's work. His achievement might be roughly divided into three areas. There are the direct accounts of life at sea, which give vitality and excitement to large sections of *The Nigger of the 'Narcissus'*, '*Youth*', *Typhoon* or *The Shadow-Line*. There are the stories in which he tries to deal with sexual relations, as in *Chance*, *Victory* or *The Arrow of Gold*. And finally there are his greatest works, from *Heart of Darkness* to *Under Western Eyes*, in which he struggles to find viable forms of sensibility and moral commitment in an apparently meaningless universe. In this last chapter I shall look briefly at Conrad's less important achievements, both as a narrator of sea stories and in his treatment of sex, and then attempt a final analysis of the vision inherent in the major novels.

During his honeymoon in Brittany in 1896 Conrad was at work on an ambitious novel, *The Rescuer* (later *The Rescue*). In this story he was trying to combine all the three elements in his imaginative life, the love of the sea, his concern with sex, and his cosmic scepticism. He soon found himself unable to continue, characteristically depressed and frustrated as he sat for hours before a blank page without completing even one sentence. In a series of letters to Edward Garnett, he described his feeling of impotence:

> I have had some impressions, some sensations—in my time:—impressions and sensations of common things. And it's all faded—my very being seems faded and thin like the ghost of a blonde and sentimental woman, haunting romantic ruins pervaded by rats. I am exceedingly miserable . . . (19 June, 1896)

> I am paralysed by doubt and have just sense enough to feel the agony but am powerless to invent a way out of it. This is sober truth. I had bad moments with the Outcast but never anything so ghastly nothing half so hopeless. (5 August, 1896) [1]

His struggle with the manuscript ended after twenty years, when he finally completed it in 1919. In 1920, after revising the novel for book publication, he was still suffering from bouts of mental paralysis. He told Garnett: 'I have done nothing—can do nothing—don't want to do anything. One lives too long. Yet cutting one's throat would be too scandalous besides being unfair to other parties. Xmas greetings.' [2] This behaviour reflects once again the oscillation between activity and stagnation discussed in my first chapter.

In *The Rescue*, Captain Tom Lingard has committed himself to fulfil a debt of honour to the romantic fugitives Rajah Hassim and his sister Immada by restoring them to their kingdom. When he arrives at the Shore of Refuge to lead his Malays into battle, he finds a stranded yacht whose company includes the beautiful Mrs Travers, with whom he falls in love. The conflict between his obligations to Hassim and his passion for Edith Travers renders him powerless. By helping Mr and Mrs Travers and their companion D'Alcacer he diminishes his authority with the natives, who want to pillage the yacht. He cannot act in the heroic manner for which he is famous, and his indecision is largely responsible for the death of Hassim and Immada. He saves the yacht and its people, but he is crushed and defeated by the collapse of his great plans. He feels his soul is dead. The yacht with Edith Travers sails away to the south. 'Steer north', commands Lingard, in the last words of the novel.

Unfortunately the published form of *The Rescue* does not fulfil the potentialities suggested by the earlier manuscript. The bewildered hero, called King Tom by his followers, lacks the complexity of Lord

Jim or Heyst. In *Conrad the Novelist*, Albert Guerard analyses the
looseness and banality of the style, which are perhaps the result of
Conrad's desire for popular commercial success. The narrative is often
little more than a conventional series of adventures, without the irony
and ambiguity characteristic of his greatest work.

But *The Rescue* has its merits. Some parts, particularly the seascapes,
are well written; and the novel as a whole throws fascinating light on
Conrad's artistic problems. When he began writing this story, he was
still an apprentice in his craft, unsure about the appropriate form for his
vision of life. In *The Rescue*, he tries to mould his ideas into a tragic
pattern, a simple conflict between romance and realism. Lingard is
depicted as a man of primitive heroic energy ruined by an uncontrollable passion. His courage and honesty are praised without serious
qualification. His plans are foiled by accident, by the unforeseen
arrival of the yacht at the crucial moment in his preparations for the
war. In 1896 Conrad was still in search for a proper medium in which
to express his cosmic scepticism. He found this only with the arrival on
the scene of Marlow as narrator in *Heart of Darkness*.

As he sails towards the Shore of Refuge, ignorant of the problems
ahead, Lingard's affections are centred upon his ship:

> Lingard's love for his brig was a man's love, and was so great that
> it could never be appeased unless he called on her to put forth all
> her qualities and her power, to repay his exacting affection by a
> faithfulness tried to the very utmost limit of endurance. Every
> flutter of the sails flew down from aloft along the taut leeches, to
> enter his heart in a sense of acute delight; and the gentle murmur
> of water alongside, which, continuous and soft, showed that in all
> her windings his incomparable craft had never, even for an
> instant, ceased to carry her way, was to him more precious and
> inspiring than the soft whisper of tender words would have been
> to another man. It was in such moments that he lived intensely,
> in a flush of strong feeling that made him long to press his little
> vessel to his breast. She was his perfect world full of trustful
> joy. (p. 54)

His sense of unity with his brig acts in a superficial way as a substitute
for a sexual relationship. The ship satisfies Lingard's romantic desire to
be at one with Nature, to feel in accord with the wind and the sea. Both
ship and master are associated with images taken from Nature. Lingard
is compared to a rugged rock in mid ocean; the brig seems at home in

the landscape 'wrapped up in a scented mantle of starlight and silence'.

The attraction of his Malay companions for Lingard, and presumably also for Conrad, is that they appear to exist in a true relation
with these natural processes, and they lack the sophisticated world-
weariness of the people on the yacht. Haji Wasub, Lingard's faithful
serang, performs his functions as if part of a natural harmony:

> His eyes travelled incessantly from the illuminated card to the
> shadowy sails of the brig and back again, while his body was
> motionless as if made of wood and built into the ship's frame.
> (p. 16)

Hassim and Immada behave with exemplary trust and devotion, like a
prince and princess in a fairy-tale. Lingard's ambitious plan to restore
them to their kingdom represents for him an attempt to conquer
reality, to impose his own heroic ideal on the warring Malay factions.
This is partly what attracts Edith Travers. After her first meeting with
Lingard and his friends, she feels transported to a more simple, youthful period of civilization. She envies Immada:

> Nothing stood between that girl and the truth of her sensations.
> She could be sincerely courageous, and tender and passionate and
> —well—ferocious. Why not ferocious? She could know the
> truth of terror—and of affection, absolutely, without artificial
> trammels, without the pain of restraint.
>
> Thinking of what such life could be Mrs Travers felt invaded
> by that inexplicable exaltation which the consciousness of their
> physical capacities so often gives to intellectual beings. She
> glowed with a sudden persuasion that she also could be equal to
> such an existence; and her heart was dilated with a momentary
> longing to know the naked truth of things; the naked truth of life
> and passion buried under the growth of centuries. (p. 153)

When King Tom visits her by night to describe his incredible schemes,
she is momentarily attracted by the temptation of savagery. The barbarous names of Belarab, Daman and Ningrat ring out for her with 'an
exceptional energy'. When she wears Immada's clothes, she feels
suddenly as if her true identity is revealed. Her husband reproaches
her: 'The matter with you, Edith, is that at heart you are perfectly
primitive.' Eventually she is unable to give up her civilized identity
and to abandon herself to her natural passion for Lingard. She seems

to fear the reality of her emotions, though the novel is not altogether clear about how far it is wise to submit to the claims of the primitive.

The idea of 'rescue' appealed to Conrad for psychological reasons. Presumably as a lonely child he had indulged in fantasies of this kind, in which an outcast is saved and redeemed in some heroic adventure. He handles the theme easily enough in straightforward narrative, and Lingard has no hesitations when his only task is to help Hassim and Immada. But, as we have seen with Heyst and Lena in *Victory*, when Conrad vicariously participates in scenes of rescue through a sexual relationship his imagination takes refuge in sentimentality, and he seems unable to understand his own conflicts. The vague generalities and stilted language of Lingard's conversations with Mrs Travers are acutely embarrassing to the reader. He behaves like a sixteen-year-old adolescent suffering from infatuation for the first time. In *Joseph Conrad: Achievement and Decline* Thomas Moser draws upon a study of the manuscripts to prove that *The Rescue* came to a complete halt in 1899 because Conrad could not cope with the sexual situation that was developing. Lingard has difficulty in maintaining self-control, but never makes love to Mrs Travers. What is most imaginatively striking is that she renders him impotent in will, and leaves him weak and broken as if a vampire had sucked his life blood.

To help her he is forced to abandon his brig, his natural relation with the outside universe. The same process is enacted in the short story, 'Freya of the Seven Isles' (1912), in which Jasper Allen is similarly in love with his brig. He tries to bring the beautiful Freya on board as his wife, and so to unite himself with Nature and woman; but his rival Heemskirk deliberately wrecks the brig. Jasper is psychologically destroyed by this event, and loses his desire to live. A similar story is told in *The Rescue* by old Jörgenson, whom Lingard has recruited to look after his stores and ammunition. Jörgenson recalls how a man named Dawson committed suicide after a Dutch official had purposely wrecked his schooner. In each case the man divided from his ship loses his potency, and often this disaster is consequential upon an overwhelming passion for a woman. The setting is usually dream-like and exaggerated, as if Conrad could only find expression for his hidden fear of sex in these terms. In both 'Freya of the Seven Isles' and *The Rescue*, the characters assume roles suitable for a melodramatic opera, aware half-consciously that their actions bear some kind of symbolic weight.

In Conrad's major fictions the romantic hero's self-confidence is broken down not so much by sexual passion as by an overmastering imaginative response to the meaninglessness of the universe. There are moments in *The Rescue* which express this fundamental scepticism, but they are insufficiently developed. Mrs Travers speaks 'from behind the veil of an immense indifference stretched between her and all men, between her heart and the meaning of events'. Before Lingard's night visit to the yacht, she has a glimpse of ultimate chaos, of the approach of apocalypse: 'She saw herself standing alone, at the end of time, on the brink of days. All was unmoving as if the dawn would never come, the stars would never fade, the sun would never rise any more; all was mute, still, dead . . .' After she leaves the yacht with Lingard, Conrad writes: 'An obscurity that seemed without limit in space and time had submerged the universe like a destroying flood.' But such typical Conradian descriptions of indifference or blackness tend to appear in *The Rescue* as a kind of self-parody, without the symbolic richness of comparable passages in *Lord Jim* and *Nostromo*. Mrs Travers appreciates that Lingard's fantasies reflect something child-like in his nature, but her criticism is not given complexity or weight.

Jörgenson is an interesting figure who might have solved Conrad's artistic problems if he had been allowed a greater part in the novel. To a certain extent he acts as an alter ego for King Tom, a mirror for the reality that will eventually destroy Lingard's romantic ideals. In his youth he has been involved in desperate adventures, and he too loved his ship, the *Wild Rose*. All was destroyed in the course of time, and he exists like a ghost, a reminder of the vanity of all earthly hopes:

> Jörgenson noted things quickly, cursorily, perfunctorily, as phenomena unrelated to his own apparitional existence of a visiting ghost. They were but passages in the game of men who were still playing at life. (p. 382)

As the story ends, Lingard has developed a similar negative stance, in Conrad's words, 'profound indifference', 'strange contempt for what his eyes could see', a 'distaste for words', an 'unbelief in the importance of things and men'. This is his reaction to Jörgenson's fanatical decision to blow up the stores and ammunition, himself, his enemies, together with Rajah Hassim and Immada. Suicidal violence is once again shown as a possible resolution for Conrad's investigations into mental paralysis.

2

It has often been argued that in Conrad's later writings there is a return to the normal after the disturbing scepticism of his great works. In *The Shadow-Line, The Rescue, The Rover* and *Suspense* there is simple trust in heroic action. In his tales of adventures at sea, Conrad could leave behind more serious artistic problems, and indulge himself in uncomplicated linear forms of narrative. He justifies this type of composition in 'A Familiar Preface' to *A Personal Record.* He has 'tried with an almost filial regard to render the vibration of life in the great world of waters, in the hearts of the simple men who have for ages traversed its solitudes, and also that something sentient which seems to dwell in ships—the creatures of their hands and the objects of their care.' Examples of this kind of writing occur throughout his career. In 'Youth' (1898), from his early period, he produced an excellent tribute to his affection for the sea. The narrative of the *Judea's* ill-fated journey to Bangkok, which ends in tragedy when her cargo of coal takes fire, is recorded with a fine awareness of the importance of direct sensations and physical actions. 'Youth' is based on his own experiences, and the writing reflects the exhilaration with which he entered upon his life at sea.

The same mood colours the style of *The Rover* (1923), his last completed novel. Peyrol, ex-pirate, ex-master gunner in the French Navy, retires to an isolated farmhouse on the coast near Toulon. In spite of his illegal activities in the past, he retains high ideals of patriotism and integrity, and at the end of the novel sacrifices his life for the lovers, Arlette and Lieutenant Réal. He takes Réal's place on a voyage across the Mediterranean carrying faked dispatches intended to deceive Nelson about the plans of the French fleet. In the final scenes Peyrol pretends to try to escape from the pursuing English sloop, and to complete the deception allows himself to be killed. *The Rover* has never been thought one of Conrad's major works, but there is a mellow dignity in the descriptions of Provence and the Mediterranean which makes this a fitting farewell to his craft. This novel, in striking contrast to those I have examined in detail, reflects accurately his credo in 'A Familiar Preface':

> Those who read me know my conviction that the world, the temporal world, rests on a few very simple ideas; so simple that

> they must be as old as the hills. It rests notably, among others, on
> the idea of Fidelity. (p. xix)

Peyrol, the outcast, returns home to find fulfilment and peace in an
heroic, sacrificial act.

Conrad's death in 1924 prevented him from completing a new novel,
Suspense, which would have given him the opportunity to express in
fictional form his interest in Napoleon. About 80,000 words had been
written, but from these it is impossible to deduce the total conception.
Cosmo Latham, a handsome Englishman, visits an old friend of his
father, the Marquis d'Armand, in Genoa during the period of Napoleon's exile to Elba. He falls in love with Adèle, the married daughter
of the Marquis; but there are hints that in fact she is his half-sister, the
child of a love affair of Cosmo's father. Their meeting is secretly
watched by Clelia, the natural daughter of Adèle's husband, a wild,
untamed girl, who succumbs to a passion for Cosmo. The atmosphere
is strained and feverish, and one wonders how Conrad would have
developed this strange situation with its suggestions of incest and
voyeurism. The best parts describe Cosmo's adventures at the harbour,
when he becomes involved with a sailor, named Attilio, who is
smuggling dispatches to Elba. The novel breaks off as Cosmo is
sailing towards Elba with Attilio, and, now the erotic problems are out
of the way, the adventures are recounted with typical speed and vigour.

The virtues of forceful narration are also characteristic of the best of
Conrad's non-fictional writings. In 1904 he had started dictating a
series of sea sketches to help to pay off his overdraft. These were
subsequently collected as *The Mirror of the Sea* (1906). In this task he
was considerably helped by his friend, Ford Madox Hueffer. Hueffer
encouraged Conrad by recalling incidents and anecdotes from his
conversation, and took these down from his dictation. In 1908 Hueffer
persuaded Conrad to continue his reminiscences for the new journal,
The English Review, and these sketches became *A Personal Record*
(1912).

Some parts of these books are badly written, such as the invocation
to the East and West Winds, and the tribute to Nelson. These sections
were perhaps those Conrad had in mind when he told H. G. Wells the
essays were 'bosh'. But he writes excellently when he describes
directly his recollections of Poland, or the *Tremolino* adventure, when
he was forced to wreck his ship while gun-running in the Mediterranean. In *A Personal Record*, Conrad offers this justification for his

autobiographical sketches: 'An imaginative and exact rendering of authentic memories may serve worthily that spirit of piety towards all things human which sanctions the conceptions of a writer of tales, and the emotions of the man reviewing his own experience.' However, it is difficult to be sure how far all these memories are 'authentic'. Conrad was the kind of man who created fantasies around the incidents of his life, and as he ransacked his memories of thirty years before he must have often confused fact and fiction. We have already noted the deliberate falsification of the duel in *The Arrow of Gold*. The most impressive scene in these non-fictional reminiscences is the winter landscape in Amsterdam where in 1887 Conrad spent weeks of waiting, frustrated and depressed, as mate of the *Highland Forest*. In this 'waste land' his imagination responded to 'the visions of ships frozen in a row, appearing vaguely like corpses of black vessels in a white world, so silent, so lifeless, so soulless they seemed to be'. Here, as in the fiction, the concretely realized visual details act as a medium for his own tensions and uncertainties. There are enough good things of this kind for us to feel grateful to Hueffer for stimulating Conrad to undertake these sketches.

Conrad first met Hueffer in September 1898 while he was visiting the Garnetts at Limpsfield in Surrey. Baines describes this as the most important event in Conrad's literary career. One result was that Conrad rented from him Pent Farm in Kent, and it was here that they collaborated together on *The Inheritors* (1901) and *Romance* (1903). Both are tedious, though *Romance* might be recommended as an adventure story in the Robert Louis Stevenson manner suitable for children. It is difficult now to assess the influence of Hueffer on Conrad during this period of his great creative triumphs. Hueffer's own reminiscences are notoriously inaccurate. Both were steeped in French literature, particularly Flaubert and Maupassant, and both were passionately interested in experimental techniques in the novel. There seems little doubt that Hueffer helped Conrad to understand the true nature of his genius. Both were highly strung and temperamental, and their relationship passed through moods of gaiety and anger more suited to a love affair. It is not surprising that Jessie took an aversion to Hueffer. A final quarrel broke off the relationship in 1909.

3

Whereas Conrad's descriptions of life at sea are admirably direct and concrete, his attempts to deal with sex usually prove disastrous. Beneath the superficially conventional relations between male and female, there are hints of the abnormal and the perverse. We have already seen evidence of this in 'The Planter of Malata', *Victory* and *The Rescue*, in which sexual passion leads to impotence or suicide. Conrad's secret fantasies take over most completely in a short story, 'A Smile of Fortune' (1911) and in the autobiographical novel, *The Arrow of Gold* (1919). Both these works falsify incidents in Conrad's own early life, telling of sexual encounters which possibly had little substance in fact.

'A Smile of Fortune' recalls details of Conrad's visit to Port Louis in Mauritius in 1888 as captain of the *Otago*, during which he made his foolish proposal to Eugénie Renouf, who was already engaged. He apparently also visited a stevedore named James Horatio Shaw who possessed a unique rose-garden, and a daughter called Alice, aged nearly seventeen. In the story, the young captain-narrator is irresistibly fascinated by the fictional Alice; Conrad allowed both his wife Jessie and his biographer, Aubry, to believe the flirtation was based on fact. But the story is so littered with Freudian images that it seems largely a product of masochistic fantasy.

As the captain approaches the island he is impressed by the beauty of this 'Pearl of the Ocean'. Later this marvel turns into 'a thing of horrors'. In these later works the attractive exterior of a woman covers places of hidden shame and disgust. On his arrival the young captain's feeling of personal inadequacy contrasts with the self-assurance of Alice's father, Alfred Jacobus, a ship-chandler. In the past Jacobus has submitted to a degrading passion for Alice's mother, a lady-rider in a circus. After he deserts his wife to follow the circus, his mistress treats him like a dog, and it is known that she even lashed him with her riding-whip. The horse, the symbol of male sex, is dominated by the lady-rider. Now she is dead Jacobus protects his daughter in his secret garden hidden away from conventional society. When the captain succumbs to Alice's fascinations, it is clear that without knowing it he wishes to replace the father and suffer a similar degradation.

The entrance to the perfumed garden lies down a grass-grown alley and through a small door. Inside, the gorgeous maze of flower-beds and the massed foliage of varied trees drowse in a warm, voluptuous silence. Alice herself, like all Conrad's *femmes fatales*, has abundant hair, in her case black and lustrous, so thick and strong that it gave 'an impression of magnificently cynical untidiness'. The captain likes her because she is an untamed slut. These images of female sex present themselves to him as magical, like something in a tapestry: 'She was like a spell-bound creature with the forehead of a goddess crowned by the dishevelled magnificent hair of a gipsy tramp.' The scented garden seems to him 'like a cemetery of flowers buried in the darkness'. As he approaches the temptress, the hidden entry to sex, he feels he is journeying towards death. He enjoys her indifference, her scorn, her curt insolence; he wants to 'taste perversely the flavour of contempt in her indolent poses'. In this manner he can enjoy sexual arousal without bringing to the test his own potency, his own masculine ability to enter into an adult relationship. She is like a child, a castaway, whom he may rescue and protect. He indulges in this pleasure with self-contempt, 'as if it were a secret vice bound to end in my undoing, like the habit of some drug or other which ruins and degrades its slave'. When he eventually embraces her, he tells us, 'the first kiss I planted on her closed lips was vicious enough to have been a bite'.

The oedipal nature of this mixture of fascination and disgust emerges clearly in a scene where the captain symbolically replaces Alice's father as her protector. After escaping from the verandah where she has been resisting the captain's embraces, Alice drops a high-heeled blue slipper. The father comes on the scene, picks up 'the fascinating object', and crushes this fetish in his hand during their conversation. The captain sends off Jacobus to wait for him on his ship, and on Alice's return buttons on her shoe for her. He has replaced the father; but immediately she begins to lose her attraction, and he experiences a 'weary conviction of the emptiness of all things under Heaven'. When he holds her close, she rewards him with a hasty, awkward kiss. As soon as she is really available, she becomes odious to him, and he escapes hastily from the island in his ship. Like Conrad himself after the actual visit to Mauritius, the captain resigns his command rather than return to his temptress in the perfumed garden.

The weakness of this story is that neither the captain-narrator nor Conrad seem fully aware of the true nature of Alice's emotional appeal. The same kind of confusion occurs in *The Arrow of Gold*. This draws on Conrad's adventures in Marseilles, which he had already used in *The Mirror of the Sea*. The main characters are M. George, based on the youthful Conrad, and a charming seductress, Rita. Many of the details, presumably in some part autobiographical, occur in a fragment of a novel, *The Sisters*, written over twenty years before. Rita has been the mistress of a wealthy patron of the Arts, Henry Allègre, but after his death she turns cold, like a woman sculptured on a monument. She suggests to M. George the wildness of unlawful sex; at the same time she responds to him like a block of marble. As she sits cross-legged on her divan in her house in Marseilles she reminds him of 'a young savage chieftain'; the image occurs to him again when in the strange house on the streets of Consuls, where he had his lodging, he sees her 'enveloped in the skins of wild beasts'. Yet when he tries to kiss her hand, she responds with violent disgust. On one occasion he kisses her throat: 'with a stifled cry of surprise her arms fell off me as if she had been shot'. Male sex nauseates her. She tells him: 'It's like taking the lids off boxes and seeing ugly toads staring at you.'

Rita's mixture of savagery and coldness reflects both the attraction and repulsion of sex. This double attitude is also expressed by the opposition between M. George and Ortega, the sadistic fanatical Carlist who loved and hated Rita when they were both children. At the climax, M. George takes Ortega to the house in the street of Consuls through Marseilles at a time of carnival. The gaiety is repellent to M. George: 'These yells of festivity suggested agonizing fear, rage of murder, ferocity of lust, and the irremediable joylessness of human condition'. When he reflects on his own unrequited passion for Rita, he recalls a visit to a lunatic asylum, where he saw a madman who believed himself betrayed by a woman: 'He was a young man with a thin fair beard, huddled up on the edge of his bed, hugging himself forlornly; and his incessant and lamentable wailing filled the long bare corridor, striking a chill into one's heart before one came to the door of his cell.' These incidents reveal how the forces of Eros frighten and intimidate M. George. This is not the only occasion in Conrad where sexual passion is associated with madness.

Rita has arrived unexpectedly at M. George's lodgings. He finds himself locked in a room with her, while the abominable Ortega bangs on the door, howling for admission. It is as if Ortega represents the brute aspects of lust M. George would prefer to repress. Like Uriah Heep and David Copperfield, Ortega and M. George personify the unsavoury and the sentimental in sex. When at last M. George might seem to have Rita in his power, he succumbs to an immense fatigue, and takes no action. Blissful repose on the breast of a protecting, maternal woman seems often the aim of the Conradian hero. In *The Arrow of Gold* he sends off the two lovers like two children to enjoy a brief idyll in a small house embowered with roses in the Maritime Alps, but M. George is forced to return, and is severely wounded in a duel. When he recovers, Rita refuses to rejoin him and so, we are told, sacrifices herself to the integrity of his life. Is it his loss or gain, M. George asks himself. Neither he nor Conrad seems to know.

In *Joseph Conrad: A Psychoanalytic Biography*, Bernard Meyer points out that when in erotic situations Conrad's heroes usually appear paralysed, devoid of excitement or aggression. Both Alice and Rita, like Natalia in *Under Western Eyes*, are described as masculine in appearance. As with the symbolic dagger Lena takes from Ricardo in *Victory*, the woman deprives the man of his potency. Rita's arrow of gold is a hair adornment which perplexes M. George's sleep: 'Often I dreamed of her with white limbs shimmering in the gloom like a nymph haunting a riot of foliage and raising a perfect round arm to take an arrow of gold out of her hair to throw it at me by hand, like a dart.' Meyer argues that whether represented by a golden hair ornament or a knife, by piercing glances or abundant hair, these women possess a phallic endowment which confers on them the capacity for active penetration of their man. In *The Rescue* Lingard tells Mrs Travers she has taken all the hardness out of him. In *The Rover* Lt Réal, when he embraces Arlette, wonders if he is about to die, and in 'A Smile of Fortune' sex is imaginatively associated with death. Thomas Moser's central argument is that in Conrad's less successful fictions inadequate males regard female sexuality as a menace, a dangerous animal power. Such episodes are presented in flabby, melodramatic prose, as if Conrad dare not scrutinize his own obsessions too closely. Bernard Meyer diagnoses in Conrad an intense castration anxiety, presumably caused by his mother's early death. In his novels he never could create a woman of virtue and maturity who was also sexually passionate. His women tend to be either like Antonia Avellanos or Natalia Haldin, proud, cold, intelligent and slightly masculine, or like Aissa in *An Outcast of the Islands*, the savage in *Heart of Darkness* or Alice in 'A Smile of Fortune', sexual, degraded, animal.

4

It is not surprising that Conrad's autobiographical writings reveal little of his inner life. Nor is there much help in the critical essays gathered together in *Notes on Life and Letters* (1921) and *Last Essays* (1926). In a review of *Notes on Life and Letters* E. M. Forster took the opportunity to assess the total quality of Conrad's character as a novelist. I too wish now to leave behind the less successful works, and to make a final assessment of his achievement. Forster starts by saying that in his non-fictional writings Conrad is interesting, stimulating, profound, beautiful, but he can scarcely be said to take us into his confidence. He guards himself by ironies and politenesses. One reason for this is that he feared intimacy, as we have seen, and had a rigid conception as to where the rights of the public stop. But, according to Forster, his character is also unclear because of essential aspects of his genius at the heart of his great novels: 'What is so elusive about him is that he is always promising to make some general philosophic statement about the universe, and then refraining with a gruff disclaimer.' [3]

Forster points out that Conrad shrank instinctively from the charge of cynicism, but yet committed himself to no creed: 'Only opinions, and the right to throw them overboard when facts make them look absurd.' Forster's analysis of this central obscurity implies a condemnation: 'These essays do suggest that he is misty in the middle as well as at the edges, that the secret casket of his genius contains a vapour rather than a jewel; and that we need not try to write him down philosophically, because there is, in this particular direction, nothing to write.' Conrad's moral standpoint is unsure because while his universal love of truth made him misanthropic, he retained a faith in the full value of the courageous deeds and dangers he had witnessed as a seaman. Human fate seems to him like that of the characters of Alphonse Daudet, poignant, 'intensely interesting, and of not the slightest consequence'. [4]

I agree with Forster's analysis of Conrad's double vision, but I do not believe the contradiction is necessarily harmful to the fiction. In my view, Forster is looking for a kind of clarity and consistency which it is the purpose of Conrad's modern imagination to resist. Conrad's best fictions often seem to be moving towards some satisfying resolution of the moral dilemmas, but then deliberately frustrate the reader's expectations. A condition of uncertainty about the precise relevance of many of the images and events is essential to our reading experience; for Conrad there can be no absolute explanations. In this respect *Heart of Darkness* is akin to *The Waste Land*, and it is not surprising that Eliot's imagination was so responsive to Mr Kurtz. The collapse of Forster's own creative vitality after the publication of *A Passage to India* in 1924 was partly due to his unwillingness to acknowledge the contradictions in his own vision of life, to realize that there can never be any reconciliation between the nihilism symbolized by the echo in the Marabar Caves and the Hindu mysticism of Godbole. Conrad's fiction admits to the validity of irreconcilable points of view, and it is this type of sensibility I have tried to describe in my analyses of the novels.

My argument is that a considerable amount of criticism of Conrad, and of other moderns, still fails to understand this art whose purpose is to reflect the precarious quality of human apprehensions of reality. For example, in an article on *Chance*, Graham Hough, a critic of the highest intelligence, suggests that the obscurity that worries Forster is because Conrad is ignorant of domestic English life, and so cannot render scenes of this kind with the intimacy of understanding he displays when writing about the sea. In his descriptions of events on land in *Chance*, 'his knowledge of circumstantial detail, detail of speech and social relationships, is not intimate enough to allow some of these critical scenes to be presented otherwise than deviously and indirectly. Where we need a scene in clear daylight we have a dissolving vista of hints and suggestions.' [5] Hough believes that 'the complexities of his narrative method are, as it were, layers of protecting covering to an essentially simple heroic vision'.[6]

Like Jocelyn Baines, whom I quoted in my first chapter, Hough is out of touch with the true nature of Conrad's imagination. I am only too aware of my own inadequacies in trying to find a language to describe Conrad's genius. Literary artefacts in this mode force us to difficult assessments of the relationship between creating and knowing. Explanation, Frank Kermode argues, involves us inevitably in a man-locked set of ideas, and so always falsifies the symbolist work of art. This also applies to the best of Conrad. Criticism of such art needs to be as open-ended as the novels themselves.

5

Like the modern scientist, Conrad does not believe that the human mind can uncover absolute truth; instead we can only substitute an ability to describe objectively the veil of appearance. We cannot describe the universe in isolation from an observer; things are seen relative to some particular individual, rather than absolutely. By placing this attitude at the centre of his work, Conrad proved himself in accord with the very essence of modern physical thought. His fic-tional stance abjures authorial omnipotence, and characteristically remains aloof and ironic. In my descriptions of the novels, I have noted several occasions when his imagination develops these attitudes towards the extremes of scepticism, and almost succumbs to the claims of the absurd. In *The Secret Agent*, he seems at times close to the view of the Dada artist, Marcel Duchamp, who believed that life is a melancholy joke, an indecipherable nonsense, not worth the trouble of investigating.

But Conrad fascinates today because of his fierce resistance to the attractions of nihilism. Ian Watt has suggested that in recent years there has been a mounting impatience, just or unjust, with Conrad's literary peers, particularly with Joyce, Pound and Eliot, while Conrad's reputation grows and grows. This change in response is because we appreciate increasingly that whereas so many moderns withdrew into some type of aristocratic isolation, Conrad desperately struggled to find satisfactory forms of commitment for the mass of humanity. The poetry of Eliot and Pound leads us away in revulsion from contemporary actuality; the novels of Joyce and Lawrence tend to focus on the breaking of ties with family, class and country. In contrast, Conrad tries to escape from the condition of individual separateness. He admired Daudet for not affecting a passive attitude before the spectacle of life, an attitude which Conrad compares to the melancholy quietude of an ape.[7] Watt suggests that this brings us to the dominating question in Conrad: 'alienation, yes, but how do we get out of it?'[8]

Although he was deeply interested in European and international politics, Conrad had no confidence that political solutions were available for the tragic isolation of human beings in the modern world. In an essay on Anatole France, he sympathizes with a sceptical view of all forms of government: Anatole France 'is indulgent to the weaknesses of the people, and perceives that political institutions, whether contrived by the wisdom of the few or the ignorance of the many, are incapable of securing the happiness of mankind'.[9] As we have seen, Conrad examined the temptation of suicide with an honesty and sense of personal involvement which broke him up mentally and eventually paralysed his creative imagination. But he refused to give way to despair, and tried to find answers to the elements in himself which found sympathetic expression in the scepticism of Decoud and Heyst. Although he rejected political solutions, he resisted complete subjection to the stoical apathy which views all human activities and ideas as akin to fictional illusions, only games towards which we must adopt an attitude of indifference. As he described the sufferings of his outcasts and solitaries, he continually sought for possible ways of commitment to life. In contrast to the typical Dada artist, he was passionately aware that his scepticism might prove reductive, that it might withdraw him from all that is most significant in human experience. He perceived the danger of the synthesis that says there is no synthesis.

6

Conrad's commitment to his art was total, and in his writing he found one answer to his despair. His aims as a novelist are best explained in the Preface to *The Nigger of the 'Narcissus'*. This was written in 1897, a few months after the novel was completed, at a time when Conrad was about to launch into his most creative period. He begins the Preface:

> A work that aspires, however humbly, to the condition of art should carry its justification in every line. And art itself may be defined as a single-minded attempt to render the highest kind of justice to the visible universe, by bringing to light the truth, manifold and one, underlying its every aspect. It is an attempt to find in its forms, in its colours, in its light, in its shadows, in the aspects of matter and in the facts of life what of each is fundamental, what is enduring and essential—their one illuminating and convincing quality—the very truth of their existence. (p. vii)

This truth, Conrad believes:

> ... speaks to our capacity for delight and wonder, to the sense of mystery surrounding our lives; to our sense of pity, and beauty, and pain; to the latent feeling of fellowship with all creation—and to the subtle but invincible conviction of solidarity that knits together the loneliness of innumerable hearts, to the solidarity in dreams, in joy, in sorrow, in aspirations, in illusions, in hope, in fear, which binds men to each other, which binds together all humanity—the dead to the living and the living to the unborn. (p. viii)

In this unusual way, Conrad moves from a position close to art for art's sake to a belief that art works in the service of 'solidarity', that it may do something to combat man's sense of isolation from his fellow men and from the visible world:

> To snatch in a moment of courage, from the remorseless rush of time, a passing phase of life, is only the beginning of the task. The task approached in tenderness and faith is to hold up unquestioningly, without choice and without fear, the rescued fragment before all eyes in the light of a sincere mood. It is to show its vibration, its colour, its form; and through its movement, its

form, and its colour, reveal the substance of its truth—disclose its inspiring secret: the stress and passion within the core of each convincing moment. In a single-minded attempt of that kind, if one be deserving and fortunate, one may perchance attain to such clearness of sincerity that at last the presented vision of regret or pity, of terror or mirth, shall awaken in the hearts of the be-holders that feeling of unavoidable solidarity; of the solidarity in mysterious origin, in toil, in joy, in hope, in uncertain fate, which binds men to each other and all mankind to the visible world. (p. x.)

The language here is highly coloured and not completely clear as a piece of rational analysis. But Conrad's main concerns emerge. As a novelist he does not intend to be overtly didactic, for he has little hope for significant political or moral progress. The business of the novel is to contemplate the world, to understand its inmost meaning, and in this assumption Conrad has much in common with the symbolists. But he takes these ideas a stage further, and argues that such contemplation has a limited social value. He will portray the truths of experience, however terrifying they may be, and this honesty will reveal to his readers the common lot of humanity. The aim of art, he says character-istically, is doubtful, obscured by mists: 'It is not in the clear logic of a triumphant conclusion; it is not in the unveiling of one of those heart-less secrets which are called the Laws of Nature. It is not less great, but only more difficult.' It is, in a paradoxical way, to let men know that they are not alone in their aloneness, that their tragic fate is shared. He will link people together in fellow feeling as they contemplate the impossibility of ever understanding their predicament.

The symbolist tends to withdraw into the self, where he feeds upon the unrealities of the consciousness in which he is imprisoned. Conrad shares such nightmares, but his experiences as a seaman supplied him with a foreground of immediate sensations in which his imagination delighted. His novels are full of colours and sounds, of people and places, whose concrete vitality works against the depression endemic in his mode of vision. Like all great artists, he imposes his unique sensibility on his readers just by expressing it so successfully.

7

Conrad, therefore, is heroic in his faith in art. Also, in spite of his pessimism, he understands the importance of trust, of care for the suffering, of honest service, and he portrays these with sympathy even when the implications of his symbolism appear alien to such values. Although he cultivates irony and withdrawal, at the same time his writings imply adherence to certain kinds of moral judgment. There is no doubt that the German Captain of the *Patna* is a despicable coward and Mrs Gould a woman of delicate and praiseworthy emotions.

At his best, Conrad practises a 'realistic kind of provisional commitment'. The phrase is from Ian Watt's article, 'Joseph Conrad: Alienation and Commitment', which provides a brilliant and definitive exposition of Conrad's warring values:

> Conrad does not see commitment as a single willed reversal occurring with dramatic clarity and violence in the individual consciousness; for him it is, rather, an endless process throughout history in which individuals are driven by circumstances into the traditional forms of human solidarity: are driven to accept the position that fidelity must govern the individual's relation to the outside world, while his inner self must be controlled by restraint and honour. This conservative and social ethic is certainly very different from the existentialist position, and embodies the main emphases of the most widely shared secular codes of behaviour over the ages.[10]

Are we to say, Watt asks, that there remains an irreconcilable contradiction between the alienation Conrad felt and the commitment he sought? Other writers seek consolation in myths of progress (Shaw, Wells, Galsworthy) or in the utopianism of the past (Yeats, Joyce, Pound and Eliot). Conrad does not evade the difficulties of his apparently contradictory stance. Watt writes: 'The way things are with our poor old planet, the time has come for bifocals.' We must acknowledge that the earth seems of minimal importance in the scheme of the universe, and that it will eventually be destroyed. We must acknowledge that all the suffering and pain and killing that took place before man came on earth make the idea of a benevolent creator seem impossible. Yet, not forgetting this pessimistic vision, we put on our bifocals, and look instead at the value of momentary sensations, and at individual examples of trust and devotion. Conrad testifies to the reality of human dignity even while admitting all those aspects of his thought which tend to nihilism. Conrad, as Watt says, justifies his bifocal vision on the simple ground that it reflects the facts of common human experience.

My purpose in this book has been to describe this courageous effort of Conrad's imagination to bring together experiences of alienation and commitment in a single work of art. As we have seen, he was not entirely successful, for reasons buried deep in his own character. His major weakness is his failure to find satisfactory expression for human love. Jim and Jewel, Decoud and Antonia, Razumov and Natalia, Anthony and Flora, Heyst and Lena, all repeat conventional gestures like puppets of sentimental romance. Conrad himself seems to have unconsciously associated sexual relationships with self-destruction for the male. But his use of two separate characters to reflect the composite nature of his own contradictory identity is responsible for a final saving grace. Marlow and Jim, Marlow and Kurtz, the Captain and Leggatt, are involved in personal relationships of commitment and concern. Conrad himself evinces a similar absorption in his characters, and there is throughout his work a deep compassion for human misfortune.

There are certain scenes that remain in my memory as supreme examples of Conrad's commitment to life, of his refusal to submit to the claims of suicide and the absurd. I recall Singleton's endurance in the storm in *The Nigger of the 'Narcissus'*, Razumov's confession in *Under Western Eyes*, and Ransome's loyal service in *The Shadow-Line*. One scene in particular gathers together my idea of Conrad's relation to his characters. After the Inquiry is over, Marlow invites Jim to his room. He sits writing letters to give Jim time to control himself as he struggles for self-possession out on the balcony against the background of rain and thunder. Marlow cannot solve Jim's problems for him, and later perhaps is foolish to interfere by promoting the Patusan adventure. But at this moment he sits quietly, considerately, submitting the self to the needs of a man who suffers.

In his essay on Henry James, Conrad praises the heroic quality of the artist, who will go on creating even at the moment of apocalypse, when the last aqueduct shall have crumbled to pieces, the last airship fallen to the ground, the last blade of grass have died upon a dying earth. 'I am inclined to think,' Conrad writes, 'that the last utterance will formulate, strange as it may appear, some hope now to us utterly inconceivable':

> For mankind is delightful in its pride, its assurance, and its indomitable tenacity. It will sleep on the battlefield among its own dead, in the manner of an army having won a barren victory. It will not know when it is beaten.[11]

Notes

Chapter 1

1. Zdzisław Najder (ed.), *Conrad's Polish Background. Letters to and from Polish Friends* (Oxford U.P., 1964), p. 176. The telegram was in French.

2. Richard Curle, *The Last Twelve Years of Joseph Conrad* (Sampson Low, Marston, 1928), p. 105.

3. *The Living Age*, 27 September 1919.

4. Najder, op. cit., p. 177.

5. Edward Garnett (ed.), *Letters from Joseph Conrad, 1895–1924* (Bobbs-Merrill, 1928), p. 56.

6. *Ibid.*, p. 141.

7. C. T. Watts (ed.), *Joseph Conrad's Letters to Cunninghame Graham* (Cambridge U.P., 1969), p. 129.

8. J. A. Gee and P. J. Sturm, *Letters of Joseph Conrad to Marguerite Poradowska, 1890–1920* (Yale U.P., 1940), letter of February, 1895.

9. Letters of 16 February 1898, 9 December 1898, and 28 July 1900.

10. G. Jean-Aubry, *Joseph Conrad. Life and Letters* (Heinemann, 1927), Vol. I, p. 322.

11. *Ibid.*, Vol. II, p. 113.

12. Jocelyn Baines, *Joseph Conrad* (Pelican, 1971), p. 127.

13. *Ibid*, p. 28.

14. *A Personal Record*, p. 121.

15. George Steiner, *Extraterritorial* (Faber, 1972), p. 11.

16. Watts, op. cit., p. 65.

17. Garnett, op. cit., p. 143.

18. Watts, op. cit., pp. 56–7.

19. J. Hillis Miller, *Poets of Reality* (Harvard U.P., 1966), p. 5.
20. Frederick R. Karl, *A Reader's Guide to Joseph Conrad* (Thames and Hudson, 1960), p. 96.
21. Baines, op. cit., p. 273.
22. *Ibid.*, p. 305.
23. *Ibid.*, p. 430.

Chapter 2

1. Royal Roussel, *The Metaphysics of Darkness* (The Johns Hopkins Press, 1971), p. 81.
2. Peter K. Garrett, *Scene and Symbol from George Eliot to James Joyce* (Yale University Press, 1969), p. 180.
3. Tony Tanner, *Conrad: 'Lord Jim'* (Edward Arnold, 1963), o. 35.
4. *Ibid.*, p. 35.

Chapter 3

1. F. R. Leavis, *The Great Tradition* (Chatto and Windus, 1948), p. 180.
2. Joseph Warren Beach, 'Impressionism: Conrad', *The Twentieth Century Novelists: Studies in Techniques* (Appleton-Century, 1932), pp. 337–65.
3. K. K. Ruthven, 'The Savage God: Conrad and Lawrence', *The Critical Quarterly* (Spring and Summer 1968), pp. 39–54.
4. Lionel Trilling, *Beyond Culture* (Secker and Warburg, 1966), pp. 20–1.

Chapter 4

1. Alan Friedman, *The Turn of the Novel* (Oxford U.P., New York, 1966), p. 97.
2. G. Jean-Aubry, *Joseph Conrad: Life and Letters*, Vol. II, p. 317.
3. Albert Guerard, *Conrad the Novelist* (Harvard U.P. and Oxford U.P., 1958), pp. 214–15.
4. Bruce Johnson, *Conrad's Models of Mind* (University of Minnesota Press, 1971), p. 111.
5. Baines, op cit., p. 373.
6. Jean-Aubry, op. cit., Vol. II, p. 296.
7. *Notes on Life and Letters*, p. 33.
8. Ian Watt, 'Joseph Conrad: Alienation and Commitment', in *The English Mind* (Cambridge U.P., 1964), edited by Hugh Sykes Davies and George Watson.

9. Robert Penn Warren, 'Nostromo', *Sewanee Review*, LIX (Summer 1951), pp. 363–91, uses this phrase.

10. Guerard, op. cit., p. 199.

11. F. R. Leavis, *The Great Tradition*, p. 200.

Chapter 5

1. 'Conrad: Order and Anarchy', in Irving Howe, *Politics and the Novel* (Horizon Press, 1957). Reprinted in Ian Watt (ed.), *Conrad: 'The Secret Agent'. A Casebook* (Macmillan, 1973), p. 144.

2. See Watt's *Casebook*, pp. 66–76, for a general account of modern critical reactions to *The Secret Agent*.

3. Avrom Fleishman, 'The Symbolic World of *The Secret Agent*', in Watt's *Casebook*, pp. 170–7.

4. *Casebook*, p. 77.

5. J. Hillis Miller, *Poets of Reality*, p. 47.

6. Frank Kermode, *The Sense of an Ending* (Oxford U.P., New York, 1967), p. 109.

7. *Casebook*, p. 116.

Chapter 6

1. Tony Tanner, 'Nightmare and Complacency; Razumov and the Western Eye', *The Critical Quarterly*, IV (Autumn 1962), pp. 197–214.

2. *Ibid.*, p. 208.

3. *Ibid.*, p. 210.

Chapter 7

1. Albert Guerard, *Conrad the Novelist*, p. 272.

2. F. R. Leavis, *The Great Tradition*, p. 208.

3. *Ibid.*, p. 209.

4. Richard E. Butler, 'Jungian and Oriental Symbolism in Joseph Conrad's *Victory*', *Conradiana*, III. No. 2, p. 52.

Chapter 8

1. Robert Rogers, *The Double in Literature* (Wayne State U.P., Detroit, 1970).

2. Edward Garnett (ed.), *Letters from Joseph Conrad, 1895–1924* (Bobbs-Merrill, 1928), p. 243.

3. Rogers, op. cit., p. 44.

4. *Ibid.*, p. 44.

5. Frederick R. Karl, *A Reader's Guide to Joseph Conrad* (Thames and Hudson, 1960), pp. 230–6.

6. *Ibid.*, p. 233.

7. Wilfred S. Dowden, *Joseph Conrad: The Imaged Style* (Vanderbilt U.P., Nashville, 1970).

8. Ian Watt, 'Story and Idea in Conrad's *The Shadow-Line*', *The Critical Quarterly*, II (Summer 1960), pp. 133–48.

Chapter 9

1. Edward Garnett (ed.), *Letters from Joseph Conrad, 1895–1924* (Bobbs-Merrill, 1928), p. 59 and p. 64.

2. *Ibid.*, p. 274.

3. E. M. Forster, 'Joseph Conrad: A Note', in *Abinger Harvest* (Edward Arnold, 1936), pp. 134–5.

4. 'Alphonse Daudet', *Notes on Life and Letters*, p. 24.

5. Graham Hough, *Image and Experience* (Gerald Duckworth, 1960), p. 218.

6. *Ibid.*, p. 220.

7. *Notes on Life and Letters*, p. 21.

8. Ian Watt, 'Joseph Conrad: Alienation and Commitment', in *The English Mind*, edited by Hugh Sykes Davies and George Watson (Cambridge U.P., 1964), p. 272.

9. *Notes on Life and Letters*, p. 33.

10. Ian Watt, op cit., p. 273.

11. 'Henry James', *Notes on Life and Letters*, p. 14.

A Checklist of the Works of Joseph Conrad

From *Joseph Conrad. An Annotated Bibliography of Writings about Him*, compiled and edited by Bruce E. Teets and Helmut E. Gerber, Northern Illinois University Press, 1971

I. FICTION

A. SEPARATE WORKS

Almayer's Folly. Lond. and New York, 1895.

An Outcast of the Islands. Lond. and New York, 1896.

The Nigger of the 'Narcissus'. New York (as *Children of the Sea, A Tale of the Forecastle*) and Lond., 1897.

Tales of Unrest. Lond. and New York, 1898. Contents: 'The Idiots', 1896; 'Karain', 1897; 'The Lagoon', 1897; 'An Outpost of Progress', 1897; 'The Return', 1898.

Lord Jim, A Tale. Edinburgh and Lond., New York, and Toronto, 1900.

The Inheritors, An Extravagant Story. (With Ford Madox Hueffer) New York and Lond., 1901.

Youth, A Narrative, and Two Other Stories. Edinburgh and Lond., 1902; New York, 1903. Contents: 'Youth', 1898; 'Heart of Darkness', 1899; 'The End of the Tether', 1902.

Typhoon. New York and Lond., 1902.

Typhoon, and Other Stories. Lond., 1903; New York, 1923. Contents: 'Amy Foster', 1901; 'Typhoon', 1902; 'To-morrow', 1902; 'Falk', 1903.

Romance, A Novel. (With Ford Madox Hueffer) Lond., 1903; New York, 1904.

Nostromo, A Tale of the Seaboard. Lond. and New York, 1904.

The Secret Agent, A Simple Tale. Lond. and New York, 1907.

A Set of Six. Lond., 1908; New York, 1915. Contents: 'An Anarchist', 1906; 'The Brute', 1906; 'Gaspar Ruiz', 1906; 'The Informer', 1906; 'The Duel', 1908; 'Il Conde', 1908.

Under Western Eyes, A Novel. Lond. and New York, 1911.

'Twixt Land and Sea, Tales. Lond. and New York, 1912. Contents: 'The Secret Sharer', 1910; 'A Smile of Fortune', 1911; 'Freya of the Seven Isles', 1912.

Chance, A Tale in Two Parts. Lond. and New York, 1913.

Victory. An Island Tale. New York and Lond., 1915.

Within the Tides, Tales. Lond. and Toronto, 1915; New York, 1916. Contents: 'The Partner', 1911; 'The Inn of the Two Witches', 1913; 'Because of the Dollars', 1914; 'The Planter of Malata', 1914.

The Shadow-Line, A Confession. Lond. and Toronto, and New York, 1917.

The Arrow of Gold, A Story Between Two Notes. New York and Lond., 1919.

The Rescue, A Romance of the Shallows. New York, and Lond. and Toronto, 1920.

The Rover. New York and Lond., 1923.

The Nature of a Crime. (With Ford Madox Hueffer) Lond. and New York, 1924.

Suspense, A Napoleonic Novel. New York, and Lond. and Toronto, 1925.

Tales of Hearsay. Lond. and New York, 1925. Contents: 'The Black Mate', 1908; 'Prince Roman', 1911; 'The Tale', 1917; 'The Warrior's Soul', 1917.

The Sisters. New York, 1928.

B. COLLECTED EDITIONS

The Works of Joseph Conrad. Lond., 1921–7. 20 vols.

The Works of Joseph Conrad. The Uniform Edition. Lond. and Toronto, 1923–8. 22 vols.

Collected Works of Joseph Conrad. The Memorial Edition. New York, 1926. 21 vols. (Several additional sets—Concord, Kent, Canterbury, etc.—are substantially the same.)

Collected Edition of the Works of Joseph Conrad. Lond., 1946–55. (Reprinted from the Uniform Edition, without the dramas.) 21 vols.

II. ESSAYS AND MEMOIRS (INCLUDED IN THE COLLECTED EDITIONS)

The Mirror of the Sea, Memories and Impressions. Lond. and New York, 1906.

A Personal Record. (Under title, *Some Reminiscences*, New York, 1908, to secure American copyright, probably only six copies printed) Lond. (as *Some Reminiscences*) and New York, 1912.

Notes on Life and Letters. Lond. and Toronto, and New York, 1921. Contents: 'Books', 1905; 'Henry James', 1905; 'Alphonse Daudet', 1898; 'Guy de Maupassant', 1914; 'Anatole France—I. *Crainquebille*', 1904;

'Anatole France—II. *L'Ile des pingouins*', 1908; 'Turgenev', 1917; 'Stephen Crane, A Note Without Dates', 1919; 'Tales of the Sea', 1898; 'An Observer in Malay', 1898; 'A Happy Wanderer', 1910; 'The Life Beyond', 1910; 'The Ascending Effort', 1910; 'The Censor of Plays', 1907; 'Autocracy and War', 1905; 'The Crime of Partition', 1919; 'A Note on the Polish Problem', 1921; 'The Shock of War', 1915; 'To Poland in War-time', 1915; 'The North Sea on the Eve of the War', 1915; 'My Return to Cracow', 1915; 'Poland Revisited', 1916; 'First News', 1918; 'Well Done!', 1918; 'Tradition', 1918; 'Confidence', 1919; 'Flight', 1917; 'Some Reflections on the Loss of the *Titanic*', 1912; 'Certain Aspects of the Admirable Inquiry into the Loss of the *Titanic*', 1912; 'Protection of Ocean Liners', 1914; 'A Friendly Place', 1912.

Last Essays. Lond. and Toronto, and New York, 1926. Contents: 'Geography and Some Explorers', 1924; 'The "Torrens", A Personal Tribute', 1923; 'Christmas Day at Sea', 1923; 'Ocean Travels', 1923; 'Outside Literature', 1922; 'Legends', 1924; 'The Unlighted Coast', 1925; 'The Dover Patrol', 1921; 'Memorandum on the Scheme for Fitting Out a Ship', 1926; 'The Loss of the "Dalgonar"', 1921; 'Travel', 1923; 'Stephen Crane', 1923; 'His War Book', 1925; 'John Galsworthy', 1906; 'A Glance at Two Books', 1925; 'Preface to "The Shorter Tales of Joseph Conrad"', 1924; 'Cookery', 1923; 'The Future of Constantinople', 1912; 'The Congo Diary', 1925.

III. DRAMA

A. SEPARATE WORKS

One Day More, A Play in One Act. (Adaptation of 'To-morrow') Lond., ENGLISH REVIEW, 1913.

The Secret Agent, Drama in Four Acts. (Adaptation of the novel) Canterbury, 1921.

Laughing Anne, A Play. (Adaptation of 'Because of the Dollars') Lond., 1923.

B. COLLECTED EDITION

Three Plays: Laughing Anne; One Day More; and The Secret Agent. Lond., 1934.

IV. LETTERS: MAJOR COLLECTIONS

Five Letters by Joseph Conrad Written to Edward Noble in 1895. Foreword by Edward Noble. Lond., 1925.

Joseph Conrad: The Modern Imagination

Joseph Conrad's Letters to His Wife. Lond., 1927.

Joseph Conrad, Life and Letters. G. Jean-Aubry. 2 vols. New York and Lond., 1927.

Conrad to a Friend, 150 Selected Letters from Joseph Conrad to Richard Curle, ed. by Richard Curle. New York and Lond., 1928.

Letters from Joseph Conrad, 1895–1924, ed. by Edward Garnett. Indianapolis, 1928.

Lettres françaises, ed. by G. Jean-Aubry. Paris, 1930.

Letters of Joseph Conrad to Marguerite Poradowska, 1890–1920, ed. by John A. Gee and Paul J. Sturm, New Haven and Lond., 1940.

Joseph Conrad: Letters to William Blackwood and David S. Meldrum, ed. by William Blackburn. Durham, N. C., 1958.

Conrad's Polish Background: Letters to and from Polish Friends, ed. by Zdzisław Najder. Lond., New York, Toronto, 1964.

Joseph Conrad's Letters to R. B. Cunninghame Graham, ed. by C. T. Watts. Lond., 1969.

Select Bibliography

BIOGRAPHY AND CRITICISM. *Joseph Conrad, A Study*, by Richard Curle, 1914; Essay in *Notes on Novelists*, by Henry James, 1914; *Joseph Conrad*, by Hugh Walpole, 1916; Essay on Conrad in *A Book of Prefaces*, by H. L. Mencken, 1917; *Joseph Conrad, a Personal Remembrance*, by Ford Madox Ford, 1924; Essays on Conrad in *The Common Reader*, by Virginia Woolf, 1925; *Joseph Conrad as I knew Him*, by Jessie Conrad, 1926; 'Reminiscences of Conrad' and 'Preface to Conrad's Plays' in *Castles in Spain*, by John Galsworthy, 1927; *The Last Twelve Years of Joseph Conrad*, by Richard Curle, 1928; *The Polish Heritage of Joseph Conrad*, by Gustav Morf, 1930; *Joseph Conrad's Mind and Method*, by R. L. Mégroz, 1931; *Joseph Conrad and his Circle*, by Jessie Conrad, 1936; *Joseph Conrad, Some Aspects of the Art of the Novel*, by Edward Crankshaw, 1936; Introductory Essay by Edward Garnett to *Conrad's Prefaces to his Works*, 1937; *Joseph Conrad, the Making of a Novelist*, by John D. Gordan, 1940; *Joseph Conrad, England's Polish Genius*, by M. C. Bradbrook, 1941; Introduction by A. J. Hoppé to *The Conrad Companion*, 1946; *The Great Tradition* (George Eliot, Henry James, and Joseph Conrad), by F. R. Leavis, 1948; *Joseph Conrad*, by Oliver Warner, 1951; *Conrad, a Re-assessment*, by D. Hewitt, 1952; *Six Great Novelists*, by Walter Allen, 1955 (Conrad is the sixth subject); *The Mirror of Conrad*, by E. H. Visiak, 1955; *The Sea Dreamer: Life of Conrad*, by G. Jean-Aubry, 1957; *Joseph Conrad*, by Thomas Moser, 1957; *Conrad the Novelist*, by A. J. Guerard, 1958; *Joseph Conrad, A Study in Non-conformity*, by Osborn Andreas, 1959; *Joseph Conrad, A Critical Biography*, by Jocelyn Baines, 1960; *A Reader's Guide to Joseph Conrad*, by Frederick R. Karl, 1960; *Joseph Conrad, Giant in Exile*, by Leo Gurko, 1962; *The Political Novels of Joseph Conrad*, by E. K. Hay, 1963; *The English Mind*, ed. by H. S. Davies and G. Watson, 1964 (see Ian Watt's chapter on Conrad); *Joseph Conrad and the Fiction of Autobiography*, by E. W. Said, 1966; *Conrad's Eastern World*, by Norman Sherry, 1966; *Poets of Reality*, by J. Hillis Miller, 1966 (2nd chapter); *The Sea Years of Joseph Conrad*, by Jerry Allen, 1967; *Conrad: A Psychoanalytic Biography*, by B. C. Meyer, 1967; *The Limits of Metaphor*, by James Guetti, 1967; *Conrad's Politics: Community and Anarchy in the Fiction of Joseph Conrad*, by A. Fleishman, 1968; *Conrad the Psychologist as Artist*, by P. Kirschner, 1968; *Joseph Conrad*, by J. I. M. Stewart, 1968; *A Study in Literary Growth*, by J. A. Palmer, 1968; *Conrad's Short Fiction*, by L. Graver, 1969; *Scene and Symbol from George Eliot to James Joyce*, by Peter K. Garrett, 1969; *Joseph Conrad's Fiction: Conrad's Western World*, by Norman Sherry, 1971; *The Metaphysics of Darkness*, by Royal Roussel, 1971; *Conrad's Models of Mind*, by Bruce Johnson, 1971.

BIBLIOGRAPHIES. *A Bibliography of the Writings of Joseph Conrad, 1895–1921*, T. J. Wise, 1921; *A Conrad Library*, T. J. Wise, London, 1928; *A Conrad Memorial Library*, G. T. Keating, New York, 1929, with 'Check List of Additions', 1938; *Joseph Conrad at Mid-century: Editions and Studies, 1895–1955*, by K. A. Lohf and E. P. Sheehy, 1959; *A Bibliography of Joseph Conrad*, by Theodore G. Ehrsam, 1969; *Joseph Conrad. An Annotated Bibliography of Writings about Him*, by Bruce E. Teets and Helmut E. Gerber, 1971.

Index